CALGARY PUBLIC LIBRARY

AUG - 2012

D0622274

TEAM CANADA 1972

Andrew Podnieks is the author of more than sixty-five books on hockey.
The following is a select list:

IIHF Guide & Record Book 2012

NHL Records Forever

Sid vs. Ovi: Natural Born Rivals

The Legend of Moe Norman: The Man with the Perfect Swing

Hockey Facts and Stats 2011–2012

The Year of the Bruins: Celebrating Boston's 2010–11 Stanley Cup Championship Season

Retired Numbers: A Celebration of NHL Excellence

Hockey Superstitions: From Playoff Beards to Lucky Socks and Crossed Sticks

Canadian Gold: 2010 Olympic Winter Games Ice Hockey Champions

Honoured Canadiens

The Complete Hockey Dictionary

World of Hockey: Celebrating a Century of the IIHF 1908–2008

A Canadian Saturday Night: Hockey and the Culture of a Country

Players: The Ultimate A–Z Guide of Everyone Who Has Ever Played in the NHL

The Goal: Bobby Orr and the Most Famous Goal in NHL Stanley Cup History

A Day in the Life of the Maple Leafs

The NHL All-Star Game: 50 Years of the Great Tradition

The Great One: The Life and Times of Wayne Gretzky

Portraits of the Game: Classic Photographs from the Turofsky Collection at the Hockey Hall of Fame

TEAM CANADA
1972

THE OFFICIAL 40TH ANNIVERSARY CELEBRATION OF THE SUMMIT SERIES

AS TOLD BY THE PLAYERS

WITH ANDREW PODNIEKS

FENN
M&S

Copyright © 2012 by Team Canada 1972

All rights reserved. The use of any part of this publication reproduced, transmitted in any form or by any means, electronic, mechanical, photocopying, recording, or otherwise, or stored in a retrieval system, without the prior written consent of the publisher – or, in case of photocopying or other reprographic copying, a licence from the Canadian Copyright Licensing Agency – is an infringement of the copyright law.

Library and Archives Canada Cataloguing in Publication

Podnieks, Andrew

    Team Canada 1972 : the official 40th anniversary celebration / Andrew Podnieks.

ISBN 978-0-7710-7119-5

    1. Canada-U.S.S.R. Hockey Series, 1972. I. Title.

GV847.7.P623 2012   796.962'66   C2012-900963-6

We acknowledge the financial support of the Government of Canada through the Canada Book Fund and that of the Government of Ontario through the Ontario Media Development Corporation's Ontario Book Initiative. We further acknowledge the support of the Canada Council for the Arts and the Ontario Arts Council for our publishing program.

Published simultaneously in the United States of America by McClelland & Stewart, a division of Random House of Canada Limited Ltd., P.O. Box 1030, Plattsburgh, New York 12901

Library of Congress Control Number: 2012932345

Typeset in Perpetua by M&S, Toronto

Printed and bound in The United States of America

Fenn / McClelland & Stewart, a division of Random House of Canada Limited
One Toronto Street
Suite 300
Toronto, Ontario
M5C 2V6
www.mcclelland.com

1   2   3   4   5   14   13   12

CONTENTS

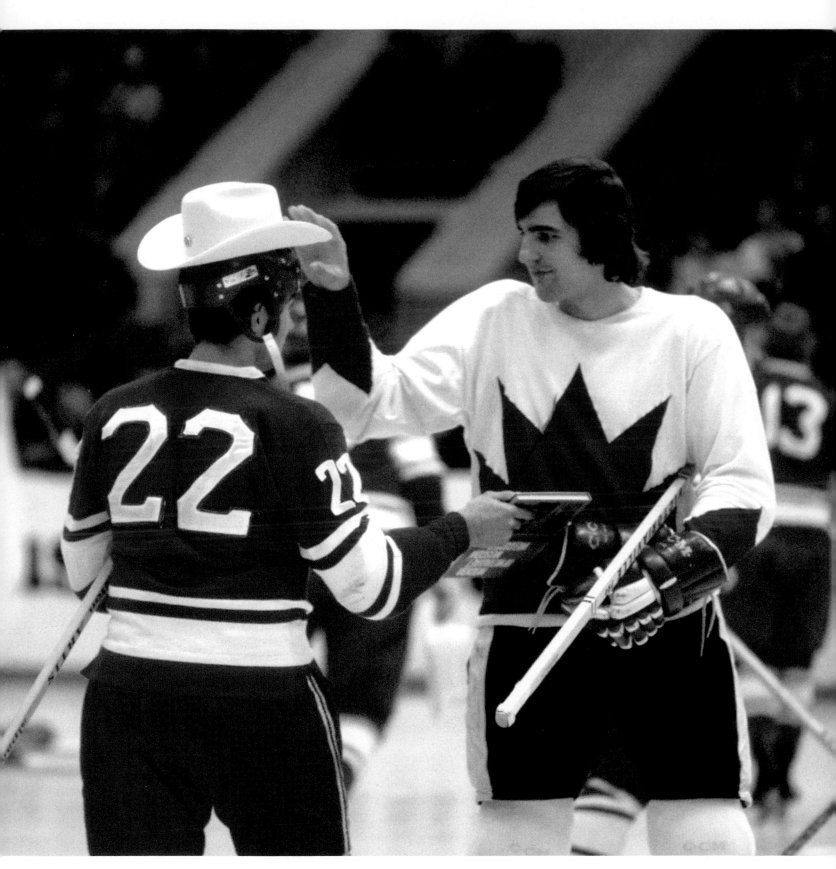

Guy Lapointe presents (right) Vyacheslav Anisin with a white Stetson during pre-game ceremonies, September 28, 1972.

INTRODUCTION

W hy was the Summit Series held? Why was it such a big deal? Why, forty years later, does it continue to play a pivotal role in Canadian history, a very cornerstone of the nation's sporting achievements?

To explain fully, we must go back to 1954 and earlier.

The International Ice Hockey Federation (IIHF) was established in 1908 when five European teams — France, Belgium, Switzerland, Great Britain, and Bohemia (now Czechoslovakia) — decided to join forces in drawing up one conclusive set of hockey rules based on the Canadian game. This version of hockey had established itself as the game of the future, usurping bandy, an outdoor winter sport played on frozen soccer fields, eleven men a side (like soccer), and using more soccer rules than hockey rules.

After 1908, European teams started competing more frequently against each other under this common set of "Canadian rules," but the culmination of these efforts didn't come about until 1920, when hockey was played as part of the Summer Olympics and the two North American nations (Canada and the United States) participated in what was the first truly international hockey tournament.

Canada won the gold in 1920 and every other gold between that first event and 1954, with two exceptions: the 1933 World Championship, when it lost 2–1 in overtime to the United States in the gold-medal game, and the 1936 Olympics, when an early round 2–1 loss to Great Britain later decided the gold.

Canada was far and away the supreme hockey country. The first Olympic Winter Games took place in 1924, largely created after the success of hockey in 1920, and starting in 1930 the IIHF held an annual World Championship in years when there was no Olympics. Canada's entry in these tournaments was usually the senior amateur champion of the previous year, that is, the Allan Cup winners. This team would leave for Europe a couple months prior to the tournament to play exhibition games, promote Canadian hockey, and prepare for the international event in which it was competing.

Everything changed in an instant in 1954. That year, the Soviet Union entered its first international event, the World Championship, held in Stockholm, Sweden. No one knew anything about the team or its players, but it performed well in the early going. Canada, represented as always by a club team, also won all its games, as the East York Lyndhursts rolled merrily along in similar manner as every previous Canadian representative for thirty-four years.

The final day of the championship pitted undefeated Canada (six wins) against unbeaten Soviet Union (five wins and a tie, against Sweden). The Soviets scored the only four goals of the first period and after an early

Canada goal in the second scored three more. Canada got one goal back in the third, losing 7–2, and the Soviets produced up to that time what was unquestionably the greatest upset in hockey history.

That score, in fact, was of such great consequence in Canada that the next year the play-by-play legend Foster Hewitt left his post during the NHL season to do radio coverage for the 1955 World Championship in Germany. The same series of events unfolded during the tournament. Canada and the Soviets each won their first seven games, setting up a gold-medal showdown on the final day. This time, a more prepared Canadian team hammered the Soviets 5–0 to reclaim the World Championship title, but it was now clear that Canada was no longer alone atop the hockey world.

The next several years produced high drama internationally. The Soviets won gold at the 1956 Olympics while Canada had to settle for bronze, the first time it hadn't won either gold or silver. Canada did not compete at the 1957 Worlds for political reasons but won in 1958 and 1959, only to finish third again at the 1960 Olympics in Squaw Valley, California.

Canada won in 1961 thanks to the Trail Smoke Eaters, but who could have predicted that Canada would have to wait until 1994 – thirty-three years later! – before it won World Championship (or Olympic) gold again.

What happened? Several things. First, Father David Bauer of St. Michael's College in Toronto came up with a brilliant strategy in 1962. Rather than have Canada send an amateur team to international events, why not gather the best senior players in the country into a training camp, have them practise for many months in advance of the tournament like the Soviets, and be ready to compete in that way? Thus was born Canada's National Team.

Although it was a revolutionary concept, the only players eligible were, for the most part, university students. Junior players were generally too young and inexperienced to play, and they, as well as all other top players, were either in professional hockey or bound for the pro ranks. And therein lay a great controversy that would soon rear its ugly head.

But first, the 1960s. Canada created a National Team. After tryouts, the players did, indeed, stay together as a group, practise, and become a team well in advance of the World Championships and Olympics throughout the decade. But the Soviets, under head coach Anatoli Tarasov, a great admirer of Canadian hockey and a key Soviet strategist, was also finding ways to improve his team through better training, diet, fitness, and virtually non-stop practice year-round. The result was that Canada finished fourth and third at the 1964 and 1968 Olympics, respectively, and finished second at the 1962 World Championship, fourth in 1963 and 1965, third in 1966 and 1967, and fourth in 1969. Sweden won gold in 1962, and then for the rest of the decade the Soviets won every gold at all top events.

The days of Canadian gold were long over as the 1960s came to a close, and the nation's amateur domination had come to an end.

The poor performances in the 1960s had political repercussions as well. When Pierre Trudeau won the federal election in 1968, he commissioned a Task Force on Sports, the goal of which was to understand why amateur hockey had failed at the international level to the degree that it had. The conclusions included a proposal to overhaul the way the game was handled below the professional level right down to grassroots hockey. The main thrust was that one organization should be responsible for everything, and so on February 24, 1969, Hockey Canada Inc. was introduced as the umbrella organization for amateur hockey.

Hockey Canada consisted of the Canadian Amateur Hockey Association (CAHA), the Canadian Interuniversity

Athletic Union (CIAU), Fitness and Amateur Sport, and representatives of the two Canadian teams in the NHL: the Toronto Maple Leafs and the Montreal Canadiens. Its mandate was summarized as follows: "To support, operate, manage, and develop a national team or teams for the purpose of representing Canadian international tournaments and competitions. To foster and support the playing of hockey in Canada and in particular the development of the skill and competence of Canadian hockey players and, in this connection, to cooperate with other bodies, groups, and associations having similar or related purposes and objectives."

Over and above internal alignment, though, Hockey Canada also sought to level the playing field between competing countries at IIHF events. Specifically, it wanted the World Championships and Olympics to be open to professional players, especially since Canada had been awarded the honour of hosting the Worlds in 1970 (Montreal and Winnipeg) for the first time. Thus, at the IIHF's semi-annual congress in Crans-sur-Sierre, Switzerland, in July 1969, the proposal to allow pros in IIHF events was at the top of the agenda.

The meetings resulted in an agreement and a compromise. The IIHF decided that Canada could name up to nine non-NHL professionals for any event for one year, after which a review would take place and a more comprehensive decision in the matter moving forward was to be made. It wasn't all Canada had hoped for, but it was a positive first step and enough to work with for the coming year.

The annual Izvestia tournament in Moscow at Christmas in 1969 was the first test for the new rule, and although Canada added only five non-NHL pros to its roster it nearly beat the best from the Soviet Union, much to the dismay of the host nation. As a result, the IIHF held an emergency meeting on January 3, 1970, at which time IOC President Avery Brundage rescinded the rule and declared that players who competed against Canada's semi-pros would be forfeiting their amateur status and couldn't compete at the Olympics or other international events. Hockey Canada was livid with the decision and withdrew the nation from international events until it could gain a favourable resolution to the widening crisis.

Jim Coleman wrote in a column in the *Toronto Telegram* on Monday, January 5, 1970: "Canada has withdrawn from the phoney world of international hockey and the vast majority of Canadians will applaud this decision. There was no point in messing around further with such hypocrites as the Swedes and the Russians. Canada couldn't gain anything from associating in such shabby sporting company. If you lie down to wallow with the pigs, you're certain to get fleas."

The CAHA's response was simple. As President Earl Dawson made clear, if the IIHF didn't continue to maintain the "nine pros" agreement that it had in place for the Izvestia tournament, Canada would refuse to host the 1970 World Championship, withdraw from all international competition, including the Olympics, and decline all invitations to play exhibition games throughout Europe.

Dawson then tabled a counter-proposal at an IIHF meeting in Geneva, Switzerland, suggesting the World Championship be replaced by a five-team invitational tournament at which Canada and all countries could put together a team of players regardless of amateur or professional status. Brundage, though, quickly shot down the idea, saying such a tournament would compromise the Olympic eligibility of amateurs who played with pros, and the idea died a quick death.

Without recourse, Canada withdrew from international hockey. Explained Dawson: "Canada will enter a team of amateurs in the 1972 Olympic Games, and we intend to question the eligibility of every other team and make ineligible any and all teams which have played professionally."

Despite the implications, reaction in Canada produced instant and unmitigated support. John Munro, federal minister of national health and welfare, was first in line to praise those who made the tough decision: "Our country has not been able to ice the best teams because of farcical regulations which made it impossible to use players with the same experience as those other countries used. Canada has some pride."

Canada was now on its own in this war against the Soviets, who declared that there were no pros in their program. As Bob Pennington pointed out in a column in the *Toronto Telegram* on January 5, 1970, the day after the withdrawal: "Olympic rules give a tremendous advantage to any communist country. It would be naive to think that Russia would voluntarily change such a sweet set-up particularly if honesty meant handing over a world crown to the fathers of hockey [Canada]."

David Molson, president of the Montreal Canadiens, was also supportive of the withdrawal. "I'm in full agreement with the decision," he said. "We should have done it ten years ago. I'm glad we stood up to them and did not compromise. It is a matter of principle."

European consensus sided with Canada as well. In Sweden, the newspaper *Dagens Nyheter* wrote that, "[IIHF president John "Bunny"] Ahearne has conducted this confused affair so badly that he should now leave his post. Otherwise there is a great risk that the cold war will be protracted." In Finland's *Ilta Sanomat*, the editors agreed: "It is no longer reasonable to distinguish between professionals and amateurs. The Russian world champions are no less professionals than the Canadians. It is unnecessary to speak of 'pure amateurs' in any country."

What was so shocking was the complete and total support the IIHF threw behind the Soviets at the expense of the Canadians. Canada was the only reason the game had established a foothold in Europe, dating back to 1920 and earlier. Every year its teams flew over months in advance and played goodwill games across the continent prior to the World Championships to the delight of thousands of fans in many countries. And now the political strength of the great U.S.S.R. trumped Canada's puck proficiency, and Europe was to have no more participation, no more games or exhibitions or anything hockey that came from Canada.

Stockholm filled in as host city at the last minute for the 1970 Worlds. At the 1969 Worlds, Canada's games drew 40 per cent of the total attendance. In Stockholm, total attendance for the championships was down – 40 per cent.

At the fourth plenary session of the CAHA's annual meeting on May 27, 1970, Dawson gave the members a detailed account of what had transpired over the past year in the wake of Canada's withdrawal:

> I attended the congress of the IIHF in Stockholm this past March, and Fred Page, your past president, the North American vice-president of the IIHF, and Gordon Juckes, who is one of the members of the council, attended as well. Mr. Hay of Hockey Canada attended as an observer.
>
> At this meeting, our position was to reintroduce a resolution that had been approved at the July meeting held in 1969 in Crans, Switzerland, and this is the resolution which gave us permission to use nine professionals on our national team. After some considerable discussion, we were finally permitted to reintroduce that resolution and had it defeated. That put us in the position that the congress, at least for the next year, adopted the position that there would not be an open tournament and Canada would not be permitted to use any professionals on their hockey team.

We had a number of meetings with practically every country that was over there. Every country approached us on the basis of having a team visit their country and return a visit to our country. Our attitude, until we left, was non-committal. We decided that we would stand pat. If we couldn't have any professionals on our team or were not permitted to have an open competition, we were not going to entertain any thought of exchanging visits or having any European team come here or us going there.

I think that the Soviets, the Czechs, Finland have not suffered the financial loss that the other teams such as Sweden suffered. Because the Swedes suffered a financial loss by Canada not appearing there for the Ahearne Trophy, plus the world tournament, they took a different stand than they had in January which was a complete about-face. Anything Canada was introducing at the congress meetings, the Swedes were prepared to support. As a matter of fact, they introduced a couple of resolutions which would have eased our position had they been passed.

As it worked out, the Russians and Czechs, as I told you, and Switzerland, Finland, most of the countries, had private meetings with us and they all wanted us to go over there and we could bring anybody we wanted on the team, including Bobby Orr or Bobby Hull, it didn't matter to them. But when we asked the question, "What happens in the world tournament?" they said that is different. You must revert to a completely amateur team. In view of that, and in view of the stand we had taken in September, we gave up the tournament on the principle of not being allowed to use the best Canadian players. It was my recommendation to the board of directors yesterday that we adopt the same stand for the next season. It was endorsed by the board with a unanimous endorsation, with two people abstaining from the vote.

What I am saying is that the board of directors of the CAHA adopted the position that there will be no exchange visits between European countries next year. Our position will remain the same. They will not come here, nor will we go there.

Despite overwhelming support for the decision, there was still worry. After all, international hockey provided Canada's young and promising players an excellent means of developing and gaining experience playing against the best from other countries. Would the emergence of the next generation of players be stunted by a lack of top-notch opposition? And, regardless of what other countries did or didn't do, wasn't it a morally and ethically strong position to play by the rules even if no one else did?

In a column for the *Telegram*, former Maple Leafs coach Punch Imlach wrote: "The national team has come a long way and it would be folly to discontinue operations just because the [world] tournament has been changed . . . I have always thought that the stronger the amateur leagues, the stronger the professionals. A good foundation is always good business."

As well, the perception of the whole mess didn't favour Canada, even if it was in the right. After all, Canada had been playing second fiddle to the Soviets for long enough that it was clear the nation was not unilaterally going to win every gold. And, with the emergence of the Czechs and Swedes, Canada was still, of course, among the very best but not categorically the best. Many felt the time had come to compete against the Soviets in a tournament outside IIHF and IOC sanctions.

After beating Canada 5–0 in the 1968 Olympics, Soviet coach Tarasov defiantly boasted that his team could beat any in the NHL. Soon he would get his chance to prove it. Hockey Canada, through negotiations led by NHL Players' Association president and player agent Alan Eagleson, arranged an eight-game tournament with the Soviets, the very best players in Canada against any team the Soviets could put together. The first four games would be played in Canada, the last four in Moscow. The dates were September 2–28, 1972.

The rosters for the two teams told a story in itself. The Soviets had thirteen players who had played at the Olympic Winter Games in Sapporo, Japan, earlier in the year and, incredibly, seven men who had played against Canada at the 1968 Olympics at Grenoble, France. Team Canada had Ken Dryden (two World Championship games in 1969), Rod Seiling (1964 Olympics), Red Berenson (1959 Worlds), and Brian Glennie (1968 Olympics) as the only players who could claim any international experience. The last three of these combined to play only five games in the Summit Series, a clear sign Canada's top NHLers and top international players were a completely different lot. Not so the Soviets.

The story of the eight-game series is not just familiar — it has become a part of Canada's cultural history alongside Laura Secord, Alexander Graham Bell, Banting and Best, the CNR, universal health coverage, the gold rush in the Klondike, and all other historical markers.

Now, forty years on, the Summit Series continues to have as its focal point the one image of Paul Henderson raising his arms in celebration as teammate Yvan Cournoyer rushes in to hug him. Canada had scored a goal with thirty-four seconds remaining in the final game of an eight-game series against the Soviet Union to win hockey's greatest showdown.

As has been told in history books and documentaries and biographies too many to count, Canada was supposed to win all eight games of what was initially billed as an exhibition series. "That was no exhibition," Frank Mahovlich said four decades later.

Canada was playing the Soviet Union in what was then a cage match, a winner-take-all, no-holds-barred contest between Canada's NHL superstars and the Soviets' so-called amateurs. Ever since the U.S.S.R. started playing internationally in 1954, the country insisted its players were amateurs, even though they did nothing else with their time, trained eleven months of the year, and were provided food and lodging and a salary (putatively because they were in the army).

The "shamateurs," as they were later called by the Canadian Amateur Hockey Association, dominated the international scene by beating university students from Canada, and as a result Canada withdrew from playing international hockey.

But out of these darkest days emerged the Summit Series. Both countries were allowed to name a roster of any players from their country, amateur/pro status be damned. The series was not just about this issue, though. It took on a much larger context of democracy versus Communism; full-throttle "north–south" hockey versus strategic, rococo play ("east–west"); tough, helmetless Canadians versus helmeted "artistes" from the Soviet Union who were far more secretive and dirty in their tactics. It pitted shooting versus passing and pride versus system. It became something no one had a clue about when the series started.

The exhibition became a war.

In 1972, NHL players and international players were different. By the time Mario Lemieux won the 1987 Canada Cup for Canada (above), Europeans had started to appear in ever great numbers in the NHL, and when Sydney Crosby scored the golden goal at the 2010 Olympics (below), NHLers and Olympians pretty much one and the same.

Yes, Henderson emerged the hero, scoring what turned out to be the game-winning goal in game six, then scoring a dazzling and dramatic game winner in game seven, and finally, to complete the greatest hat trick ever, banged home a loose puck at 19:26 of the final minute of the final game to give Canada the series win.

But there were plenty of heroes in the series, players who one never imagined would be called upon to become heroic, players who had no concept of the road ahead of them when they waltzed into training camp at Maple Leaf Gardens one sweltering day in August 1972.

Phil Esposito became a hero off ice and a leader on ice, a superstar scorer but so very much more. Bobby Clarke – young, a rising star – became coach Harry Sinden's key faceoff man and centred the best line in the series with wingers Henderson on the left side and Ron Ellis on the right. Gary Bergman was a rock on the blue line and Yvan Cournoyer a blazing patroller of the right wing. Brad Park was just as Orr-like in the series as he was back in the NHL, and no one could overestimate the value of Serge Savard on the blue line, a calm presence who never played in a loss during the eight games.

The Summit Series became the Summit Series only after game one. Canada rattled in two early goals to take a 2–0 lead, and the players laughed as they skated on and off the ice, believing the "exhibition" was going exactly as planned. But then the nervous Soviets found their footing, tied the game before the end of the first period, and skated to an easy 7–3 win that humiliated the home team and stunned the packed house at the Forum in Montreal.

Suddenly, game two in Toronto became a must-win game, and thanks to a superb short-handed goal from Peter Mahovlich early in the third, Canada did, indeed, win 4–1 to even the series. But Canada blew a two-goal lead in game three and had to settle for a tie, and it was embarrassed again in game four, losing 5–3 and skating off the ice to a chorus of boos from the Vancouver fans.

Right after the game Phil Esposito did an on-ice interview with Johnny Esaw of CTV, and Espo produced a speech that rallied the nation and created unity from coast to coast. The team then had two weeks off to prepare for the final four games, in Moscow, using much of that time to train and play two exhibition games in Stockholm, Sweden, to adjust to the bigger European ice. These were the days the players became a team, but you wouldn't have known it from game five. That night, Canada built an impressive 4–1 lead through two periods, but the vaunted Soviet attack counted the only four goals of the third period to win 5–4.

There was no margin for error remaining. The Soviets had won three and tied one of the five games, so Canada would need to win all three remaining games to win the series. Game six was a nail-biter, but Canada came out on top 3–2. In game seven, the score was tied 3–3 late in the game and a tie seemed inevitable, a result that would have given the Soviets the win. But with less than three minutes left, Paul Henderson had the puck at centre ice, one man surrounded by four Soviets. He managed to get around all of them to beat goalie Vladislav Tretiak while falling to the ice. It was a spectacular goal of extraordinary drama, and it kept Canada's hopes alive.

In game eight, Canada trailed 5–3 heading into the final period, but Esposito was unstoppable, scoring early and setting up Cournoyer for the tying goal midway through. In the final minute, Henderson was the hero again, smacking home a shot with just thirty-four seconds left in the game. Canada won the Summit Series by the narrowest of margins in what proved to be the greatest hockey series ever played!

The Summit Series had an extraordinary influence on the development of hockey. The Soviets based their training on fitness and diet under Coach Tarasov, but he – irony of ironies – was influenced by Canadian Lloyd

Percival, a man well ahead of his time. Percival had published *The Hockey Handbook* in 1951, a tome that promoted conditioning, diet, and skills as the fundamental principles to hockey success. Although the book was ridiculed in NHL circles, Tarasov swore by it: "I have read it like a schoolboy," he once confessed to Percival.

Tarasov trained his players eleven months of the year and created five-man units that skated together rather than change defence partners and forward lines independent of each other. He employed a soccer style of play in which possession was most important. Players skated in circles to create a hurricane-like rush, but if it didn't work they would retreat and try again – they never shot the puck into the offensive end and chased it down.

As the Soviets closed in on goal, they didn't believe in shooting the puck until they had a clear and superb scoring chance. They passed and passed again, often giving up a good scoring chance in an attempt to create a great scoring chance.

The Canadians played with a heart and intensity that improved every game and reached its crescendo at the times it was needed the most. The Soviet "method" had no answer for that intensity. And Canada's attack was based on the simple mandate that any shot is a good shot. You never know if the goalie will make a mistake or give up a rebound, and if the puck is at the goal, that's the best place for it to be.

The Summit Series proved a number of things: Canada had better players, and many more of them, than the Soviets; the Soviets' "pro" team was the same as their "amateur" team; and the gap between them and the Canadians wasn't as great as the latter had thought.

After 1972, the two styles and systems merged as each country adapted and learned and stole liberally from the other to create a hybrid game better than either individual nation's style in '72.

Despite the unparalleled success of this head-to-head matchup, the IOC and IIHF were no closer to allowing professionals to join the Olympic ranks than they were before 1972. Canada continued to pass on the Worlds and Olympics, and the Soviets continued to win. When the 1976 Olympics came along, both sides hadn't altered their feelings one iota. Canada wanted to use professionals; the IOC was adamantly opposed. Canada again did not send a hockey team, but this time it was not alone. Sweden, Norway, and East Germany also passed on the Games, a protest that was recognized by the IIHF – but not the IOC – as significant.

In response, the IIHF announced that beginning in 1977, the World Championships would be open to professionals. Canada immediately announced its intention to compete that year. No such declaration came from the IOC, however, in time for the 1976 Olympics, and this time Eagleson organized a true world championship, the inaugural Canada Cup. And, just to make sure the taint of "amateur," or, more rightly, "shamateur," would never darken the Canada Cup's doors, Eagleson announced that $150,000 in prize money was to be won, in addition to the beautiful trophy and international prestige!

The Canada Cup differed from the Summit Series in that six nations – Canada, the Soviet Union, Czechoslovakia, Sweden, Finland, and the United States – would compete in a round-robin, Olympic-style tournament, culminating with an NHL-style, best-of-three finals. This time, the dubious Soviets sent an "experimental" team and didn't even make the finals. Canada won handily and dramatically over the Czechs 6–0 in game one and then 5–4 in overtime of game two after Darryl Sittler faked goalie Vladimir Dzurilla with a slap shot and slid the puck into the open net.

At the opening of the 1977 World Championship in Vienna, IIHF secretary Walter Wasservogel openly defied the IOC, saying, "It's a big lie. They [the hockey players] are all professionals . . . the people want to see the best athletes in the world, and the best athletes in the world are professional. My personal opinion is that if the Olympic Games aren't open in the next, let's say eight years, they are finished."

Perhaps the most significant event in the process of reconciliation between Canada and the IIHF came in the summer of 1975 when the IIHF replaced Bunny Ahearne with Gunther Sabetzki as president. Sabetzki immediately announced that getting Canada back on side was his top priority, and to this end Eagleson represented Hockey Canada in meetings intended to solve the amateur–pro rift. Negotiations focused on two events, the inaugural 1976 Canada Cup and Canada's participation in the 1977 World Championships in Vienna.

The IIHF agreed to sanction the Canada Cup and was, in turn, given a flat fee of $25,000, 5 per cent of television revenues generated by the five non-Canadian entries in the tournament, and a $100,000 bond guaranteeing Canada's commitment to the '77 Worlds. This agreement was definitely a trade-off. Canada got its Canada Cup, which it won in dramatic fashion, but even though it could now send pros to Vienna, the tournament was still held in early spring, from April 21 to May 8, 1977, a time when the NHL playoffs were in full swing.

Thus, the only professionals who could participate were those on NHL teams that did not make the playoffs or were eliminated quickly. They would be playing at the end of a ninety-game season (exhibition and regular season), have virtually no time to gel as a team and become a unit, and have to adapt almost instantly to jet lag and a significant culture change.

Furthermore, while the team left Toronto on April 5, 1977, for an eight-game exhibition tour beginning in Gothenburg, Sweden, nine more players arrived a week later in Dusseldorf after their teams had been eliminated from the first round of the playoffs. Thus, most of what was positive about the tour was offset by the infusion of new, unfamiliar players who had little time to learn how to fit in. As well, it introduced an enormous controversy among the players. The ones who were with the team in the early going were often replaced by "better" players who became available at a later date. Thus, after just a few days some were sent packing or just never played again, damaging team morale and endangering future participation of players who didn't want to be treated like interchangeable parts.

All in all, the gesture of allowing pros to participate at the World Championships was as hollow as it was generous. It was a sign of progress, but not much more. The IIHF refused in future years to push the date of the Worlds back so as to allow better players to represent Canada, and the dates for submitting final rosters was, in reality, a precarious gamble for whomever coached the Canadian entry.

As well, for 1977, the IIHF refused to allow Canadians to play without helmets, which, at the time, virtually all of them had done their entire careers. Team Canada beat the teams it should have beaten – the United States, Czechoslovakia, Finland, West Germany, and Romania – but lost to Sweden 4–2 and were hammered 11–1 by the Soviets in the preliminary round. In the medal round, Canada clobbered the Swedes 7–0 and the Czechs 8–2, but were again thrashed by the Soviets 8–1. At the end of Canada's last game, Phil Esposito famously tossed his helmet into the stands in both relief and disgust.

Thanks to the two exhibition games Team Canada played in Sweden during the Summit Series, another advancement in the game occurred. Two players on that Swedish all-star team were Borje Salming and Inge Hammarstrom, and a year later they were signed by the Maple Leafs. Hammarstrom didn't have great success in the NHL, but Salming became the first European superstar in the league, paving the way for general managers in the 1970s to draft and sign Swedes and then Finns, both in the NHL and WHA.

In the 1980s, several high-level defections occurred, most notably the three Stastny brothers, Peter Ihnacak, and Jiri Crha (Vaclav Nedomansky had defected to the WHA in 1974, the first hockey player to do so.) Later in the decade, the first Soviets formally were allowed to leave their country to play in the NHL (Sergei Priakhin being the first) and the two greatest Soviet stars of the future left of their own devices, shocking the hockey world. Sergei Fedorov and Alexander Mogilny had established their reputations at the World Junior Championships, but left their country for Detroit and Buffalo, respectively, and with the advent of perestroika in 1992, the Iron Curtain fell and dozens of players from Russia, the Czech Republic, and Slovakia also came to North America.

By the mid-1990s, virtually all of the best hockey players in the world played in the NHL. Canada, which represented 99 per cent of the league into the early 1970s, was now at about 55 per cent, but the league was stronger and expanding from twelve to fourteen up to twenty-one and later thirty teams. The Original Six in 1967 was five times larger by the year 2000.

Because the NHL was both the best league in the world and also fully international, it made sense that the league would shut down to allow its players to participate in the Olympics, in Nagano, Japan, in 1998. This gave the league and its players the ultimate platform to perform and promote the game, and it was seen as a litmus test for 2002, when the Olympics would be held in Salt Lake City, Utah.

In 1970, not even minor pros could play for Canada at the World Championship, but in 1998 the entire Olympics tournament was professional!

It is clear that the 1972 Summit Series represented the birth of modern hockey. Out of it came the Canada Cup series, the influx first of Swedes and then Finns, and later other Europeans to the NHL, to the participation of NHL players at the Olympics and modern rules emphasizing speed and skill. After 1972, Canada took from the Soviets a greater appreciation for training and passing and skill, and after 1972 the Soviets learned that heart and desire can conquer as much skill as any team could offer.

In 1972, the two greatest hockey planets in the constellation collided, producing a new planet and new form of hockey life superior and majestic in every way. This book tells that story forty years on, a celebration of what happened then and how we remember the greatest eight games ever played.

TRAINING CAMP

The collection of superstar players who reported to Team Canada's training camp at Maple Leaf Gardens on Sunday, August 13, 1972, would hardly be recognized by the team that arrived in Montreal and then Toronto on Sunday, October 1, 1972, after the fifty most harrowing and heroic days of their lives.

As players filtered in for their medical exams, some were nicely tanned, others peeved at having had their summer cut short, others looking forward to a little casual shinny prior to the more important matter of their 1972–73 NHL seasons. That attitude was smacked hard in the face once the Summit Series began.

Coach Harry Sinden had the difficult and unique task of running the camp with assistant coach John Ferguson. They had thirty-five NHL players and three junior stars (goalie Michel "Bunny" Larocque, defenceman John Van Boxmeer, and forward Billy Harris). The idea was that the players would form two teams and scrimmage in the morning, and in the afternoon they'd be broken into two groups for practice and drills.

"The first week will be mostly devoted to getting their skating legs back," Ferguson explained at the time. "We'll go on stamina the second week."

Red Berenson, one of the few players with previous international experience, realized the importance of the camp far more than most of his teammates. "The disadvantage our team faces is that we're going against superbly conditioned athletes who have played as a team unit in competition and who have a much greater national stake in what they are doing. They have a lot more to prove."

How right he was about the first point – and how wrong about the second!

Sinden himself remained optimistic, even though he would live to regret his words after the first game on September 2. "I think our guys will be in adequate shape," he boasted. "I've been very impressed with their determination to get this job done and to do it right."

Peter Mahovlich takes a break from practice. Brother Frank is in the background.

Goalie Tony Esposito makes a save off Vic Hadfield as Serge Savard looks on.

In some respects, Sinden didn't have much to worry about at camp. He stuck to the obvious combinations wherever possible, keeping teammates as partners up front and on the blue line. That's why, for instance, Ron Ellis and Paul Henderson, two Leafs, played together, why the GAG (Goal-A-Game) line for the Rangers stayed together (Vic Hadfield–Rod Gilbert–Jean Ratelle) and why Black Hawks partners Bill White and Pat Stapleton skated on defence together.

What made things less complicated in the immediate future and much more so over the course of the series was that Sinden had promised all thirty-five NHLers they would play in at least one game. Thus, his lineup wasn't that important so much as having an obligation to keep to his word. It was only when the series was a hair's-breadth away from being lost that he had to make tough decisions, bench some star NHL players, and go with a set roster of seventeen skaters who he thought could beat the Soviets.

After just two days of practice, Ferguson declared with confidence that "they're going to be ready." There was little concern for the fact that Yvan Cournoyer was traipsing back and forth between Canada's camp and Montreal, where his hockey school carried on; ditto for Gary Bergman and Red Berenson, who missed a day to return to Detroit for their school; Phil Esposito, who took one morning off to fly to New York to film a television commercial; Brad Park, who missed a day in the hospital after taking a puck to the face; players who were overly relaxed and enjoying each other's company in the off hours; several members of the team who didn't arrive until several days later than most.

Undeterred, Sinden was delighted with the progress in an update he offered on August 22. "I had the camp broken down into stages," he said, reiterating Ferguson's words. "The first week was to work out the kinks. The second week [upcoming] is perhaps the most important because we'll start rather intense preparation. The third week the concentration will be aimed at mental readiness for that first game."

The team held the first of three Red-and-White intra-squad games on August 22. Using the two American referees who would work the first four games of the series itself, Len Gagnon and Gord Lee, the games were a good way to become familiar with international rules as much as sort out lines and team chemistry. White beat Red 8–5 before a crowd of 5,571 at the Gardens.

The next day, Bobby Orr arrived at camp, limping with his thrice-operated left knee in full recovery mode, clearly not ready to do any serious skating but desirous to give the players an emotional spark. His intentions were noble, and his opinions prescient.

"I had the itch to get started, just to be here with all the guys," he began. "I wanted to play in as many games as possible because this will be the greatest experience any of us likely will have in our careers. Maybe it's corny, but helping Canada win this series is important to me."

The second intra-squad game occurred on August 27, White again winning by a lower-scoring 4–2 count in front of 6,734 fans at the Gardens. A day later, the players gathered at the south end of the Gardens ice for the official team portrait, the mood still light and jovial, ignorance in this case truly being bliss.

The team's final warm-up game was played on August 29, and 8,742 fans watched White prevail by a 6–2 score. The most impressive performances came from the line of Henderson and Ellis with Bobby Clarke as the centreman. Sinden had put this troika together on the first day, and they impressed every practice since, clinching a starting role for game one as a result.

Team Canada travelled to Montreal on September 1 and held its final practice that afternoon leading to the first game of the series the next night. The Soviets had arrived a day earlier and were also ready. The teams had made their preparations in different ways, but they were ready for a head-on collision at the Forum on September 2, the start of the greatest eight games ever played.

Who on Team Canada knew?

The Red vs. White exhibition games were the only preparation Team Canada had before facing the Soviets.

COACH HARRY SINDEN – HOLDING IT ALL TOGETHER

There is no question the most difficult job at the Summit Series belonged to head coach Harry Sinden. He had made a name for himself as coach of the Boston Bruins from 1966 to 1970, a hugely significant period of the team's history. Bobby Orr was a rookie in Sinden's first year, and in his last year he led the Bruins to the Cup. He was out of hockey for the better part of two years, thus being available for a series at a time when all other NHL coaches were at training camp with their teams.

"Alan Eagleson contacted me," Sinden began. "What happened was that, unfortunately at the time, the company I was working for in upstate New York went into bankruptcy. I was down on vacation in Cape Cod, and I got word that the company was going out of business, and I had to get right back. So I was out of work. I got this call from Alan [Eagleson] asking me if I wanted to be the general manager and coach."

Although training camp was tough, Sinden would soon find out this was the easiest time of the whole experience. He invited thirty-eight players to camp, enough for two full teams, and he had two main tasks: to get the players in shape and to make lines and defensive pairings.

"It was August, and the players in many instances were reluctant to play. At first, it didn't seem all that important. They weren't on our payroll or anything, so in many ways it was a volunteer situation. To start a training camp with forty players who weren't trying out for a team in the middle of the summer, I had to get them in shape in a short period of time. So, the workouts were extremely strenuous. I thought it was the toughest two or three weeks of training I had put any of my teams through. We were very fortunate because they were all star players, and the very elite of the star players were the ones who worked the hardest, so that helped when we were trying to get everyone to cooperate."

Sinden had one fortuitous experiment work at camp, and many others that didn't. He put Bobby Clarke at centre on a line with two Maple Leafs wingers, Ron Ellis on the right side and Paul Henderson on the left, and the threesome stayed together the whole series. But other players went in and out of the lineup, on and off every imaginable line combination possible.

"A lot of the stuff you're led to believe is somewhat mythical; that coaches look at their team and know exactly who will play well with whom isn't true," Sinden explained. "You may have a scrimmage or exhibition game, and you see if they complement each other, and you leave them together. Other times, we tried to put a couple of players from the same team on the same line because even though they might not have played on the same line on their team, they might have some familiarity. Those lines were put together through a lot of experiment and through game-type situations. I wouldn't say they were formulated in my mind. We had three very competitive games in exhibition, and we started to figure out who were the players we were probably going to have to use the most, and in some instances what lines they'd be on."

Then there was the problem of keeping a training camp promise in light of ever-increasing pressure to win at a time when the series, now not assured by any means, was slipping away.

"We promised that every one of the players would play in at least one game. I don't think anyone realized the significance of the series, in Canada in particular, at that time, and I don't think anyone, except me, realized how good the Russians were going to be when we made that promise," Sinden acknowledged. "I had played and been involved in many games and watched them play a lot and knew how good they were, but I now had the best players in the NHL going to play against them, and even as impressed as I had been all those years, I thought the best NHL players would be able to beat them. So, it wasn't too difficult to promise thirty-five pretty darned good players that they'd play in a game. But I think when we finished in Vancouver is when we realized we had to pick the best nineteen players. We had to pick our team. And if somebody had not yet played, we're just going to have to break our promise."

In one sense, Sinden was victim of his own experience. He had played at the 1958 World Championship and won gold with the Whitby Dunlops and silver at the 1960 Olympics. He knew the international game, and knew the Soviets, but he was still overconfident.

"I had seen them play a lot, but against amateur teams, so you think, what would they be like playing against pros, and you don't have a high regard for the way they were piling up wins. But that was misleading. It didn't take long in Montreal to find out how misled I was because when that game was over, I don't think any of us didn't believe this was going to be really, really difficult. And it was."

Sinden really started to coach after game one. Training camp was done, the first game was an unmitigated disaster, and now he had to roll up his sleeves and figure some things out. He did.

"We made some adjustments after the Montreal game that kind of took us away from the general way that we played in the NHL in those days," he started. "We kind of changed the rules that we played by because of the opposition. The normal way was that the two wingers were responsible for the two point men, and your centreman in the NHL would come back and help out the defence in our end. We changed that somewhat, and we asked our centreman – because the Soviets did not shoot the puck from the point as often as we did in the NHL, and probably not as well – to play out somewhere between their two point men, freeing up our wingers to go back toward the corners to help our defencemen, so they wouldn't be caught in two-on-one situations down low too often. We made that adjustment after game one, and that stuck pretty much the rest of the series. Another thing had to do with them using the centre of the ice coming out of their own zone a lot more than we did in the NHL. In the NHL, the *modus operandi* was to come up the boards with the puck. They were an excellent passing team, a tremendous skating team, and as they broke out of their own end, their pass up through the centre was leaving us pretty vulnerable. We tried to shut that off."

These changes worked like a charm, but they were still only pieces of the winning puzzle, not the entire thing. One other strategy he employed was to have Clarke take almost every faceoff when Phil Esposito wasn't on the ice. Clarke was a master of the draw – and the Soviets were not – and he often ensured puck possession right off the bat.

"He was a tremendous player on that team," Sinden said of Clarke enthusiastically. "His numbers were great in the NHL, but not Gretzky-like. But he has to go down as one of the really top centres, from all aspects of the game, that the league has known. He was a top player."

While the rest of the country may have heaved a huge sigh of relief after game two, Sinden knew the battle was far from won. "I came to the reality of how difficult it was going to be to beat them when we were in Winnipeg and we had a 4–2 lead going into the third period and we ended up tying the game," Sinden revealed. "They played a fourth line that we hadn't seen before, and they absolutely dominated the period. We had outstanding goalkeeping that period, but it was all we could do to survive. We were only allowed one coach behind the bench, so John Ferguson couldn't stand behind the bench with me. But he could sit in the first row behind us. I can remember halfway through the third period turning to him and saying, 'My God, where did these guys come from?' It hit me then how good they really were, and it might be that we might not win this series."

The good and bad of the four games in Canada were the toughest aspects of Sinden's job. The home crowds expected glorious victories every night, and when they didn't get these they blamed the Canadians rather than praised the opposition. Within the team, though, Sinden still tried to keep his promise of getting every one of the players into a game, even though to do so was at the risk of forming a team worthy of its opponents.

"We had a lot of unrest on that team during the series," he conceded. "People weren't playing and were upset about it. We had fifty-goal scorers in the NHL who couldn't make the team. It was a tough act to deal with. We spent a lot of time addressing that. We split the team every day into two. Normally, I'd practise the team that was going to play that day or the next and John practised the others."

One significant sign that Sinden took positives from was the performance of the two teams over the course of the series. As Mickey Redmond noted, the Soviets never got better – or worse. They were consistently great the whole series. Canada, however, started poorly but got better and better. The coach agreed, even at a time when panic might have been the order of the day.

"Game five was the best game we played, or close to it, and we lost," he rationalized. "But I didn't see any noticeable change in the Soviet team from game one to game eight in terms of the way they played, their conditioning, their discipline, their skill set, which was better than ours. It was tough to cope with, but I didn't see a lot of change in the way they played."

After game five, Sinden focused on a set lineup, but he still had to contend with the goalies, who were the focus of the team and under extraordinary pressures of their own. "Neither of the goalies was so outstanding in any of the eight games that they won the job," Sinden explained of how he handled them. "They played quite well, but neither overshadowed the other at all. John and I felt that as the series went on and things looked pretty gloomy for a while, the pressure on the goaltender was immense. That would have been the case anyway. They are kind of a separate entity from the rest of the players, and they kind of live in their little cocoon before the game and have a different mountain to climb every night. We felt that with so much pressure that to ask them to get ready for every game, with only one day in between games, was

Coach Sinden behind the bench at the Luzhniki Arena in Moscow.

just going to be too much for them. We might have done that had one goalie shown that he was in much better form than the other, but that didn't happen. So, we went on the basis that it would be easier for a goalie to be ready if he had a couple of days off before he had to play."

Thus, Ed Johnston was the backup for games two through seven, so that the goalie not starting wouldn't have to dress, take warm-up, or even think at all about playing, making him mentally, physically, and psychologically that much sharper for when he did have to play.

In the end, while the players praised Sinden for being able to control the team off ice and coach it on ice to victory, he shot the praise right back.

"The players themselves were absolutely tremendous," he enthused. "When you're a pro hockey player and you only get a couple of months off a year, it's precious to you. We took it away from them. Their behaviour was sensational, I thought. They deserve the credit for sticking together. And that's one reason I had John Ferguson there. He was more apt to understand their problems and what they were going through than I was because I had been out of for a couple of years. He was a player just a year before. He had a lot to do with that."

Sinden had a job waiting for him upon his return, one that had been quietly discussed in the little free time he had in Moscow.

"When I got back, I was still living in upstate New York, but the Bruins had hired me. I spent a few days at home and then became their general manager. It happened during the series itself. The Bruins had Eagleson speak to me about it, and we talked about it during the series, and we made a deal."

There were two notable highlights for Sinden in Europe, and they are closely connected. As fate would have it, only he and Ferguson celebrated birthdays in the month of September, and in Sinden's case he turned forty while the team was in Sweden. "The Canadian Embassy in Stockholm threw a party for me at the embassy," he said with glee. "We had a great party. It was a beautiful palace. We all went there to celebrate my fortieth."

And did the players buy him a present? Sinden laughed. "They gave me a present with thirty-four seconds to go in game eight!"

#39 BILLY HARRIS – TAKING IT ALL IN

The expansion era Billy Harris (not to be confused with the Original Six Billy Harris) was the first overall draft choice by the New York Islanders in 1972, the team's inaugural season. He had an outstanding junior career in the OHL with the Toronto Marlies, culminating in 1971–72 when he led the league in scoring with 129 points.

"They invited me to training camp. They needed bodies. I'm from Toronto," he started. "There wasn't much of a chance I'd be playing in any of the games, but I wasn't in very good shape. About two weeks before training camp, I had two separate operations, one on my nose, one on my feet – both feet, in fact. I didn't have a chance to workout because I had trouble running. My nose had been broken so many times I had a deviated septum and needed a procedure to clear the air so I could breathe. But I could barely walk, let alone put my foot in my skate. I had Plantar warts removed from both feet, so that's the one thing I was disappointed about, that I couldn't have been in better shape at camp. But there was nothing I could do about it."

Harris was one of three pre-NHLers invited to camp along with defenceman John Van Boxmeer and goalie Michel "Bunny" Larocque.

"There were the three of us they invited just to help make the practice run more smoothly," he explained. "I played with Bunny later in Toronto. He was a great junior goalie. And that's why he was there because we needed four goalies to make two full teams. There were a lot of guys who were there for a couple of days and would then go away. I remember Cournoyer was commuting back and forth from Montreal. Several players had business deals or family obligations. But for us [juniors], it was a courtesy invitation because Eagleson was our agent. It was a great experience."

Of course, to a twenty-year-old at a camp with the finest players, the memories are many. "My first roommate was Eddie Johnston, one of the greatest guys of all time. It was my first meeting with all of these guys, but I knew some of the younger guys like Dale Tallon and Marcel Dionne from junior. About halfway through camp Bobby Orr shows up and rooms with Eddie, so I move down the hall to a room of my own, which is pretty neat. I'm at Team Canada's camp, living at the Sutton Place Hotel in a single room. How good is that?"

One lesser known fact about the invitations to the three juniors is that it included the entire tournament in Canada, not just training camp. "We spent another ten days after camp travelling across the country with the team, practising with them, talking to them off ice. After the Vancouver game, we all came back to Toronto, and I packed up and drove to Peterborough for the Islanders training camp. I had been the first overall draft that summer, and I was about five days late."

Harris's highlight came in Vancouver, a city not high on the list for members of the team itself.

"After game four we were in a bar and who was there but Bobby Hull! He had jumped to the WHA and couldn't play, but there he was! He was my idol growing up – I was a huge fan of the Chicago Black Hawks, and I got to meet him in Vancouver."

That gee-whiz thrill of meeting and playing alongside his heroes even for a short time continued throughout the 1972–73 season as the rookie Harris made his way through NHL cities for the first time.

"I remember my first time in the Chicago Stadium," he boasted. "The Islanders were a team of misfits then. We lost seven or eight guys to the WHA, and we were awful. In the warm-up, I'm talking to Dennis Hull, and he's asking how I'm doing. For a kid to go into the old Chicago Stadium and talk to Dennis Hull was huge. So then my teammates come over later and ask how the hell I know Dennis Hull! I explained I played with him at Team Canada. It was the same in every town where I knew players from Team Canada – Mickey Redmond in Detroit or Bobby Orr in Boston."

Harris got his own sweater, number 39, and although he isn't the first name one recalls from the Summit Series, make no mistake – he was there. "I learned more spending time with the guys off ice, talking to them, seeing how professionals behaved. On ice, it was drills and practise, so there wasn't as much learning. I got a plaque from Premier Bill Davis for being on the team, so it's pretty cool."

#40 JOHN VAN BOXMEER – PARTNERS WITH ORR

Drafted fourteenth overall by Montreal in 1972, John Van Boxmeer was the oddest name on the Team Canada training camp roster because he hadn't even played junior hockey. "I was playing Tier II hockey in Guelph," he explained. "Guelph wasn't even a major junior team at the time. I didn't even have an agent when I was drafted, but then I heard my name on the radio. My GM in Guelph told me that I couldn't go and see [Canadiens GM] Sam Pollock without an agent. I'd be playing for nothing. So he called Alan Eagleson for me. That's how the whole thing started."

That summer of 1972, Van Boxmeer was working for his general manager but not with the team. "I was working in Guelph at the time for the team's general manager who had a car dealership. I worked in the parts department driving parts around."

"I recall that the team wanted to get Jim Schoenfeld to come, but they had had so much difficulty with Buffalo getting Perreault and Martin in, and as well Alan Eagleson was my agent by then. I think everyone assumed we were just filling out the roster so we had thirty-eight guys. Bunny and I roomed together during the camp because we were both Montreal draft picks. It was a little different for Bunny and I because Billy had played for the Marlies, so it was his hometown, but for us everything was new and strange."

His first memory of camp speaks to the nature of what was then considered an exhibition series.

"The first thing I recall was driving to the Sutton Place Hotel on Bay Street in downtown Toronto, and as I pulled into the parking area, Tony and Phil Esposito were arriving as well. They were unloading beer from their car."

Van Boxmeer was the great unknown on the team, but he made an impression on day one.

"The player I remember most is John Van Boxmeer," recalled goalie Ken Dryden of the three junior recruits. "He was a sensation the first couple of days in camp. And, of course, he was more particularly one because nobody knew the name at all. The other guys were junior stars, but Van Boxmeer played Tier II. He had a great shot. He wasn't that big, but he had a really hard shot. He was somebody on the first two days of scrimmaging who looked like he really belonged."

Perhaps it didn't hurt that the defenceman had a good partner early on – Bobby Orr. "I was just in awe," Van Boxmeer said of his start. "It was an unbelievable treat. Bobby Orr was always my idol, and on the first day I was paired with him."

Reality set in quickly, though. While a talented kid playing in Guelph, his style of play was not going to translate well to the NHL right away. "I was kind of an offensive defenceman," Van Boxmeer described. "I was a pretty good skater, but I didn't have much knowledge of the game. Every time I got the puck, I'd just rush up ice. I remember John Ferguson told me, 'Son, I'm going to tie a rope to the crossbar and tie it around your neck with enough rope so you can reach centre ice.'"

Van Boxmeer and everyone else not playing in game one sat in the stands in Montreal, a night he remembers vividly. "We were up 2–0 early on. And the Russians had these old skates and beat-up gloves. I turned to Billy Harris and said, 'Geez, we might even get a chance to play.' Wrong!"

"We went right across Canada with the team. We were supposed to go to Moscow as well. That was the plan, but then Montreal wanted me to come to training camp. But for me, I'll always remember the goal Pete Mahovlich scored in Toronto."

Van Boxmeer made the jump straight from Tier II to the AHL's Nova Scotia Voyageurs for the 1972–73 season after the Habs' training camp. It was a remarkable leap, and one that soon led to a lengthy and successful NHL career.

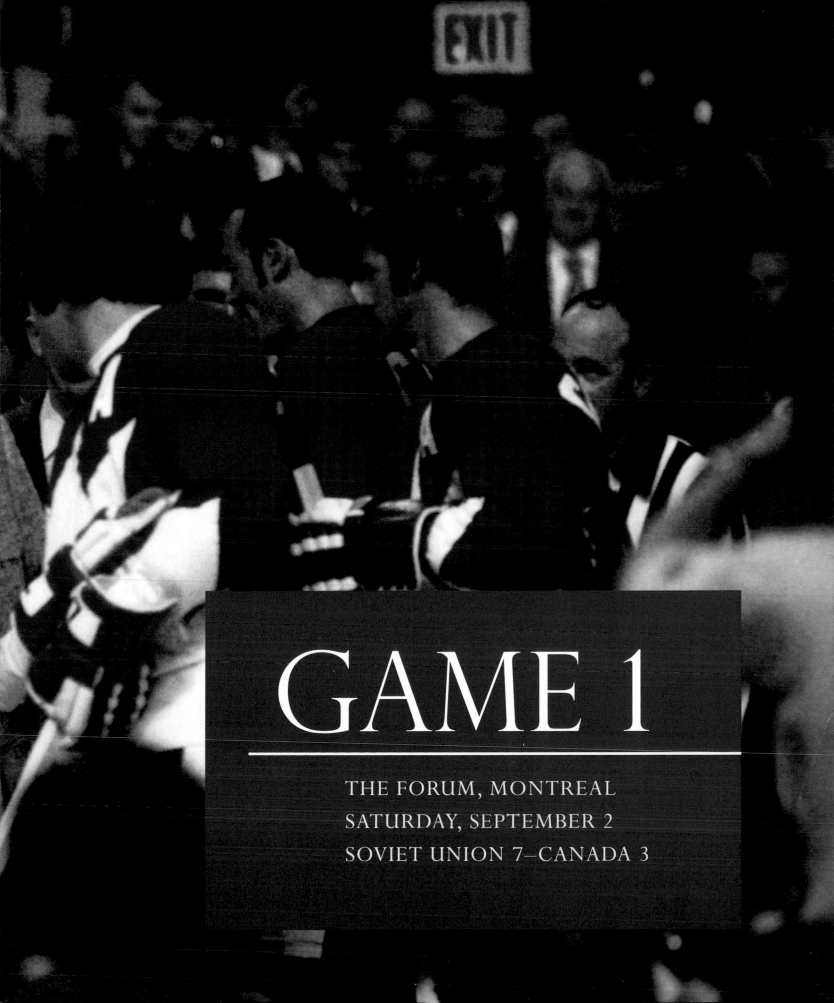

GAME 1

THE FORUM, MONTREAL
SATURDAY, SEPTEMBER 2
SOVIET UNION 7–CANADA 3

"One thing is very noticeable tonight, and that is the Canadian team have yet to produce a leader."

—FOSTER HEWITT

Soviet star Valeri Kharlamov is checked by Ron Ellis (#6) and Bobby Clarke as fog rolls through the Forum in game one.

SHOCKING START

Perhaps defenceman Rod Seiling said it best after the game, one of the most shocking results in hockey history: "It was like playing the seventh game of the Stanley Cup finals in our first pre-season game." Indeed, Team Canada was rocked by the superior conditioning and training of the Soviets, who started slowly but cruised to a flying 7–3 win to start the Summit Series.

Canada's prime minister, Pierre Elliott Trudeau, took part in a jovial pre-game ceremony, and the mood continued after Phil Esposito scored the first goal just half a minute after the opening faceoff when he batted a Frank Mahovlich rebound out of the air. Paul Henderson made it 2–0 just a few minutes later on a great play with his linemates. Bobby Clarke won the draw cleanly to Ron Ellis to the right of the Soviet goalie, Vladislav Tretiak, and Ellis moved the puck to Henderson at the top of the circle in one quick motion. His shot beat Tretiak under his glove, and Canada held a seemingly comfortable 2–0 lead.

Esposito had a glorious chance to make it 3–0 with a chance in close, but Tretiak was in perfect position to make the save. Soon after, both Jean Ratelle and Frank Mahovlich also had great scoring chances from in close, but it was Alexander Zimin who made it a 2–1 game.

Vladimir Petrov tied the game when he backhanded the puck in on a two-on-one rush while the Soviets were short-handed. Ironically, Petrov was one of only two right-handed shots on the team (the other being Yuri Lyapkin).

Esposito, the dominant player of the opening period, had another great chance to put Canada ahead late in the period, but again he was foiled by Tretiak.

The ice became foggy in the second period, one dominated by the Soviets' best player, Valeri Kharlamov. He put his team ahead on a sensational rush, beating defenceman Dow Awrey to the outside and then having his shot deflected by Awrey through Ken Dryden's pads. Kharlamov made it 4–2 later in the period with a bullet shot low under the glove of the tall Canadian goalie, sending the fans in the Forum into a state of shock.

Frank Mahovlich led a three-on-one but decided to shoot, and again Tretiak was there to make the critical save. Play-by-play commentator Foster Hewitt made several ingenious observations in the period, including: "I think it's more of a team effort against a group of individuals," he said of the Soviets' superior team play.

Esposito had two more chances to bring the score closer early in the third period but was unable to beat Tretiak. Canada got a goal all the same thanks to the Clarke-Henderson-Ellis line when Henderson made a great pass off the boards to Ellis in the high slot. He spotted Clarke to the side of the goal and made a sensational shot-pass to Clarke, who redirected the puck in.

This brought about several minutes of Canadian domination, and it seemed a matter of time before they would tie the game. However, Boris Mikhailov snuffed out the rally when he beat Dryden with a backhander between the pads as the goalie came well out of his net to challenge the shooter.

Less than a minute later, Yevgeni Zimin put the game out of reach when he fanned on a shot, bringing Dryden out of his net, and got the rebound with an open cage. Alexander Yakushev closed out the scoring with another backhand, again drawing Dryden down and out of his crease before scoring with a high shot.

"We were outplayed in every department by an excellent hockey team," Team Canada coach Harry Sinden said after the game. "We knew the Russians were good, but we had no idea they were that good."

Ken Dryden smothers the puck as Alexander Yakushev looks for a rebound.

LINEUPS

CANADA – Ken Dryden, Tony Esposito (did not play) – Brad Park, Don Awrey, Yvan Cournoyer, Phil Esposito, Frank Mahovlich, Bobby Clarke, Mickey Redmond, Peter Mahovlich, Gary Bergman, Ron Ellis, Rod Gilbert, Vic Hadfield, Red Berenson, Rod Seiling, Jean Ratelle, Paul Henderson, Guy Lapointe

SOVIET UNION – Vladislav Tretiak, Viktor Zinger (did not play) – Alexander Gusev, Vladimir Lutchenko, Viktor Kuzkin, Alexander Ragulin, Gennadi Tsygankov, Yuri Blinov, Alexander Maltsev, Yevgeni Zimin, Yevgeni Mishakov, Boris Mikhailov, Alexander Yakushev, Vladimir Petrov, Valeri Kharlamov, Vladimir Vikulov, Vladimir Shadrin, Yuri Lyapkin, Yevgeni Paladiev

GAME SUMMARY

FIRST PERIOD

1. Canada, P. Esposito (F. Mahovlich, Bergman) 0:30
2. Canada, Henderson (Clarke, Ellis) 6:32
3. Soviet Union, Zimin (Yakushev, Shadrin) 12:40
4. Soviet Union, Petrov (Mikhailov) 17:28(sh)
Penalties: Henderson (CAN) 1:03, Yakushev (URS) 7:04, Mikhailov (URS) 15:11, Ragulin (URS) 17:19

SECOND PERIOD

5. Soviet Union, Kharlamov (Maltsev) 2:40
6. Soviet Union, Kharlamov (Maltsev) 10:18
Penalties: Clarke (CAN) 5:16, Lapointe (CAN) 12:53

THIRD PERIOD

7. Canada, Clarke (Ellis, Henderson) 8:22
8. Soviet Union, Mikhailov (Blinov) 13:32
9. Soviet Union, Zimin (unassisted) 14:29
10. Soviet Union, Yakushev (Shadrin) 18:37
Penalties: Kharlamov (URS) 14:45, Lapointe (CAN) 19:41

SHOTS ON GOAL

Canada:	10	10	12	32
Soviet Union:	10	10	10	30

IN GOAL

Canada:	Dryden
Soviet Union:	Tretiak

REFEREES

Len Gagnon (USA) and Gord Lee (USA)

OUTSTANDING PLAYERS

Canada:	Bobby Clarke
Soviet Union:	Valeri Kharlamov

#8 ROD GILBERT – A TIMELY GOAL

Although Rod Gilbert was an obvious choice to play for Team Canada in 1972, his participation was not so easily assured. Gilbert had finished his twelfth NHL season, all with the New York Rangers, by the time the summer of 1972 rolled around, and he had had his best season in 1971–72. Playing on the GAG (Goal-A-Game) line with longtime friend Jean Ratelle at centre and Vid Hadfield on left wing, Gilbert scored a career-best forty-three goals and ninety-seven points. There was just one problem – he was being recruited for the WHA, and Team Canada insisted a player had to be under an NHL contract for 1972–73 to play in the Summit Series.

"It was a very confusing time for me when I accepted the invitation," Gilbert admitted. "I was at a crossroads in my career. The WHA had just been formed, and I was in the same position as Bobby Hull. He was named First All-Star for left wing, and I was named First All-Star for right wing for the past season. And then I was asked to go to Toronto for the Team Canada training camp. Jean Ratelle and Vic Hadfield had signed with the Rangers and we had the best line that year. [GM] Emile Francis didn't acknowledge that I had been offered five times my NHL salary to play with the Cleveland Crusaders, and so had defenceman Brad Park, who also had an outstanding year for us. We were negotiating five-year contracts with Nick Mileti, a billionaire. He wanted to raid the Rangers, I think because he had wanted an NHL expansion team and didn't get one. He had built a beautiful arena for the Cavaliers in the NBA and wanted a hockey team. I was almost there signing, but at the end of July we went to Toronto and Vic and Jean had signed with the Rangers. I was really conflicted. But when I got back to New York, Emile had changed his mind and signed me and Park and Ed Giacomin and a few others to much bigger salaries. That was emotional, but that's how I became eligible for Team Canada."

Over and above that, Gilbert was a typical veteran and community member who needed to work in the summers. "It was also tough because I had a hockey school in New York with Brad Park for two months, July and August, and we had to disband that," he explained. "We had two hundred kids, but we had to give that up. This was our vacation. Brad and I were playing golf and teaching at the school. But it was exciting to join Canada and to see all the other great players who were chosen."

The GAG line was the only forward line chosen in its entirety, and given their incredible season one would have thought they'd be the lynchpin to the team's offence. Not so. Not after game one, in Montreal.

"We were not in shape, and we were not prepared to counteract their style of play," Gilbert readily admitted. "They brought to us a style we hadn't seen before, all five guys moving up ice at the same time and not giving up the puck. On our first shift, we were out maybe a minute and a half, and we came back to the bench and none of us had touched the puck. With the Russians, if they couldn't carry the puck in, they went back, reorganized, and tried again. We played against Kharlamov's line, and we were wondering where this guy came from. He was that good."

As Gilbert confirmed, the opening-game disaster was in part because the Canadians were playing against a completely unknown entity. "We didn't know anything about international hockey," he said. "I didn't even know Canada had a team at the Olympics. I never watched the World Championships on television. I did not know one name on that team. Not one. Our scouts came into the room maybe once to tell us how bad they were and how poor their goalie was. It was very disorganized and unprofessional."

And after game one, Gilbert experienced another, more personal shock. "It was tough for me after game one," he said. "My brother, Jean, who is six years older and was my mentor, asked me in Montreal, 'What happened out there?' I said, 'You had a ticket. You saw. Did you see how good they were?' He said, 'They weren't that good. You were all a bunch of bums. And furthermore, you're a disgrace to your country.' He's my mentor, my brother. He directed my career. I went to Guelph when I was sixteen. My parents didn't want me to go, but he told them I was going. He persuaded them. And he's telling me that."

"When we got to Toronto, things went bad," Gilbert continued. "Vic Hadfield is from just outside Toronto, and Harry decided to bench the whole line for game two at Maple Leaf Gardens. It was embarrassing for Vic, who had all his family and friends there, and he was very angry with Harry. That was the beginning of the trouble for Vic. He told Harry that he was blaming our line for the loss in Montreal. Sinden said he had thirty-five players, and he wanted to see everyone at least once. It didn't satisfy Vic. That was very difficult."

Gilbert didn't play in game three either, but Ratelle did, and in game four Ratelle and Gilbert were reunited, playing on a line with Peter Mahovlich. Hadfield played as well, but not much.

Rod Gilbert was a member of the Rangers' high-flying GAG line.

"By the time we got to Sweden, we were in much better condition and the three of us played as a line for both games," Gilbert noted.

The two games in Stockholm were the first such experience for Gilbert on the much larger European ice. "We'd never been exposed to big ice like that before," he admitted. "We weren't invited to the Olympics. I was concentrating on the Rangers in my career. There's a lot more room behind the net. We could make some plays back there. That's what impressed me about the bigger ice."

"But in Moscow, Harry took Vic out and put in Frank Mahovlich. Frank had been sick in Vancouver and hadn't played in ten days, so he needed to play." The result was that Hadfield had had enough. Despite protestations from his linemates, he flew home. "We tried to persuade him not to go," Gilbert said. "We said, 'Vic, this is only one game.' But it stemmed from the Toronto game. He was still angry. He said if they didn't need him, he didn't want them. The atmosphere in Moscow was very stressful. Imagine if we had lost that series."

Gilbert excelled in Moscow. In fact, he and Paul Henderson were the only Canadians to register at least one point in all four games at Luzhniki Arena. "I played on a line with Jean and Dennis Hull," he began. "I had played with Ratelle since we were eight years old, so whoever they put there it was a matter of him complementing us. Dennis played pretty much like Vic. He had a big shot, and he was a digger in the corners, so it worked out well. But by that time, we weren't the offensive line. Our job was to make sure the other team didn't score. Although Ratelle and I are two Hall of Famers for offensive reasons, we changed our style when we got to the sixth, seventh, eighth games. We weren't in scoring mode anymore. We were fighting for our lives. We just wanted to make sure they didn't score on us. We had learned our lesson. We backchecked, played well in our end. And we were in good shape then, too."

One of the greatest differences in the series was team play and strategy. Gilbert noted the difference between Canada's innate improvisation and the almost chess-like puck movement of the Soviets. "We never played a technical game in Canada," he described. "We dropped the puck and tried to score goals. There was no communication between players to say, 'If you play here the puck will go there.' Nothing. It was all instinctive. The Russians were all technical. They planned what to do with the puck and how to move it."

Gilbert's only goal of the series came at a critical time. In game seven, with the score tied 2–2 early in the third period, he beat Tretiak from in close to give Canada the lead. "I brought the puck toward the front of the net and got off a really good backhand. It was pretty exciting." Although the Soviets tied the game three minutes later, Paul Henderson scored the best goal of the series late in the game to give Canada the crucial 4–3 victory. That set the stage for game eight and the miraculous win in the final minute.

"We celebrated at the hotel," Gilbert finished, "but it was disappointing in one way. The Russians were also there with their wives, but we couldn't talk to them. There were some speeches, and then they all disappeared. They weren't allowed to talk to us. I would have liked to exchange some thoughts with them. It took a lot of years for that when they came to Ottawa to play three games for the fifteenth anniversary in 1987. I remember it was in Ottawa because both teams took the same bus after the game and went to drink some beers. Everything in Ottawa closes at 11:00 p.m., so we went across the river to Hull. And the Russians were drinking vodka on the bus. We get to the town and there's a big sign that says, 'Entering Hull,' and Dennis was telling all the Russians they named a town after him because we kicked their ass!"

#11 VIC HADFIELD –
FROM TEE TO (CANADIAN) RED

Vic Hadfield was the left-winger on the New York Rangers' GAG line and had finished fourth in NHL scoring in 1971–72 with 106 points and tied with Bobby Hull for second in goals with fifty (behind only Phil Esposito's sixty-six). Although his being invited to training camp was a no-brainer, the series didn't go as he had hoped.

"I was in the golf business in Oakville, Ontario, when I got the call," he related, "and it was an honour to represent Canada. I had just signed a five-year contract with the New York Rangers, and then to have an opportunity to play for Canada with only thirty-five other guys, and two of them being my linemates, Jean Ratelle and Rod Gilbert, there was no hesitation. We had been together quite a few years and had a couple of outstanding years, in my estimation. They broke us up a couple of times, but to be selected as a line was quite an honour."

In fact, they were the only complete line invited, so it was memorable. But they were still just three players of a much larger, and very talented, group. "With thirty-five guys, we also knew that we can't all play in the same game, so we all knew that at some point there would be lineup changes, which is fine. It's part of the game."

Unfortunately for the Rangers' trio, they had a tough start in game one, in Montreal, and when Coach Sinden made changes for the second game, all three were scratched. "We weren't prepared to play them the way it ended up that we had to play them," Hadfield theorized. "We weren't going to run those guys or scare them. They were hard as nails. And they certainly had the skill. Here we are trying to knock them through the boards, and it backfired. We were set back. I'll never forget that first game. We had to change our thinking, and we had to do it fast or we would really be in trouble. That's when they started to change things."

Change came out of necessity and desperation, but it was clear almost from the first minute of play that two different ways of playing the game were colliding. "Our hockey was always the left-winger goes up the left wing and the right wing goes up and down the right wing, but those guys were all over the place with their drop passes and circling," Hadfield explained. "We had to change. We had to use our head, be a bit more disciplined, and not try to play a style we didn't know."

Hadfield didn't play in game two, a huge disappointment given he was born and grew up just west of the city. "Growing up in Oakville, the Leafs were always my favourite team," he noted. "The biggest amateur team to win at the World Championship was probably the Whitby Dunlops, so we were a little bit aware of international hockey, but my focus was on the NHL and the Leafs."

The Rangers threesome was reunited for game four in Vancouver, and that also turned out to be a dubious evening of hockey. The team had a few days off, flew to Stockholm for practice and two exhibition games, and the GAG line was reunited, but only briefly. The team then flew on to Moscow for game five.

"Before we left Sweden, we had an idea how the Russians would treat us," Hadfield said of the Soviets' intimidation tactics. "We flew into Moscow, and arrived late at night. We looked out the window and saw all the lights and realized we were in Moscow. We landed and sat at the end of the runway for about an hour. Then, they moved in, took our equipment off, put it on the bus – and we couldn't find the bus driver. We got to our hotel, and we all had little cots about two feet wide. They all had blankets with holes in the middle. We wondered if we had to crawl through the hole to get into bed. They had to find us different rooms with proper beds. When we woke up in the morning, we discovered they'd taken all of our food and beer. We went down to practice, and after had a shower, but there was no hot water. The hot water came on a while later, and then we couldn't find the guy who had the towels. They did all these things to throw the guys off, but what it did was made the guys stick together more."

Things went downhill after that for Hadfield, and he reacted badly when he wasn't named to the lineup for game five.

"We had a team meeting before game five, and the coaches decided to go with eighteen guys, which was probably the way to go. We were there as a team. The thing that bothered the thirteen or fourteen guys who weren't going to get the opportunity to play was that we couldn't practise as a team. Meanwhile, our teams in North America were at training camp. If I wasn't going to play, and as captain of the Rangers I had just signed a new contract, we were all told we could go home. It was decided we'd have a press conference to announce the team the rest of the way and the other guys were going home. The guys going home were supposed to go on two flights, one in the afternoon and the other at night, and the press conference was supposed to take place between the flights. So, three of us jumped on the early plane, but they cancelled the press conference. The other guys saw what was going on, and decided to stay, and the three of us got skewered. Johnny Esaw ended up calling a press conference in Toronto to explain what happened, which I attended, and then the rest of the team realized we supported them from day one."

Hadfield was trying to see the big picture in 1972 when he flew home early, and forty years later his philosophy hasn't changed. "We probably didn't play as well as we should have," he said of his line's performance in games one and four. "But I certainly wasn't going to just sit there and not stay in shape at a very important time of my career and for the New York Rangers. We should have won the Stanley Cup in the spring of 1972, and you don't get too many of those chances. We had a good team, but I thought I should get home. It was my decision as captain."

Of course, Hadfield found a television in New York to watch the final games, and he remained an integral part of Team Canada ever after. "I congratulated every player as I met them during the season. And I made friends. I stayed close to Fergie 'til the day they put him in the ground. Right through to today we all get together and support each other. We've built some pretty good relationships over the last forty years by being a part of Team Canada."

Vic Hadfield skates near the Soviet goal of Vladislav Tretiak.

#18 JEAN RATELLE –
A CLASS ACT EARNS MORE RESPECT

As centreman for the New York Rangers' top-scoring line, Jean Ratelle was both a scorer and passer. Think Bryan Trottier after him or Jean Béliveau before. His wingers were Rod Gilbert on the right side and Vic Hadfield on the left, and in 1971–72 the threesome finished 3–4–5 in league scoring, Ratelle on top with 109 points (forty-six goals).

"Our line did a little bit of everything," Ratelle explained. "We were able to make plays, and I had great shooters in both Rod and Vic. They could score goals, and I could score goals, too, but they were the guys with their slap shots. I didn't do that. They were also both very good in the corners. The three of us complemented each other, and we always knew where we were going to go on the ice. When you play with the same players for a long period of time, you know where they're going to be and what they're going to do most of the time. That was our best asset, that we had played together for so long."

As a result of their remarkable chemistry, the entire line was invited to training camp, the only threesome so honoured. "It was just like a regular training camp. Everyone got invited and then some players were elected to play. Our line had a great year the previous year, so there was a good chance we'd be elected to play."

"I lived in Montreal in the summers, in Brassard. I was working at a golf course three days a week as an assistant pro. I had been doing that for a few years. If I wasn't going to make it in hockey, maybe I would have been able to make it in golf. As it turned out, things kept going in hockey, so I didn't have to worry about golf."

Ratelle was physically fit in a general sense, but like his Team Canada teammates was by no means ready for a gruelling series. "I jogged about three times a week for a month before I got to training camp," he said. "That's not too much, really, compared to what the Russians were doing. They trained all year and were in really good shape. Our summers are for resting. And besides, there was no place for me to train anyway. In the '60s and '70s, there were no gyms around. I would have had to go to the YMCA in Montreal to work with the weights."

Typically, Ratelle's knowledge of the Soviets and the international game was minimal at best. "When I was growing up, I knew we sent amateur teams to the World Championships and Olympics, like the Whitby Dunlops, I remember. I think Harry Sinden played for that team. That was an amateur team, so there was

The smooth-skating Jean Ratelle was a fierce competitor and sportsmanlike superstar rolled into one.

nothing to look forward to for me. I had signed a contract with the New York Rangers, so you couldn't think about international hockey."

The terrible result of game one spelled the end for the line in the Summit Series. All three sat out game two, and only Ratelle was back for game three, in Winnipeg. He missed game four, but then played all the games in Moscow. "We got pretty badly beat, and our line didn't do much," Ratelle admitted of the opening-game loss. "They broke our line up. It was a game we wanted to forget, but we couldn't at the time."

Ratelle's only goal of the series came in Winnipeg, late in the first period, to give Canada a 2–1 lead after a sensational pass from Yvan Cournoyer to spring him free. "I had a breakaway against Tretiak and scored. Shot off the post, left side, and in. I saw a little opening. In those days, goalies didn't play the butterfly; they stood up more. They usually gave you a little more room on one side than the other, but Tretiak didn't give much. He was a great goaltender."

The GAG line was reunited in Sweden, and the three played together for both games. "It was good to go to Sweden because it gave us some time to play together a little more and play some games that didn't matter too much," Ratelle noted. "We could relax a bit and get in good shape. That's why we played better in Moscow — we were in better shape."

Perhaps, but Hadfield was not in the plans. He was scratched for game five and decided to fly back to the Rangers' training camp. "He came to tell us he'd be leaving," Ratelle recalled. "For me, if I didn't play, I didn't play, but I was going to stay. I think Rod said the same thing. I mean, we hadn't played in a couple of games anyway. It was a great trip. As it turned out, I played all the four games in Moscow."

Hadfield's departure left Harry Sinden scrambling, but he put Dennis Hull on the left side and he fit right in, albeit in a different role. "It was a little different playing with Dennis," Ratelle acknowledged. "We weren't as offensive as we had been with Vic, but I think that's why were put together. We were more defensive. But with Dennis you just got him the puck and he'd shoot. He had a great shot, too."

Ratelle had a different and interesting hypothesis for the success of Henderson's success in the series. "He knew that he could score on Tretiak, and Tretiak knew that Henderson could score on him. Sometimes that happens, a player feels he can score on a particular goalie. Paul felt he could score on him. Paul had a really good wrist shot. Tretiak probably didn't want Paul Henderson to shoot on him. He was so good."

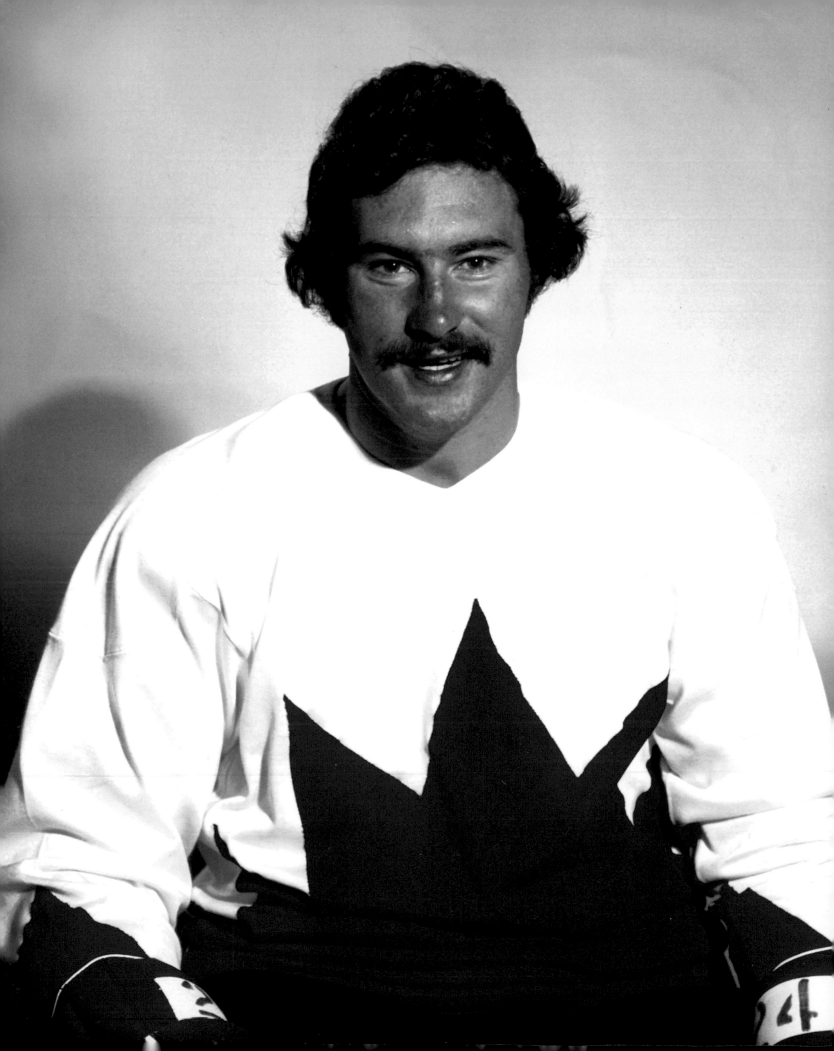

#24 MICKEY REDMOND – YOUNG MAN'S GREAT STRIDES

ichael "Mickey" Redmond said it best: "We were in pretty good shape for the shape we were in!"

That captures the essence of what Canada faced when it began the Summit Series, a team rounding into shape playing a team in peak physical condition, from best player to worst.

"We finished a season the first of May or so, and then our skates went against the wall and they weren't picked up until September 15 when we went to camp with the purpose of getting into shape. When we were asked to go to camp mid-August, the first thing we thought about was, 'Oh, man, this is interrupting my summer, my down time, my good times.' But, when you realize what you're into, meaning representing your country, that supersedes your down time. However, that didn't make us competitive – we had done nothing before training camp. Zero. When you think about it, it's amazing that we won the series. As I've described it, it's like me taking my left hand and putting it on my eyebrow. The Russians started there and ended there. We started about our elbow and ended just above the eyebrow. The ability of Canadians to reach down, to the heart, the commitment that we have as Canadians, allowed us to come back and win that series. It was the only reason we won."

Redmond grew up in a hockey family. His brother, Dick, had a long career in the NHL, and their father was both a player and executive. Although Mickey hadn't much knowledge of the Soviets from on-ice experience, he had plenty of anecdotal evidence from paternal influences.

"My dad had a lot of interaction with the Russians over the years, not only through the Whitby Dunlops at the World Championships in 1958 in Oslo, Norway, but he was on and off over the years the president of the Peterborough Petes for perhaps twenty of the next thirty years," he explained. "It was only after my brother and I left that he became directly involved. He didn't want any conflict. The Petes played the Russians on a pretty much annual basis for several years. I remember him telling me that the Russians were well prepared to play us in 1972, and that they'd been studying us for fifteen years. They're not going into this blind. And he was right. They were something that none of us expected. It was ridiculous how good they were."

Redmond was one of the league's bright young stars. He had played three and a half years with the Canadiens before being traded to Detroit in a deal that brought Frank Mahovlich to the Habs, and in 1971–72 he had a breakout season with the Wings, scoring forty-two goals. The next two years he reached fifty, but his career ended halfway through 1975–76 because of a chronic back injury.

Mickey Redmond only played the first game in Montreal, but stayed with the team for the entire series.

"It was a very competitive training camp," he recalled from his perspective. "I don't think there were any givens. There were six or seven right-wingers, six or seven left-wingers, so you just busted your rear end to be as good as you could be and be the right person for the kind of player they wanted."

Redmond must have done something right because he was in the lineup for game one, in Montreal, but it wasn't the wonderful outcome he had hoped for when he skated off the ice three periods later.

"I felt like a boy back in Peterborough on the pond, a boy playing against men. That's what it felt like. I remember being completely outclassed. We chased them around. We couldn't catch them. I tried to hit two or three guys out of frustration – never got them. They were so nifty and nimble. I remember coming in after the game completely beaten up and drenched and thinking, 'Holy crap, what are we going to do about this?' We got our dinner handed to us – breakfast, lunch, and dinner."

As fate would have it, game one was all that was in the cards for Redmond, but he has nothing but great memories of the series.

"They changed the lineup. We won. Stuff happens," he says philosophically. "You can look at it and say, 'Geez, I only got into one game,' but I don't look at it like that at all. I was chosen one of the best thirty-eight players in the world to play in this thing and play for your country, and then to make the opening lineup was incredible. What a great honour."

Part of Redmond's status was determined by an illness he contracted in Stockholm that persisted in Moscow – with hilarious results.

"I got very sick in Sweden," he explained. "I got the flu. In Moscow, I slept in late and missed the team bus. I don't know how I got to the arena, but that arena was on lockdown, and there were two ladies who were at least 250 pounds guarding the front door. It was snowing out. I had Peter Mahovlich's trench coat on, which came down to the ground on me because he was six-foot-five. I was freezing and sick, and I had to find a diversion of some sort to get in, and I did. I was standing between two sets of doors trying to keep warm, and had no ID, and I bolted through the door and into the arena. I was running down the corridor as these two women chased me. I went down by the Zamboni entrance and ran for safety into our dressing room. If they had caught me, I would have been in jail."

Redmond wasn't married at the time, so wives' privileges weren't necessary, but he got an equally happy treat when his mom flew over for the Moscow leg of the series.

"I had the great fortune of my dad having been a Whitby Dunlop and going around the world, so he said to me, 'Why don't you take your mom over there? I've already been.' So I did. And my mom and Mrs. Mahovlich roomed together and became known as Monty Hall because they were bartering and exchanging over there with Mars bars and blue jeans like nobody's business. They had a ball. It was a great time in her life to be there."

While recovering, Redmond got to watch the best hockey ever played, and he appreciated every minute of what he witnessed. The evolution of the Summit Series from an exhibition to an historic matchup left him in awe.

"When you take thirty-eight of the top players in the world who played in the best league in the world, and they go out and get into shape and play together, there's an awful lot of raw talent there. When you put Canadian heart with that talent in the toolbox, you get what happened – the ability to reach down the way we couldn't get before because we weren't able to because of conditioning. The mother of invention is necessity. It was all about reaching down. Once we realized we were in a very, very tough spot, when we felt that an eight-point sawoff would have been a win for them, and after game five we couldn't afford a hiccup – that was it. You couldn't script what happened after that. We got closer together as a group."

He expanded: "Before the series, we were used to being guys who somewhat hated each other. It wasn't love at first sight. The Bruins and Canadiens used to have brawls all the time. Then you go into the dressing room and wonder, 'How do I interact with Wayne Cashman? He tried to take my head off a couple of months ago.' You have to do a lot of growing up. You have to put that stuff aside, but it doesn't happen instantly. It takes time for a large group to bond together, which is why Sweden was really crucial for us. It's remarkable that we got that good that quickly, but it's also remarkable that we were able to stand shoulder to shoulder as one so quickly, having been archrivals just a few weeks ago, and having each other's backs, and that was the key. We had to forget that one guy was a Bruin and the other guy was a Black Hawk or Canadien. Egos had to be put aside for the better of the country – and they were. It's still amazing to me that what we thought was a skate-about, so to speak, turned into what it did."

Of course, as he well knew, though, it wasn't just about bonding and getting into better shape and putting egos aside. "I wouldn't go far as to say we were in great shape by the time we got to Moscow. It's more about the heart. There was no way even at the end we could compete with those guys physically. They were way ahead of us."

As Redmond sees it, that heart still factors into the equation lo these four decades later. "The whole experience makes you a better person, and that's the key. I think we were all the same players [after returning home], but we were different people, better people for the experience. And to have that bond forty years later is pretty special. I made some very good friends that I never thought I would, like Cashman and Esposito. Getting to know those guys and being a teammate taught me a lot about professionalism."

And for Redmond, the bond carries on to the next generation. After his early retirement, he remained in Detroit and worked in radio and television for the Red Wings, a job he loves and continues to do more than thirty years later. The Red Wings had a terrible team for many years, but in the mid-1990s they started to challenge for the Stanley Cup with seeming annual consistency, and they have been the class of the NHL ever since. Part of their success was the integration of Soviet players into the Detroit roster at the undertaking of coach Scotty Bowman, who created a "Russian Five" much as the old Soviets did. Among their number were Igor Larionov and Vyacheslav Fetisov, two veterans who were small children in the Soviet Union, watching their heroes lose in the Summit Series in which Redmond played!

"Larionov and Fetisov knew that I played for Team Canada in '72," Redmond said with a playful wink. "They watched those games. I'd mention some of the old Russian names and said I'd played against them, and those were their idols. We had some laughs about that."

Redmond earned his start in Montreal thanks to an excellent training camp, but coach Harry Sinden revamped the roster for game two and Redmond found himself on the outside looking in.

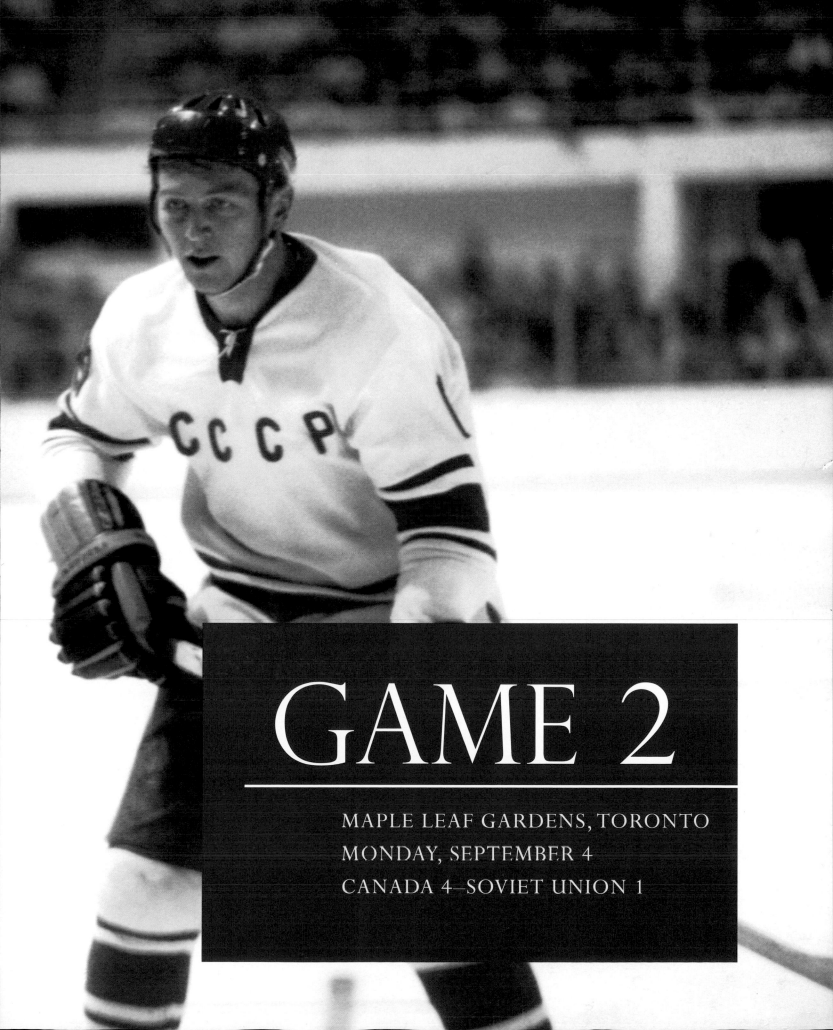

GAME 2

MAPLE LEAF GARDENS, TORONTO

MONDAY, SEPTEMBER 4

CANADA 4–SOVIET UNION 1

"I was always under the impression that international rules wouldn't allow any rough stuff in the game, but I don't think I've ever seen an NHL game with more of the old gusto than this one."

—FOSTER HEWITT

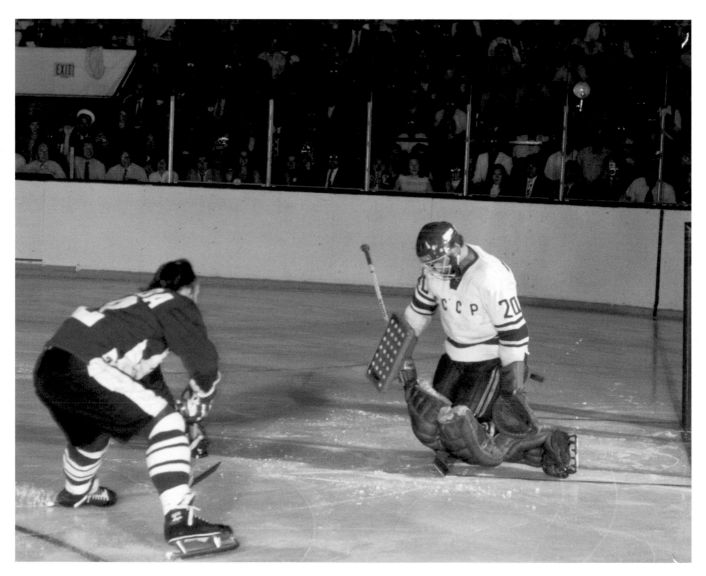

Yvan Cournoyer scores a breath-taking, game-winning goal on Tretiak in game two.

CANADA WINS MUST-WIN GAME

While Soviet coach Vsevolod Bobrov made two lineup changes for game two, Canada's coach, Harry Sinden, completely revamped his roster. He had goalie Tony Esposito in net, and seven of seventeen skaters were switched to produce a lineup more conducive to physical play. The crux of the changes saw centre Phil Esposito with two new wingmen in the form of Bruins teammate Wayne Cashman and J-P (Jean-Paul) Parise. As well, Sinden dressed six defencemen instead of the five he used in Montreal.

The result for Canada was a sensational turnaround from shocking defeat to remarkable victory, or, as Milt Dunnell wrote in the *Toronto Star* with alliterative panache: "The difference [between the two games] was about the same as between a wedding and a wake."

And the best man for Canada at this wedding was none other than Peter Mahovlich, who scored one of the finest goals the game of hockey has ever witnessed, a short-handed gem early in the third period to more or less seal the victory.

An interesting pre-game ceremony featured former prime minister Lester B. Pearson coming out on the ice to give Team Canada player Jean Ratelle (another of the scratches in that night's lineup) the eponymous NHL award for top player as selected by his peers. After a brief speech in English and French, Ratelle left the ice and the game began.

The first period was dominated by the coaches. Rules made clear the home team gets last change for putting players on the ice, but the referees didn't seem to know which was designated home team and were unable to administer the rule properly. The result was often two or three line changes on one whistle as coaches jockeyed to match lines and avoid matchups simultaneously.

Esposito had the best scoring chance of a scoreless opening period, but Canada got plenty of momentum from that physical play Sinden was looking for as well as from the penalty-killing brothers of Frank and Peter Mahovlich. They were sensational in a period in which Canada had the only two minors.

As well, Tony Esposito was excellent when he had to be, and brother Phil opened the scoring early in the second on a delayed penalty. He was dumped in the Soviet end, but got up just as Cashman did the spadework and got the puck in front. A great move with quick hands to get the puck from backhand to forehand fooled Tretiak, and Espo beat the goalie with a quick shot.

"Let's just say that Cashman was one of our leaders in changing the tone of this game from the one in Montreal," Sinden offered after the victory.

Canada controlled play in the period, using the body to break up the Soviet rushes and circling passing plays that marked their style. Sinden used Bobby Clarke for most key faceoffs, but it was still a 1–0 game after forty minutes. The game changed irrevocably in the first half of the final period. Brad Park made a sensational pass to Yvan Cournoyer, streaking down the right wing, and Cournoyer blazed past defenceman Alexander Ragulin and rifled a shot between Tretiak's pads for a 2–0 lead.

Alexander Yakushev made things close again when he was left alone in front and converted a nice pass from Yuri Lyapkin on a power play, but then the Mahovliches went to work. Canada got another penalty, but on the penalty kill Phil Esposito backhanded the puck off the boards out to centre ice. Peter Mahovlich got control and went one-on-one with defenceman Yevgeni Paladiev.

Mahovlich froze the defenceman when he wound up to shoot, but he kept the puck and moved in alone on goal. Tretiak slid to the ice in the direction Mahovlich was skating, but the Canadian stopped and knocked the puck in the open near side. It was one of the most spectacular goals ever scored, and was the key to victory. Brother Frank added the final goal two minutes later, and Canada left Maple Leaf Gardens with greater confidence, knowing they could beat the Russians.

One fan's sign in the end Blues proclaimed, "This is our game," and on this night Team Canada confirmed as much.

Named the Canadian player of the game, Phil Esposito was interviewed on ice by Johnny Esaw after, foretelling the historic interview in Vancouver just four nights later. On this night, Phil was all smiles: "This is bigger than winning the Stanley Cup as far as I'm concerned," said Espo, who was qualified to draw the comparison because he had won the Cup just a few months earlier with the Boston Bruins. "This is as excited as I've ever been in my life. I was excited Saturday night in Montreal, but this is even bigger."

Peter Mahovlich puts the finishing touches on his sensational short-handed goal early in the third period of game two.

Team Canada had skated off the ice after game one not knowing international decorum called for handshakes after the game, a protocol the players made sure to follow after game two.

LINEUPS

CANADA – Tony Esposito, Ed Johnston (did not play) – Brad Park, Yvan Cournoyer, Phil Esposito, Frank Mahovlich, Bobby Clarke, Peter Mahovlich, Gary Bergman, Ron Ellis, Paul Henderson, Guy Lapointe, Pat Stapleton, Bill Goldsworthy, Wayne Cashman, Bill White, Stan Mikita, J-P Parise, Serge Savard

SOVIET UNION – Vladislav Tretiak, Viktor Zinger (did not play) – Alexander Gusev, Viktor Kuzkin, Alexander Ragulin, Gennadi Tsygankov, Alexander Maltsev, Yevgeni Zimin, Yevgeni Mishakov, Boris Mikhailov, Alexander Yakushev, Vladimir Petrov, Valeri Kharlamov, Vladimir Shadrin, Vyacheslav Anisin, Yuri Lyapkin, Yevgeni Paladiev, Vyacheslav Starshinov, Vladimir Lutchenko

GAME SUMMARY

FIRST PERIOD

No scoring

Penalties: Park (CAN) 10:08, Henderson (CAN) 15:19

SECOND PERIOD

1. Canada, P. Esposito (Park, Cashman) 7:14

Penalties: Gusev (URS) 2:07, URS bench (served by Zimin) 4:13, Bergman (CAN) 15:16, Tsygankov (URS) and Kharlamov (URS – misconduct) 19:54

THIRD PERIOD

2. Canada, Cournoyer (Park) 1:19 (pp)
3. Soviet Union, Yakushev (Lyapkin, Zimin) 5:53
4. Canada, P. Mahovlich (P. Esposito) 6:47 (sh)
5. Canada, F. Mahovlich (Mikita, Cournoyer) 8:59

Penalties: Clarke (CAN) 5:13, Stapleton (CAN) 6:14

SHOTS ON GOAL

Canada:	10	16	10	36
Soviet Union:	7	5	9	21

IN GOAL

Canada: T. Esposito
Soviet Union: Tretiak

REFEREES

Steve Dowling (USA) and Frank Larsen (USA)

OUTSTANDING PLAYERS

Canada: Phil Esposito and Tony Esposito
Soviet Union: Vladislav Tretiak

#5 BRAD PARK – A WELCOME ADDITION

One of the greatest rushing defencemen the game has known, Brad Park was on the cusp of superstar status when the Summit Series began. Perhaps more than any other player, though, his training camp at Maple Leaf Gardens was fraught with incident, both good and bad. A native of Toronto, this is where he spent his summers, so the arena was just a drive away from his house.

"I ran a hockey school out in Pickering," he said in reference to the Toronto suburb. "I lived in West Hill. I didn't know anything about the series until I got a call from Harry Sinden asking me to be a part of it. I told him I'd play so long as my wife got a free trip to Russia because going there was so uncommon I knew it would be a great experience for her."

But even as Park boasted of the negotiation – which Sinden happily promised all the players – his situation – or, more to the point, his wife's – was tenuous because she was late into her first pregnancy.

"It was touch and go," he explained. "By the time the series started, she was overdue. We ended up losing the first game in Montreal – which was a real shocker – and chartered back to Toronto that night and got back to the hotel. I thought I better call my wife – it's two o'clock in the morning. I called and the first thing she said was, 'You better get home quickly.' I jumped in my car and drove like a madman out to West Hill, took her to Scarborough General Hospital, and at 4:52 a.m. my first son was born. So it went from being the worst day of my hockey life to being the best day of my family life."

The boy was named James Edmund in honour of the boy's two great-grandfathers, and the mother did make the trip to Moscow. "My wife did come over," Park said. "Her mother was a registered nurse, so she stayed with our son."

If the Summit Series were to have been played today, however, it's not so certain Park would have participated, not because of a lack of talent but because of a bad mishap in camp. "We were doing line rushes," he started, "and Dennis Hull was coming down the wing. It was nine o'clock in the morning, and there's Dennis Hull coming down, winding up for a slap shot. It was just a light scrimmage, so I slid to my left so I didn't get in the way of the shot. He's shooting from the blue line. As he starts to shoot, Yvan Cournoyer comes back and puts his stick in the way to deflect the shot. The puck changed direction and almost took my face off. It hit me flat on my left cheek. It didn't cut me, but I was out cold. There was a picture in the newspaper the next day of two guys carrying me off with my arms around their shoulders. They took me to the hospital. At about 10:30 that night, everything cleared for me, but I was pretty much out all day. The next morning, I was back at practice. I wouldn't be if I played today."

Coach Sinden paired the rushing Park with the more defensive-minded Gary Bergman, a partnership that lasted

Tenacity is writ large in Brad Park's efforts against Soviet star Alexander Maltsev.

the entire series. In fact, the two almost combined to beat Paul Henderson for end-of-game heroics in game eight. In an odd situation, the two charged ahead on a three-on-two rush with three minutes left in the final game.

"First off, you never want two defencemen to lead the rush," Park said with wit as dry as desert sand. "In the back of our minds, though, was that we were told at the end of the second period, when it was 5–3 for the Soviets, that if the game ended in a tie they'd claim to win the series because they scored more goals. So in the last five minutes of the game, the score was 5–5, but we weren't sitting back. We were attacking. We wanted that sixth goal. Usually in a 5–5 game, the defencemen are sitting back, but Bergy and I had the same idea. We've got to get another goal."

Impressive but not surprising, Park had five points in the series, all in the two most important games of the series. He had two assists in game two, a crucial win in Toronto, and he had a goal and two assists in the final game.

"Game eight was spectacular," he enthused. "If you ever want to know what pressure is, that was it."

Park scored the tying goal late in the second period to make it a 2–2 game, partnering with his New York Rangers teammate. "The second goal was the result of a play with Jean Ratelle," Park said. "He knew what I was going to do and I knew what he was going to do. There was a quick turnover at centre ice, and we went on the attack and went boom-boom. I saw Tretiak there and shot stick side."

That "boom-boom" was Park making a pass to Ratelle and then charging ahead to get the return pass. In alone, he made no mistake with his quick shot under Tretiak's blocker.

Park has a friendly score to settle with Phil Esposito, the great leader who scored the first goal for Canada in game eight. "Actually, I had two goals in game eight," Park relates. "The first one, Lutchenko put it in off my rebound. That's the one Espo took credit for and never said anything. I saw that twenty-five years later. I never knew about it. It came out on DVD and I saw the goal and thought that SOB didn't touch it! I told Phil, twenty-five years later. I went through the whole series not worried about getting points. The first goal of the series, in Montreal, I set it up, but they gave the assist to Bergman. I didn't think much of it, but then Red Fisher writes that I'm not producing!"

Park is also part of an answer to a pretty good Summit Series trivia question: Who are the only three Canadians to play all eleven games (including the two in Sweden and one in Prague)? Answer: Park, Phil Esposito, and Yvan Cournoyer.

"I thought I was going to get the night off in Prague, but I guess that wasn't in the cards," he deadpanned before adding, "and don't forget the three exhibition games in Toronto. I played those as well."

For a rushing defenceman such as Park, the bigger ice of Luzhniki Arena was both good and bad. "I thought the bigger ice was more difficult to defend, especially in our zone. So, as a defenceman, I liked the NHL ice. But on offence, the bigger ice was better because you had more room to make a pass."

Park summed up the pre-series attitude of the players toward their opponents. "We knew the Russians beat our amateur guys, but in the back of my mind that didn't matter. We're pros. We have the best players in the world. We were overconfident, absolutely."

As for personal highlights, Park doesn't look to games two or eight. Instead, he recalls the first must-win game. "I think the thing I remember the most was game six," he said. "The one thing we were told was not to look ahead. We play shift by shift, period by period. That was all we think about. That was our strategy. When game six started, I must have knocked four or five guys to the ice on my first shift, just to let them know that we weren't going to go quietly. I was out to prove a point."

#20 PETER MAHOVLICH – A SHORTY FOR ALL TIME

I
t's incredible the number of players from Team Canada who point to Peter Mahovlich's short-handed goal as the third greatest moment of the Summit Series. First, of course, is Henderson's winner in game eight, and second is his one-on-four game winner in game seven. But the "Little M" scored a highlight-reel goal for the ages to ensure victory in a crucial game.

"I was used specifically as a penalty killer," he started. "We knew that the Russians' power play was about puck possession and passing. We knew they'd wait for a really good scoring opportunity. They passed to the backside of the goal quite a bit. We were up 2–0 in the second period, and all of a sudden we got a penalty. They got a power play goal to make it 2–1, and the next shift we get another penalty. All of a sudden, we're thinking, 'What's going to happen now?' I can still remember sitting on the bench and Phil saying to me, 'Look, if we go out on the ice together, and we get possession of the puck, we're going to hold on to it. We're going to rag it for as much time as possible rather than just shoot it down the ice.' So, we go out and we're killing the penalty, and Phil gets the puck inside our blue line. Now I know he doesn't want to shoot it down the ice, so I break out on the wing, and he bounces the puck off the boards and gets it to me just outside our line. Now I'm carrying it up ice, and I'm thinking that I'll fake a shot and carry the puck laterally and wait for Phil, to pass him the puck so we can hold on to it for a little longer. So I go to take the shot and the defenceman just froze – he just froze! – so I went around him at their blue line and I ended up having a partial breakaway going in on Tretiak. And, of course, from there I made a move and it was 3–1. It was one of those things that came at a critical point, and then Frank [Mahovlich] scored another goal in the period to make it 4–1. But that proved to be a turning point of that game and maybe the series, because if they had scored another power-play goal to make it 2–2, who knows what would have happened?"

Indeed, we'll never find out thanks to Peter's great goal. After the game, he had all the players sign the stick he scored the goal with, but over time it has gone missing. "I don't have the stick. I don't have the sweater. I don't know what happened to them," he said despondently.

Mahovlich was just reaching the prime of his career when the Summit Series was played. Twenty-five years old, he had been in the league seven years and won the Cup with the Canadiens in 1971. He had had two straight thirty-five-goal seasons leading up to the summer of 1972 before getting the call to attend Team Canada's training camp.

"Everything happened pretty quickly that summer," he explained. "The WHA was being formed, and players were signing there. Of course, those players weren't allowed to play. For me, I was back in Toronto, after playing for Montreal in the winter. My wife's family was in Toronto, and my mom and dad lived there as well, so we were there and then spent a lot of the time at Rice Lake. We had a place up there. It was a big surprise for me to be selected to that team. I think John Ferguson, when he was named assistant coach, wanted a couple of guys in particular on the team, and I was one of them. I was really thrilled and thought it would be a great experience. Nobody thought it would be the kind of series that would have the impact that it would have and for as long as it has had. For me, to be part of the team in the first place was a great honour. I was happy playing one game, let alone seven."

The only game he missed was game four, and that was more because of injury and circumstance than poor play. "I blocked a shot in game three and had to have an X-ray," he explained. "I didn't skate the next day, but I could have played in Vancouver. Harry decided to give other players an opportunity. He really wanted to try to get everybody into a game. The coaching staff initially promised that everyone would play at least one game. Well, that never happened because of what transpired in the games in Canada. As things went along, the team started to gel, and those guys who were playing were getting better, and you couldn't expect to put in three of four new guys every game and expect some cohesiveness. As the series went on, the coaches started to go with the same lineup more and more."

Mahovlich was part of the core that played every game in Moscow, thanks largely to his efforts as a penalty killer. Big and strong, but also a good skater, he was very tough to knock off the puck. As a result, he usually opted to rag it rather than just smack it down the ice.

"Throughout my career I always preferred to hang on to the puck, and I'm sure I drove a lot of coaches crazy doing that," he admitted. "But I always felt that if I had control of the puck, I'd rather carry it a little, move it around, look for an open man, even if I had to pass it back. If there was a man who was wide open. If you can waste an extra ten or fifteen seconds when the other team can't move the puck, you're killing valuable penalty time, which is critical. They were terrific with the puck."

Peter Mahovlich was both a physical presence and a gifted stickhandler for Team Canada.

But as Sinden narrowed his lineup and Mahovlich continued to excel, he earned more ice time and responded with a solid performance. "I continued to do a lot of penalty killing in Moscow," he noted. "They tried to get you to move side to side and get you out of the box, so we tightened it up and didn't chase them as much. I got an occasional shift five-on-five, but not many, until the second period of the last game. Then I started to play quite a lot with Phil Esposito and Yvan Cournoyer."

Mahovlich played junior with the Hamilton Red Wings in the 1960s at a time when European teams first started to come to Canada to play exhibition games. He was right in the thick of things.

"When I played junior hockey there were teams from Russia and Sweden that came over and played some exhibition games against all-star junior teams. I played against a Swedish team in my last year of junior at Maple Leaf Gardens. It was quite an experience."

Mahovlich recalls how quickly the series changed after the result in game one. "At the start, I don't think the fans understood what we were trying to represent, and I don't think the players did either. The first five minutes of game one looked like the series would be a rout, and everything was fine. But all of a sudden, the Russians showed up, and after they won the first game so easily, we understood that these guys felt they could win this series. Then things changed. In the second game, Harry made a lot of changes in the lineup, and the same for the next two games, but when we got to Russia and gelled, there weren't so many changes."

One of the keys to team morale was the appearance in Moscow of wives and girlfriends and families. They supported the players, allowed them to enjoy their time off, and created a homey feeling in an inhospitable environment. "We had a two-year-old son, and my wife didn't want to leave little Peter behind. I took my mother over. She and Mickey Redmond's mother roomed together, and they had a great time."

What Mahovlich recognized about the series over time, though, was its importance not just to the cultural and sporting fabric of Canada but as a catalyst to an ever-changing, rapidly expanding sport. In 1972, 99 per cent of the players were Canadian. In 2012, that number is down to 55 per cent while Americans and Europeans make up the other 45 per cent in about equal numbers.

"When you're going through the series, you don't have a chance to say, 'Oh, this is going to have an impact on Canada; this will have an impact on the game,' Mahovlich said. "When you look back, it is a life-changing event for a lot of Canadians. And in hockey, too. In 1974, the WHA played a series against the Russians, and in 1976 there was the Canada Cup, and we played not only the Russians but the Swedes and Finns and Czechs. That had never happened before with the pros. And then you get all these Europeans coming over to play in the National Hockey League. That was all because of what happened in 1972. And look at the Russian conditioning in 1972 – that also had a tremendous effect. Players started to come to training camp in better shape and not get into shape at camp."

Personal memories merge with nationalistic ones for Mahovlich looking back forty years later and thinking about what transpired in September 1972. "For me, the greatest thing was how the people of Canada acted and reacted in the first four games, and then the tremendous support we got when we went to Moscow, the outpouring of telegrams that we got, pages and pages of telegrams from a town with names on it. Thousands of names on these sheets. We'd paste them up on our dressing room walls and the hallways that went into the room. That to me, and the three thousand fans who travelled to Moscow and were chanting "Go Canada Go!", was fabulous. It was a tremendous feeling to be part of all that."

#27 FRANK MAHOVLICH – ELDER STATESMAN FIGHTS RAGWEED

"This was supposed to be an exhibition series," began the "Big M," Frank Mahovlich. "There wasn't that much exhibition, certainly not by the time we got to Vancouver. And then we played exhibition games in Sweden, but that was no exhibition either. That was a rough series. Wayne Cashman got his tongue cut really badly."

And so it was, a friendly set of games turned into the most contested hockey battle ever waged, and Mahovlich, at thirty-four years of age, was the oldest player on the team (technically, Boston goalie Ed Johnston was the oldest, at thirty-six, but since he didn't play in the games against the Soviets, Big M can claim being the elder statesman). He had played sixteen years in the NHL with Toronto, Detroit, and, most recently, Montreal, and his place in the Hockley Hall of Fame was already assured.

Still, he wanted to be there.

"The Rangers beat us in the playoffs, so I was just resting at home," he started. "Our cottage was up at Lake Simcoe at the time. It was strange that in the middle of summer you're getting together to play this series and starting training camp in August. It wasn't easy because there were so many players, and we were playing against each other in practice. We never did that. Even for an All-Star Game we might have played with each other, but we never practised. Getting to know your teammates wasn't easy."

There was a double whammy for Mahovlich, though, who had a long and running battle with ragweed. "I can remember it being very hot when training camp started. And in the fall, I always got an allergic reaction to ragweed. Toronto is one of the worst places for it because of the dampness around Lake Ontario. In Timmins, it's not so bad. It's a lot drier up there. And Moscow is pretty good. After my career, my wife and I would always take a trip to the ocean – maybe Nova Scotia – because the ragweed wasn't so bad there. I've grown out of it, thank God. But I remember the practices with Team Canada – I was labouring all the time."

"I also played on the Team Canada that played the Soviets in 1974, and the ragweed was bad. I remember my eyes swelling up. We got to Winnipeg, which is a pretty good place – not much ragweed there – and my eyes started to blacken as the swelling subsided. Somebody asked me what happened, and I said, 'I met two Russians in the back alley.'"

But back to 1972. Mahovlich was in the lineup for every game in Canada, so he saw the ebb and flow of the series, from shock to comeback, anxiety, and embarrassment.

"I don't think we were ready for them like they were ready for us," he suggested. "They were used to playing in a series like the Olympics. They trained for that. They were in better condition. That's what stands out in my mind about the first game, how ill prepared we were. At the morning practice before game one, we didn't come in as a team. One guy came in, then another trickled in. And I remember there were three Russians on the ice and they wouldn't get off. I had to call the Zamboni driver and tell him to get on there because it was time for our practice. But our guys were so casual."

Game one ended badly. "Because we had so many players, our timing was off. We played four lines when we usually played three. Before we knew it we had lost 7–3."

In game two, the Mahovlich family had reason to celebrate. Clinging to a tenuous one-goal lead early in the third period, Canada got a tremendous short-handed goal from Peter Mahovlich, and then a few minutes later Frank added a nail into the coffin to make it 4–1, the final score. "Mikita passed me the puck near centre and I fired a low shot that beat their goalie," Frank recalled.

Frank also has a clear recollection of a goal that Valeri Kharlamov scored to give his team a 3–2 lead in the next game. "Kharlamov scored a goal in game three that stands out in my mind. Esposito and I went into their corner to check a defenceman. We were really going to ram this guy. He turned around and fired the puck blindly off the boards at the blue line. It bounced to the red line, right to Kharlamov, and he was in full flight! He took it and put it in the net. Esposito and I hit the defenceman in the corner, turned around, and saw the puck in our net. It happened that quickly."

A bit weary from the travel and ragweed, and nursing a leg injury, Mahovlich didn't play in games six and seven, but he also had a good view for two key moments in game eight. "First, there was the incident with Alan Eagleson. Peter was sitting beside me and tying his laces. I said to him, 'Hey, they're taking Eagleson away! They've got him! Soldiers are taking him away!' He couldn't see. It was across the ice, in the penalty box. Peter grabbed his stick, jumped over the boards, and then jumped over the boards on the other side. He raised his stick up and shook it at the soldiers, and they let him go. Eagleson went onto the ice, white as a sheet, and sat beside me on the bench. I told him he'd be all right if he just sat there and was quiet. He was complaining about the goal light not coming on when Cournoyer tied the game. He was upset about that."

Just a few minutes later, he was witness to history. "Here's what happened," Frank said, his voice rising with excitement. "I was on the bench, sitting beside Henderson. My brother was coming up ice, and Henderson was screaming at Peter to come off! So, I'm looking at Henderson thinking, 'What kind of a crazy man is this?' So Peter comes off, and Henderson goes out and gets the goal!"

More than most players, Mahovlich was affected by the Soviet regime and all things KGB to a humourous degree. As Stan Mikita related: "Big Frank thought we were always being followed by spies. When we were in Vancouver, he'd look behind every picture that we passed thinking we were bugged. He said, if they wanted to have a football team, it could beat the Cowboys. He was a great guy, but boy was he intense."

Mahovlich has few warm and fuzzy memories about Moscow as well. "In meetings before we left, we were warned by the RCMP about our phones being bugged," he explained. "Things were different over there. My wife and I got into our hotel room, for instance, and the beds were toe to toe. The first thing we did was put them beside each other. We brought our own steaks, but they cut them in half, so we only had half a steak. So we complained. Before the third game, they cut the thickness in half. We complained again. It wasn't until the last game that we finally got a whole steak."

The Big M carries the puck over the Soviet blue line during the Moscow half of the series.

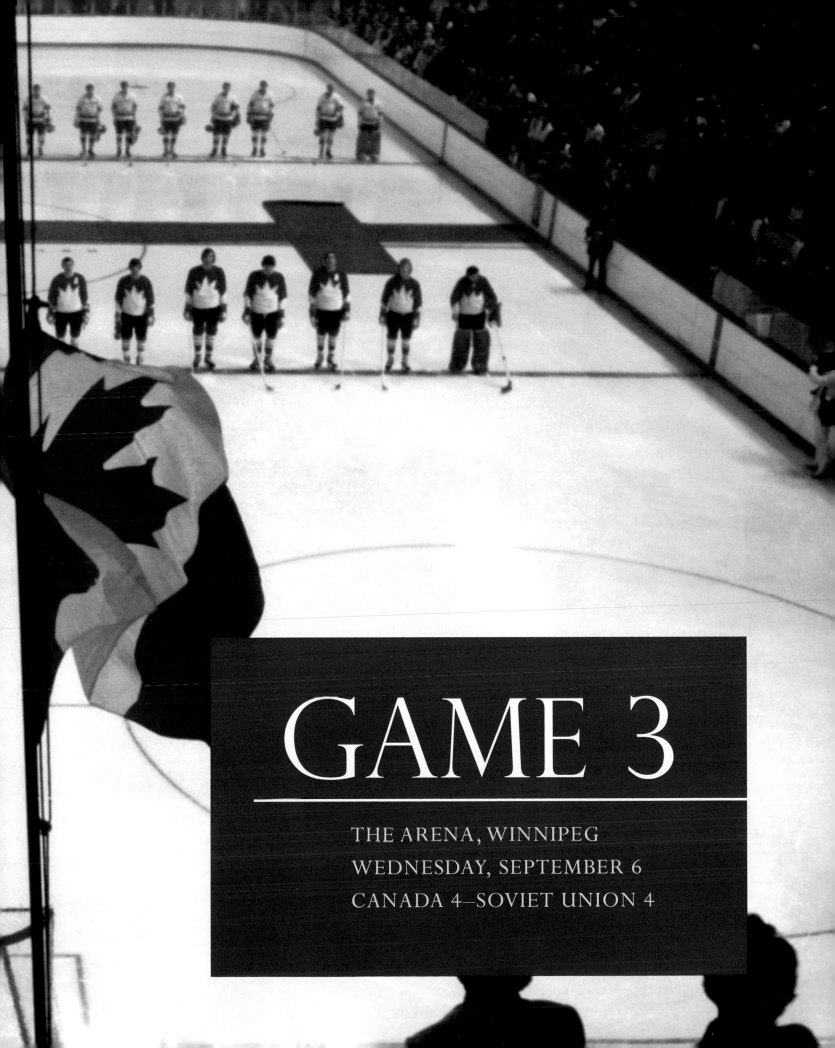

GAME 3

THE ARENA, WINNIPEG
WEDNESDAY, SEPTEMBER 6
CANADA 4–SOVIET UNION 4

"And the game is over! Canada 4, the USSR 4, and this is fair appraisal of a tremendous struggle."

—FOSTER HEWITT

An exhibition became a war and hockey cultures collided ever more intensely as the eight games of the Summit Series progressed.

A BLOWN LEAD

Now that the teams knew each other's strengths and weaknesses, game three was played as evenly as one might expect between two hockey powers. Canada twice had two-goal leads, but the Soviets rallied in a second period in which five of the game's eight goals were scored. And although the third period was scoreless, it was not without many great scoring chances at both ends of the ice.

The pre-game ceremonies featured Father David Bauer presenting the two coaches with gold medallions, and the player introductions were highlighted by a long and loud ovation for Bobby Clarke, a Flin Flon native and the only Manitoban on Team Canada. After all players were introduced, a moment of silence was observed for the Israeli athletes killed the previous day at the Munich Olympics.

Harry Sinden made only one coaching change, taking out Bill Goldsworthy and inserting Jean Ratelle, while Soviet coach Vsevolod Bobrov made six changes, most notably inserting two youngsters into his lineup, Yuri Lebedev and Alexander Bodunov. They played on a "kid line" with Vyacheslav Anisin, the three twenty-one-year-olds giving the Soviets needed spark as the team tried to recover from a convincing 4–1 loss in game two. They had taken the Soviets to victory a year previous at the World Student Games in Lake Placid, and they were the best threesome this night in Winnipeg despite their youth.

Canada was lucky to come away from the hard-hitting first period with a 2–1 lead because it was only the second-best team in the opening twenty minutes. J-P Parise opened the scoring when he tapped home a rebound off a Bill White point shot that Tretiak couldn't control, but two minutes later Vladimir Petrov tied the game while short-handed. He intercepted a lazy Frank Mahovlich pass at the Canada blue line and beat Tony Esposito between the pads.

Ratelle gave Canada the lead again when he took a sensational pass from Yvan Cournoyer and beat Tretiak to the stick side with a terrific shot. Canada seemed to take control early in the second. The cornermen of Parise and Wayne Cashman got the puck deep in the Soviet end, and Cashman made a great pass to Phil Esposito in the slot. Phil drilled a one-timer over the glove of Tretiak.

Valeri Kharlamov made it 3–2, though, when he got a loose puck in centre ice and simply outskated Canadian defencemen Pat Stapleton and Guy Lapointe, beating Tony Esposito with a deke after the goalie had come way out of his net.

But again Canada upped its lead to two goals off a lovely pass from Bobby Clarke and a little luck. His pass through centre was badly missed by Soviet defenceman Viktor Kuzkin, and Paul Henderson zipped in to get the puck and snap a quick shot to Tretiak's stick side.

The only goal of dubious quality came with 5:01 to go in the second when a Valeri Vasiliev point shot was deflected in front by Yuri Lebedev to make it 4–3. Then, just like Esposito in the slot, Bodunov took a pass from Anisin in the corner and fired a quick shot past Tony O to tie the game.

Both teams had excellent chances in the third period, but no finer play occurred than one in which Clarke made a perfect pass from behind the Soviet net to Henderson all alone in front. He let the shot go immediately and raised his hands to celebrate the goal — but at the same time Tretiak was snapping his glove in the air to catch the puck, making a save that helped establish his reputation as one of the greats.

"Henderson thought he had that one in the net," said Foster Hewitt with his usual succinct brilliance.

Not to be outdone, Valeri Kharlamov got the puck in the slot and made a clever play to slide it past Tony Esposito, but as it rolled through the crease Brad Park swept it away and averted possible disaster.

The game ended in a tie, and after three games there was little to separate the two teams in the series.

Frank Mahovlich runs a little goalie interference in Winnipeg, much to the surprise of Vladislav Tretiak.

LINEUPS

CANADA — Tony Esposito, Ed Johnston (did not play) — Brad Park, Yvan Cournoyer, Phil Esposito, Frank Mahovlich, Bobby Clarke, Peter Mahovlich, Gary Bergman, Ron Ellis, Paul Henderson, Guy Lapointe, Pat Stapleton, Jean Ratelle, Wayne Cashman, Bill White, Stan Mikita, J-P Parise, Serge Savard

SOVIET UNION — Vladislav Tretiak, Viktor Zinger (did not play) — Alexander Gusev, Vladimir Lutchenko, Viktor Kuzkin, Valeri Vasiliev, Gennadi Tsygankov, Alexander Maltsev, Yevgeni Mishakov, Boris Mikhailov, Yuri Shatalov, Alexander Yakushev, Vladimir Petrov, Valeri Kharlamov, Vladimir Shadrin, Vyacheslav Solodukhin, Vyacheslav Anisin, Yuri Lebedev, Alexander Bodunov

GAME SUMMARY

FIRST PERIOD
1. Canada, Parise (White, P. Esposito) 1:54
2. Soviet Union, Petrov (unassisted) 3:16 (sh)
3. Canada, Ratelle (Cournoyer, Bergman) 18:25
Penalties: Vasiliev (URS) 3:02, Cashman (CAN) 8:01, Parise (CAN) 15:47

SECOND PERIOD
4. Canada, P. Esposito (Cashman, Parise) 4:19
5. Soviet Union, Kharlamov (Tsygankov) 12:56 (sh)
6. Canada, Henderson (Clarke, Ellis) 13:47
7. Soviet Union, Lebedev (Vasiliev, Anisin) 14:59
8. Soviet Union, Bodunov (Anisin) 18:28
Penalties: Petrov (URS) 4:46, Lebedev (URS) 11:00

THIRD PERIOD
No Scoring
Penalties: White (CAN) and Mishakov (URS) 1:33, Cashman (CAN – minor, misconduct) 10:44

SHOTS ON GOAL

Canada:	15	17	6	38
Soviet Union:	9	8	8	25

IN GOAL
Canada: T. Esposito
Soviet Union: Tretiak

REFEREES
Len Gagnon (USA) and Gord Lee (USA)

OUTSTANDING PLAYERS
Canada: Paul Henderson
Soviet Union: Vladislav Tretiak

#6 RON ELLIS – HIS CROWNING GLORY

To steal from Rodney Dangerfield, if you look up unsung hero in the dictionary, you'll see a photo of Ron Ellis. Not noticeably big or noticeably strong, not blessed with a whammy of a Hull-like slap shot or speed, he nevertheless barrelled up and down the right wing with a consistency and rate of success that few have given the game.

Ace Bailey recognized at least a little of that when he offered his retired number 6 to a young Ellis, and coaches Sinden and Ferguson must have agreed to some extent because he was invited to camp. But few could know of the prominent role Ellis would go on to play in the series.

"The only reason I thought that it might happen," Ellis said with due humility of his invitation, "is the fact that they had to invite so many players so they could have intra-squad games. So, I thought I might be in that group of thirty-five. To be honest, if they had picked only nineteen guys, I wasn't on that team."

Even better for Team Canada, he arrived in pretty decent shape, unlike many teammates. "I did some work. I was a partner with my parents at a tourist resort just north of Huntsville. We had a place up there for years, and that's where I spent a lot of my summers when I played junior. When I turned pro, my parents and I formed a partnership. We had cottages and campgrounds and a marina."

All of this is prelude to the really special time for Ellis, which was the result of a bit of common sense, a bit of blind luck, and a lot of tenacity. On day one, coach Harry Sinden decided that Ellis and Toronto Maple Leafs teammate Paul Henderson (left wing) would play with young Philadelphia centre Bobby Clarke. As it turned out, the threesome had the same ambitions, played well, and stayed together from the opening day on August 14 to the final day in Prague, September 30, the only line to survive so long.

Ellis explained, "We looked at a list that the coaches had prepared for the first workout, and we were put together as a line on that first day. Paul made a comment to the effect that he wasn't overly excited. We thought he and I might stay together because we played on a line with Norm Ullman with the Leafs, but when you looked at the centres, we thought Stan Mikita would be great. But here's this young kid Clarke. It turned out this was the break we needed to gel as a line. Clarke was a young Norm Ullman — great forechecker, good on faceoffs, good playmaker and playing at both ends of the ice. We didn't have any major adjustments to make, which is the main reason why we played well early at training camp and scrimmages."

More incredibly, the line became successful both for producing offence and for being the team's top checking line, a remarkable combination of skill sets at the best of times. "Initially, no one indicated to us we were going to be a shut-down line," Ellis admitted. "In fact, we enjoyed some offensive success during the Red-and-White games. Paul and I were known as players who could score. But after game one, in Montreal, that's when things changed. Our line did well in that game. Paul and Bobby both scored, but Kharlamov also had a pretty good game."

"After that game, Harry told me he'd like me to skate with that guy. If that's my role, that's my role. And we were successful in keeping him off the scoreboard, and Paul was successful scoring. It was an assignment I was given quite often. Every time we played the Chicago Black Hawks, coach Punch Imlach said, 'You've got Bobby Hull.' So I was known for that, and my style was to play at both ends of the rink. I tried to check him just by skating with him, not hacking and whacking him. Kharlamov was a gifted player. I'd put him on a level with Hull. He wasn't quite as big, but he was very strong. And he had a great shot. We all had to change our roles a little, and if you didn't change your role, you didn't play."

Ellis related a story about linemate Clarke that summed up nicely Team Canada's frame of mind heading into the series. "I think Clarke said it best. He said, 'Sure, maybe the Russians have been winning world championships and defeating our top senior teams almost at will, but,' he said — and he looked around the dressing room — 'how can anyone beat this team?'"

His teammates couldn't have agreed with him more, and chaos ensued. Canada won only one of four games on home ice and headed to Sweden, tail between its collective legs, looking for answers. But as Ellis noted, those answers were there in spades.

"One thing I've thought about for many, many years is why did we enjoy the success we did over in Moscow? Even the first game we were in control until we lost momentum. But here's one important factor. In the Canada games, we were basically an all-star team, not a hockey team with a lot of chemistry, and maybe a team which had animosities floating around from NHL teams. Once we got to Moscow and realized the challenge ahead of us, we became a hockey team. The egos and animosities had to be left outside the dressing room. That all started with those games in Sweden, where we became a real team, not an all-star team. In my estimation, we wouldn't have won if we hadn't had those days in Sweden to recover. When we left Vancouver, we were rock bottom. If we had gone straight to Moscow from Vancouver, we wouldn't have won. We needed that time to recover, practise well, skate on the larger ice surface. That's one of the advantages of Canadian hockey players. We know how to adjust. In the six arenas we played in during the Original Six, not one was the same. Each rink had different boards, different corners. In the end, the fact that we could make adjustments of all kinds as the series went along and the Russians were not able to was a factor."

There was another element to the camaraderie that helped create this "team." "There were two things we were promised at training camp," Ellis revealed. "One, that everyone at camp would play in at least one game. Of course, that was easy to promise then because we were supposed to win all eight games, so moving players in and out was no big deal. As it turned out, that didn't happen. The other thing was that our wives would be able to join us in Moscow. It wasn't a big deal for guys in Toronto, but the other guys gave up most of their summer and hadn't seen their wives since before camp. So for them to be able to explain to their wives that they could come to Moscow was important to get some of the guys to come to camp."

A little-known fact about the four games in Moscow is that they were almost never played!

"Just before we left Sweden, the Russians told us the wives would have to stay in one hotel and the players in another. Most people don't realize that if they hadn't changed that, we were potentially going to get on an Air Canada plane and come home and not go to Moscow. But the Russians did not want us to go home. They thought they had us."

Every hockey rink has its own personality, a smell and feel and temperature that makes it both one of a kind and particular to hockey. Luzhniki was no different, but for Team Canada, the dressing room became an important hostel, a home away from home where the players had to live for a tense and nerve-wracking week. In this case, it wasn't a dumpy room but rather a series of rooms.

"I remember we had to change in about three different little rooms," Ellis described. "We couldn't all fit in one room. There was a very long hallway with these little rooms off it, and then before we went on the ice we all crammed into one room. But the positive of all this was that long hallway. When we started getting all of the telegrams and postcards from Canadians back home, we nailed them all up along that hallway. I think Phil's speech really brought the fans around that we were in a really tough series. By the time we got to Moscow there were mailbags full of cards and telegrams. When we left Vancouver and left Toronto to go to Sweden, there was nobody. We got booed off the ice in Vancouver. When we flew out of Toronto, there wasn't a soul at the airport."

Game six was a must-win game for Canada. A loss or a tie would give the Soviets the series. Henderson had scored the third goal for Canada in the second period, and the score stayed 3–2 throughout the final period – with one tense moment near the end.

"Game six, 3–2, two minutes left in the game. Ellis takes a penalty," number 6 described self-referentially. "I was sitting in the box knowing if the Russians tie this up, the series is over. It was one of those questionable penalties. To be honest, I do not take penalties at the end of a game. I'm the one who kills penalties at the end. It might have been part of all that talk about giving the Russians one last chance here to tie the game. I'll never forget it. But Phil and Peter went out and killed most of it off."

Redeemed, Ellis played a key role in game seven and eight, both victories. "One of the greatest honours I ever received from a coach was to be out there for the final thirty-four seconds," he said of the final shift of the final game to win the series. "I remember it very well. The Russians could score three goals in that length of time, so it wasn't over yet. We had to regroup. I was honoured that Harry put me out. Paul said to me after, 'Ron, that left-winger wasn't going to touch the puck anyhow, anyway.' I had him so wrapped up. He wasn't going anywhere!"

One of the fascinating elements of the series was that players from a variety of NHL teams who never socialized came together as a team and for seven weeks developed a bond that lasted a lifetime. For some players, facing them later in NHL games proved difficult, but for others, it was business as usual.

Ellis and Henderson returned to the Maple Leafs as teammates, of course, but the Leafs and Clarke's Flyers were to wage many a nasty battle during the rest of the 1970s, the nostalgia of the Summit Series long forgotten by the Flyers captain once the puck dropped.

"Bobby Clarke was the kind of player you loved to have on your team and didn't like playing against," Ellis explained. "When that series was over – and we went through war together, really, and became very close – and we were back in the NHL, all of that was forgotten. And I respect him for that."

#25 GUY LAPOINTE – PARTNER, TANDEM, BACK-END ROCK

Although he had played only two full seasons in the NHL by the summer of 1972, Guy Lapointe turned out to be one of the team's best players, a fast and smooth skater like Brad Park and a quick and reliable defenceman in his own end. Partnered with Serge Savard, his Canadiens teammate, most of the time, Lapointe matured and became a better player from his experience with Team Canada.

"I was very excited to get the call from Harry, but I told them I had to talk to my wife first because she was expecting our first child. So, of course, in the end I went, but while we were in Moscow, my son, Guy Jr., was born, on September 25. That's why I didn't go on to Czechoslovakia. As soon as the series was over, I flew home to see my wife and son. So when Harry called, I was getting the house ready for our first child."

"It was kind of a surprise because it was only my second year in the league, so it was quite an honour to be invited even though I didn't know how much I'd play or if I'd make the team at all," he added.

Lapointe was a standout at training camp and played in every game in which he was healthy, notably the first one in his hometown. "I was a little nervous before the first game in Montreal," he admitted, "but we sure found out quickly how good they were. At the end of the first period there were a lot of red faces, and we knew we had a tough game on our hands. Those guys are skilled. They can skate. They meant business. It was a pretty intense game, high tempo."

Although Coach Sinden changed almost half his lineup for game two, Lapointe was back on the blue line for the win and again two nights later for the 4–4 tie.

"I got slashed on the ankle in game three and couldn't put my skate on. I didn't play in Vancouver. Serge and I flew back to Montreal. He had a cracked ankle, much worse than I had. But I flew to Sweden."

Lapointe was one of the few players on the team who was no novice to the European ice. "In 1968, we had a team that flew to Moscow for some games and I was on it. Jackie McLeod was coach, and there were some other pros there like Jean Gauthier, Wayne Carleton, Phil Roberto, Al MacNeil, and Bob Berry, who became my coach later on. So I had that experience playing overseas."

By the time the team arrived at Luzhniki Arena, Lapointe had gone from a shy, two-year player in training camp to a player who was mature and contributing to the team in ways expected by the top stars.

"I was more comfortable in Moscow with the team after knowing the players for a few weeks," he agreed. "It was only my second year. So I was pretty quiet in the beginning. There was never any friendship between players on different teams in those days, so we became way stronger as a team in Moscow. And it was tough because Harry had to deal with players who weren't playing, and all of us were like top-four defencemen or top-six forwards on our NHL teams, playing power play, penalty killing, and now some were playing and some were watching, just being cheerleaders. That was not an easy thing to do. And the guys who weren't playing also had to be ready to play if the call came."

Not surprisingly, the five players on the ice at the time of the historic goal included forwards Paul Henderson, Phil Esposito, and Yvan Cournoyer – and defencemen Serge Savard and Guy Lapointe!

"It was crazy. We were all tired, but when you win, you forget the fatigue. There was joy, and I was crying. All the pressure we had. If we were to lose that game, we were aware of what would happen. The emotion, the thousands of fans in the crowd who were louder than all the Russian fans. What a relief!"

What struck Harry Sinden about the series looking back was that much had remained the same, but one thing was markedly different. Immediately after, players talked about the certainty of winning all eight games had they been in great shape. But with time, they realize they might well have won with greater ease – but all eight games? Never.

"I honestly believe if the team had been in good shape at the start of the series the way we were at the end," Lapointe commented, "the series wouldn't have been that close. But we wouldn't have won all eight games either."

Lapointe settled into his role with the Canadiens and became one of the "Big Three" with Savard and Larry Robinson, helping the Habs win the Cup four years in a row (1976–79). He retired in 1985 and was inducted into the Hockey Hall of Fame in 1993.

"That series definitely did a lot for my confidence," he said. "Playing with all those guys gave me the push to become the player I became for all those years after. The attitude that I had was like those guys – I hate losing. I was glad to have played with all those guys, but once we played against each other, I put that aside while we were on the ice and did whatever I had to do to help my team win."

But the last word goes out to his buddy Savard, without whom Lapointe, like many others, would have been a lesser player.

"I was happy to be a teammate with Serge. I think a lot of him as a hockey player. He was always the calm person, never panicked. For me, he was the best partner to play with. He was a big part of our team. He cracked his ankle but came back to play. I'm sure he wasn't 100 per cent, but he was a solid guy. And he played five games and never lost one!"

Guy Lapointe (left) has a little fun with Marcel Dionne away from the rink in Moscow.

GAME 4

PACIFIC COLISEUM, VANCOUVER
FRIDAY, SEPTEMBER 8
SOVIET UNION 5–CANADA 3

"The Soviets are hanging on to [the puck], and they don't shoot until they think they have a good chance. They're always passing the puck. Whereas the Canadian team has been carrying the puck up and shooting it in and trying to recover it. What a difference in style."

—FOSTER HEWITT

Phil Esposito comes out of the corner and goes hard to Tretiak's goal, but the goalie follows the play and stays low to take away the shooter's options.

A NIGHTMARE OF BOOING

Who knows how history might have changed had Soviet coach Vsevolod Bobrov been able to ice the lineup he wanted. In Winnipeg, he hoped to start backup goalie Viktor Zinger, but Zinger was fighting the flu. Again this night in Vancouver, Zinger was supposed to start, but he was still too weak to make an appearance. Tretiak started again, of course, and was sensational.

Discipline was one of only several storylines to this game, but it might have been the most important. For whatever reason, Canada started the game in an ornery mood, one marked by many, many cheap shots that the Soviets received without retaliating, their discipline verging on the timorous, but Canada's aggression verging on stupidity.

Sinden again made eight lineup changes to his roster, and such a high turnover for three games now produced a lack of cohesion and teamwork. Two key changes were made by necessity because the Montreal tandem of Serge Savard (cracked bone in his ankle) and Guy Lapointe (charley horse) were unable to dress. Worse, Bill Goldsworthy, in the lineup for the first time since game two, took two senseless penalties early in the game, and the Soviets capitalized on both. Indeed, both goals were very similar, a Vladimir Lutchenko shot being deflected in front of goalie Ken Dryden by Boris Mikhailov.

And so Canada fell behind 2–0, a deficit it couldn't overcome. Worse, Dryden struggled and the fans started to boo, first with impatience, then with anger. Goldsworthy, who started the game with a helmet, took it off after the first penalty, but played no better without one as the game progressed.

The Soviets dominated the first period and were full measure for their two-goal lead after twenty minutes. Canada's best chances to get into the game came early in the second. Newcomer Gilbert Perreault went end to end on a dash, and as he ran out of room he slipped the puck in front of the Soviet goal. It hit defenceman Alexander Ragulin and went past Tretiak to make it a 2–1 game.

Moments later, Ron Ellis made a great rush and was stopped by Tretiak, who slid well out of his crease and lost control of the puck. But Gennadi Tsygankov checked Bobby Clarke inches from the goal line before the Canadian could slide the puck into the open net to tie the game. The play was soon followed by a third Soviet goal. Pat Stapleton lost the puck at the Soviet blue line, and Vladimir Petrov broke out with Yuri Blinov on a two-on-one. They converted the play perfectly for a 3–1 lead.

If Canada were going to get back into the game, a sequence of plays a short time later decided the outcome. Phil Esposito set up Yvan Cournoyer for two breakaways in a matter of seconds, but Tretiak was there to make the save on both occasions. The result was never in doubt after that.

Dryden struggled with some routine shots, causing the fans to cheer him derisively as he fought the puck in a game that looked lost from the outset. The Soviets more or less put the game out of reach later in the second when Valeri Kharlamov found Vikulov alone in front, and his quick shot beat Dryden.

In the third period, the booing by the fans in Vancouver intensified with every missed pass by the Canadians, every good piece of forechecking by the Soviets, and every play that indicated this would be a bad loss for the home side.

Canada made it a 4–2 game when Phil Esposito's long shot rang off the crossbar and Goldsworthy knocked in the rebound. Initially, Espo was credited with the goal, and things were so bad that when the PA announcer corrected the scoring and gave the goal to Goldsworthy, the crowd booed lustily.

Vladimir Shadrin scored the final Soviet goal on a nice play. Alone in front, his backhand was stopped by Dryden, but as both players fell to the ice Shadrin managed to get his stick on the puck and push it in. A late score from Dennis Hull only made the score a bit closer.

After the game, only one Canadian didn't go straight off. Phil Esposito went to the far corner of the ice where a small red carpet had been rolled out for interviews with the players of the game. CTV's Johnny Esaw was there with microphone in hand, as was the Soviet player of the game, Boris Mikhailov, who had scored those two early power-play goals for the visitors.

Espo shook hands with his opponent, and then spoke to Esaw, sweat pouring off his face, producing one of the great speeches in Canadian history, one that inspired the nation's people to take pride in themselves and to support, not ridicule, the players.

"To the people across Canada, we tried. We gave it our best. For the people that boo us, geez, I'm really … I'm really … all of us guys are really disheartened and we're disillusioned and we're disappointed in some of the people. We cannot believe the bad press we've got … the booing we've gotten in our own buildings, and if the Russians boo their … their players … if the fans … if the Russians boo their players like some of the Canadian fans – I'm not saying all of them – some of them booed us, then I'll come back and apologize to each one of the Canadians, but I don't think they will. I'm really, really … I'm really disappointed. I am completely disappointed. I cannot believe it. Some of our guys are really, really down in the dumps. We know. We're trying. Hell, I mean, we're doing the best we can, and they've got a good team and let's face facts, but it doesn't mean we're not giving it our 150 per cent because we certainly are."

Esaw commented, "I think, Phil, the disappointment is a natural thing because the whole thing was an unexpected thing. We all live with the National Hockey League. We've all been so proud over the years how great we are – "

Esposito cut him off. "Fans expect it because of the press that said we're so good. Not one of guys said we're so good – "

"No, no, this is the thing," Esaw said, reclaiming the microphone. "This is the thing on behalf of the fans, I must say that, ah, probably, since everything is relative – we know how good you people are, but the people didn't realize how good the Soviet team was. And now we've found out how good they are, I think we can appreciate how good both teams are."

Esposito continued as if he hadn't heard Esaw's last remarks. "… I'll tell you, we … we love, I mean, every one of us guys, thirty-five guys that came out and played for Team Canada, we did it because we love our

Goalie Vladislav Tretiak arrived in Canada an unknown and left Vancouver after game four as the Soviet Union's star player.

country and not for any other reason, no other reason. They can throw the money for the pension fund out the window. They can throw anything they want out the window. We came because we love Canada. And even though we may play in the United States and we earn money in the United States, Canada is still our home, and that's the only reason we've come. And I don't think it's fair that we should be booed."

Before leaving the ice, Esposito promised, "We're going to get better," a promise he and the team kept in Moscow.

Canada now had the difficult task of regrouping before the final four games in Moscow. The players flew back to Toronto and after a two-day break moved on to Stockholm, Sweden, for two exhibition games, game five against the Soviets scheduled for September 22 at the Luzhniki Arena.

"I most certainly think we can make it tough for them in Russia," Sinden said. "You don't write off a team in the Stanley Cup playoffs when it's behind 2–1, do you?"

Guy Lapointe goes hard to the Soviet goal, colliding with Vladislav Tretiak as Paul Henderson looks on.

LINEUPS

CANADA – Ken Dryden, Ed Johnston (did not play) – Brad Park, Yvan Cournoyer, Phil Esposito, Frank Mahovlich, Bobby Clarke, Gary Bergman, Ron Ellis, Paul Henderson, Pat Stapleton, Bill White, Don Awrey, Rod Seiling, Vic Hadfield, Rod Gilbert, Dennis Hull, Gilbert Perreault, Bill Goldsworthy

SOVIET UNION – Vladislav Tretiak, Viktor Zinger (did not play) – Vladimir Lutchenko, Valeri Vasiliev, Gennadi Tsygankov, Yuri Blinov, Alexander Maltsev, Boris Mikhailov, Alexander Yakushev, Vladimir Petrov, Valeri Kharlamov, Vladimir Vikulov, Vladimir Shadrin, Vyacheslav Anisin, Yevgeni Paladiev, Yuri Lebedev, Alexander Bodunov, Viktor Kuzkin, Alexander Ragulin

GAME SUMMARY

FIRST PERIOD

1. Soviet Union, Mikhailov (Lutchenko, Petrov) 2:01 (pp)
2. Soviet Union, Mikhailov (Lutchenko, Petrov) 7:29 (pp)
Penalties: Goldsworthy (CAN) 1:24, Goldsworthy (CAN) 5:58, P. Esposito (CAN) 19:29

SECOND PERIOD

3. Canada, Perreault (unassisted) 5:37
4. Soviet Union, Blinov (Petrov, Mikhailov) 6:34
5. Soviet Union, Vikulov (Kharlamov, Maltsev) 13:52
Penalties: Kuzkin (URS) 8:39

THIRD PERIOD

6. Canada, Goldsworthy (P. Esposito, Bergman) 6:54
7. Soviet Union, Shadrin (Yakushev, Vasiliev) 11:05
8. Canada, Hull (P. Esposito, Goldsworthy) 19:38
Penalties: Petrov (URS) 2:01

SHOTS ON GOAL

Canada:	10	8	23	41
Soviet Union:	11	14	6	31

IN GOAL

Canada:	Dryden
Soviet Union:	Tretiak

REFEREES

Len Gagnon (USA) and Gord Lee (USA)

OUTSTANDING PLAYERS

Canada:	Phil Esposito
Soviet Union:	Boris Mikhailov

#17 BILL WHITE – THE LONGEST THIRTY-FOUR SECONDS

"That summer we went to the cottage in Muskoka as usual, and it was while I was there that I got the call to come down to training camp for the series. I was really surprised and honoured. There were a lot of great defencemen around, and to be chosen for that team was an honour."

What an incredible story of perseverance it was that led to White's being invited to play for Team Canada. The Toronto Marlies grad couldn't make the NHL during its Original Six days and had to play in the AHL for eight years until expansion in 1967. He played for the Los Angeles Kings for three years starting in 1967, but a trade brought him to the more hockey-mad city of Chicago in early 1970.

His defence partner with the Black Hawks was Pat Stapleton, and the two continued their partnership with Team Canada. Nary an odder pair ever took to the ice, though. White was tall and angular, partly bald. Stapleton short and stocky with a full head of hair so blond he was nicknamed "Whitey."

"Harry and Johnny Ferguson knew how Pat and I played together," White said. "We seemed to complement each other naturally on the ice, to help each other out. I can't explain it. We were like Mutt and Jeff out there. He had his side and I had mine. Going out there with Patty, I felt very comfortable."

Unlike most players on the team, White had some knowledge of the international game and the Soviet style of play. "I knew about Father Bauer and the National Team because I had a friend, Ross Morrison, who was on that team. I played junior with him. I knew about the Whitby Dunlops and Lyndhursts. And as far as the Russians, I knew they were good because of all the Olympics and World Championships they won. The guy I played for in Springfield, Eddie Shore, had a sort of similar system as the Russians. He told us never to advance the puck unless we knew we could. We'd come back into our end and advance as a group of five. If it didn't look right, don't get rid of it. It's tough to get the puck back."

In some respects it was a blessing in disguise White and Stapleton didn't dress for game one. First, of course, it was a bad loss. Second, it gave them a chance to size up the enemy from the comfort of a seat.

"We saw the lineup for that game and we weren't playing. We weren't offended by it. Unfortunately, we came up short in that game, and Harry told Pat and I that we'd be going into the second game and played the rest of the series. What we saw from the seats, the thing that was most obvious, was that as the game wore on, our conditioning started to fail. We weren't at the same level that they were. Pat and I went into

Bill White watches his man carefully as they go into the corner in Moscow.

the dressing room after the second period, and our guys were pretty whipped. It wasn't until Sweden that our shots were starting to get harder, and we were skating better. It took a while."

The two played in game two and never missed another in the series. It was clear they played better with each other and better as a pair than they might be given credit for individually. And even when they got to Sweden and then Moscow, the larger ice didn't faze them one bit.

"We practised with Chicago in West Point one time before we played the Rangers, and that was a big rink, but in Sweden, you'd throw a pass and it would take forever to get there. It's funny how you adjust. In Springfield, we had a very small rink. The Boston Garden was a small rink. You adjust your whole life. On the big ice, you had a lot more room. You couldn't commit completely."

White got hurt in game five, but managed to play the rest of the series. "I took a puck off my heel," he said. "Aggie Kukulowicz took me to the hospital to have an X-ray. I didn't know whether it was cracked or not. They said it wasn't broken. But once I got the foot in my skate I was fine."

Good thing, too, for although White was hardly known for his offence, he did score one goal in the series — and that came at a great time. The scene was game eight. Second period. Soviets leading 3–2.

"I remember Rod Gilbert had the puck in the left defenceman's corner and had nowhere to go, so I just came in from the point, and he put the puck right on my stick. To the surprise of all the Soviet defencemen, who probably wondered what I was doing there, I scored. It was one of my best goals."

The crowning glory came in the last half-minute. In the mayhem and insanity that was the Canadian bench after the Henderson goal, Coach Sinden had to have the presence of mind to realize there were still thirty-four precious seconds remaining in the game.

"We were out for the last thirty-four seconds after Paul had scored," White noted with pride. "We were in the middle of a change when he scored, and then just before the faceoff Patty and I looked over and no one was coming on for a change, so we got the idea we were out there for the rest of the game. It was a long thirty-four seconds. There was one play when the puck came just inside our blue line. I picked it up and wanted to lightly get it out, but the puck kept going and going, and I thought we'd be called for an icing. But to my surprise a Russian defenceman got to it before the icing. Thank you very much."

After the game and celebrations in the dressing room, the Canadians returned to their hotel.

"There was supposed to be a reception. We were really disappointed because only three or four of the Soviet players showed up. The rest apparently got the flu," White said with an appropriate chuckle. "So, we carried on with our celebration on our own."

#26 DON AWREY –
NO ORR, NO PROBLEM

Few defencemen in NHL history can put on their résumés that they were the defence partner for Bobby Orr. Don Awrey was one, and he had the best spot in the house to watch the great Orr fly up the ice time and again – and he was happy to stay back and mind the goal during these incredible forays that defined the game for a generation.

Yet, with Orr unable to play in the Summit Series, coach Harry Sinden revised Awrey's role more than somewhat. Instead of pairing him with another skating defenceman, Sinden put him with Rod Seiling to create a shutdown unit that focused entirely on defensive play.

"I was a great skater, but for me, being a defensive defenceman who didn't carry the puck a lot, I always felt that when I had the puck on my stick I had to get rid of it. That's when I got into trouble, when I held on to the puck," he noted.

"I had no idea that I'd ever be included," Awrey said humbly of his invite to training camp. "It was like being named to play in an All-Star Game, and I didn't put myself in that category of being an all-star. I thought of myself as not a bad hockey player, and we had just come off winning the Stanley Cup and thinking I must have played well and held my own, but I never thought I'd be asked to play in this series."

Although Awrey had been on the Cup-winning Bruins in 1971–72, he also missed half that season with a bad injury from which he fought hard to recover. "I broke my leg in a fight," he explained. "I was fighting Phil Roberto in St. Louis. It was just the way that we grappled. I fell back and my right leg went out underneath me and I heard it snap. I knew that didn't sound like a good thing."

Recover he did, and he played well enough at camp to be included in the roster for the opening game in Montreal, a game that went particularly poorly for the tandem.

"I don't know how it happened, but I got paired with Rod Seiling in training camp. You couldn't find two more defensive-minded defencemen. The reason we started game one in Montreal was that we played so well at training camp. Now I don't want to throw anybody under the bus, but I didn't think we got the best goaltending in that first game. There was one time when somebody went around me to the outside and that didn't happen to me too often, but I didn't think that was a good goal. I've had to take a lot of ribbing from my friends for forty years for that goal. Ken was always a good friend when I was in Montreal, but it's not the kind of thing you say to him: 'Ken, that was a bad goal to give up.'"

Awrey and Seiling were in the press box for games two and three and back for game four, another loss. He never played in Moscow, but that didn't upset him one bit.

"I think there were ten defencemen on the team. Here's the way I looked at it. I certainly wasn't in the top six. I know that. Deep down, I knew I wasn't one of the best six who went to training camp, but I was more than pleased to be one of the ten, and if I was number seven, eight, nine, or ten, that was still quite a feather in my hat to be thought of by Harry Sinden. If they were going to go with their six best in games that meant the most, I certainly was not insulted by not being one of those."

Although Awrey's focus was always the NHL as a kid, he knew plenty about international hockey because of where he lived. Still, he was as surprised as anyone the series became the hard-fought battle it became. "I don't know how I thought about this series at the start, at training camp. I look at the Olympics because I lived in Waterloo and the Kitchener-Waterloo Dutchmen went to the Olympics and then the Whitby Dunlops with Harry Sinden and the Belleville McFarlands. But I never gave it a thought that it could be the great series that it ended up to be. Who ever thought it was going to be as exciting as it ended up being? We were supposed to win all eight games. We didn't realize how good the Russians were. We won by the skin of our teeth."

In all, Awrey played twice against the Soviets and once against the Swedes, and the experience was one of the greatest memories of his life.

"Being a member of Team Canada '72, to be asked to be a member of the series, was my highlight. I can pat myself on the back to playing well enough in training camp that the powers to be thought that I should play in the first game. It didn't turn out the way we wanted to, but that's beside the point."

Don Awrey's reputation was built on strong play in his own end. His physical ability combined with an ability to move the puck out quickly and effectively made him one of the best defenders of his day.

GAME 1

JOHANNESHOV ISSTADION,
STOCKHOLM
SATURDAY, SEPTEMBER 16
CANADA 4- SWEDEN 1

GAME 2

JOHANNESHOV ISSTADION,
STOCKHOLM
SUNDAY, SEPTEMBER 17
CANADA 4–SWEDEN 4

Ken Dryden had a tough time in games one and four in Canada, but he made amends with a superb performance in game six and was the winner in game eight as well.

GAME ONE – COMING TOGETHER

Team Canada flew to Toronto after game four in Vancouver, and the players were given three days off to see their families and pack for a lengthy European sojourn. On September 12, everyone left for Stockholm, the team flying in two planes at the insistence of NHL owners. The only player not with the team was Frank Mahovlich, whose allergic reaction to ragweed in Vancouver had caused excessive swelling around his eyes (not to mention an unrelated knee injury). He flew directly to Moscow on September 20.

The players arrived on September 13, held an intra-squad game the next day, and then played back-to-back games against a collection of Swedish all-stars on Saturday and Sunday. They practised again on Monday and Tuesday and flew to Moscow on Wednesday, September 20.

Having been in Stockholm for three days to practise on the much wider European ice, Canada took to the ice knowing it had a monumental task ahead in Moscow. The focus wasn't on their Swedish opponents, but soon enough scenes of dirty play and violence got the attention of everyone in the arena.

Coach Harry Sinden inserted several players in the lineup who hadn't played at all against the Soviets in the first four games in Canada, notably Jocelyn Guèvremont, Brian Glennie, and Marcel Dionne.

Canada won the game, but it was by no means a creative or artistic triumph. Nonetheless, it was a great game for getting the players to think of one another as a team – us against the world – instead of a collection of all-stars.

LINEUPS

SWEDEN – Christer Abrahamsson – Stig Ostling, Borje Salming, Arne Carlsson, Thommy Abrahamsson, Bjorn Johansson, Lars-Erik Sjoberg, Kjell-Rune Milton, Tord Lundstrom, Hakan Wickberg, Inge Hammarstrom, Dan Soderstrom, Mats Ahlberg, Dan Labraaten, Ulf Nilsson, Ulf Sterner, Bjorn Palmqvist, Anders Hedberg, Dick Yderstrom

CANADA – Tony Esposito – Gary Bergman, Brad Park, Bill White, Pat Stapleton, Jocelyn Guèvremont, Brian Glennie, Yvan Cournoyer, Phil Esposito, Wayne Cashman, Ron Ellis, Bobby Clarke, Paul Henderson, Rod Gilbert, Jean Ratelle, Vic Hadfield, Mickey Redmond, Marcel Dionne, J-P Parise, Peter Mahovlich

GAME SUMMARY

FIRST PERIOD
1. Canada, Henderson (Ellis) 1:45
Penalties: none

SECOND PERIOD
2. Canada, Clarke (Ellis) 1:20
3. Sweden, Sterner (Sjoberg) 3:51
Penalties: P. Esposito (CAN – minor, major, misconduct), Bergman (CAN), Clarke (CAN), P. Mahovlich (CAN), Hadfield (CAN), Abrahamsson (SWE), Salming (SWE), Sterner (SWE)

THIRD PERIOD
4. Canada, Park (unassisted) 9:15
5. Canada, Cashman (Parise) 16:04
Penalties: Cashman (CAN), Carlsson (SWE)

SHOTS ON GOAL
Sweden:	20
Canada:	32

IN GOAL
Sweden:	Abrahamsson
Canada:	T. Esposito

REFEREES
Franz Bader (FRG) and Josef Kompalla (FRG)

GAME TWO – A TEAM IS BORN

Coach Harry Sinden started Ed Johnston in goal for the first time, and the netminder responded with a terrific performance. Indeed, he was Canada's best player in a game that devolved into mayhem on several occasions, none worse than at the end of the second period when Wayne Cashman received an horrific spear to his mouth from Ulf Sterner, cutting his tongue for eighteen stitches and forcing him to miss the rest of the Summit Series.

Not to be outdone, Vic Hadfield broke the nose of Lars-Erik Sjoberg with a nasty high-stick that was, in the eyes of the Canadians, due comeuppance for Cashman's injury.

The game ended in a tie, and players questioned the purpose of playing two games in a country that had nothing to do with the Summit Series at a time when focus was critical.

Said Sinden right after the second game: "Obviously our players were not motivated for these games in Sweden. How could they be? They're thinking about the Russians, not the Swedes."

Nevertheless, the players to a man later agreed that the days in Sweden were essential to success in Moscow.

Tony Esposito had a win and a tie in the Canadian half of the series and then came up big in game seven, a must-win game for Canada.

LINEUPS

SWEDEN – Curt Larsson – Stig Ostling, Borje Salming, Arne Carlsson, Thommy Abrahamsson, Bjorn Johansson, Lars-Erik Sjoberg, Karl-Johan Sundqvist, Tord Lundstrom, Hakan Wickberg, Mats Lindh, Ulf Nilsson, Ulf Sterner, Bjorn Palmqvist, Anders Hedberg, Mats Ahlberg, Hans Hansson, Dick Yderstrom

CANADA – Ed Johnston – Dale Tallon, Brad Park, Don Awrey, Pat Stapleton, Rod Seiling, Jocelyn Guèvremont, Yvan Cournoyer, Phil Esposito, Wayne Cashman, Rod Gilbert, Jean Ratelle, Vic Hadfield, Bill Goldsworthy, Red Berenson, Dennis Hull, J-P Parise, Gilbert Perreault, Rick Martin

GAME SUMMARY

FIRST PERIOD

1. Canada, Hadfield (Gilbert) 10:30
Penalties: Parise (CAN), Goldsworthy (CAN – minor, major)

SECOND PERIOD

2. Sweden, Nilsson (Sjoberg) 1:12
3. Canada, Awrey (unassisted) 9:15
Penalties: Tallon (CAN), Salming (SWE)

THIRD PERIOD

4. Sweden, Lundstrom (Hammarstrom) 3:16
5. Canada, Martin (Perreault) 3:32
6. Sweden, Hansson (Hedberg) 7:09
7. Sweden, Hammarstrom (Lundstrom) 11:17
8. Canada, P. Esposito (unassisted) 19:13
Penalties: P. Esposito (CAN), Ratelle (CAN), Parise (CAN), Hadfield (CAN – major), Tallon (CAN) and Sterner (SWE)

SHOTS ON GOAL

Sweden: 31
Canada: 23

IN GOAL

Sweden: Larsson
Canada: Johnston

REFEREES

Franz Bader (FRG) and Josef Kompalla (FRG)

#1 ED JOHNSTON –
PROVING HIMSELF IN SWEDEN

Although goalie Ed Johnston never played in the Summit Series, he did play in one of the exhibition games against Sweden and was the backup goalie for six of the eight Summit games. At thirty-six years of age, he was the oldest player on the team, but age didn't matter. In 1971–72, he split the goaltending duties with Gerry Cheevers in Boston, both in the regular season and playoffs, as the Bruins won their second Stanley Cup in three years.

"When we won the Cup in May," Johnston began, "everyone was so ecstatic, but when we beat the Russians in the eighth game, the emotion and the tears were unbelievable, the hugging and crying. That will never happen again in this lifetime. It was both a relief and a celebration. To be able to come back after the position we were in after we left Vancouver, and to come back after being down three games to one, was phenomenal."

It was clear that coach Harry Sinden brought Johnston in as insurance, and he wasn't likely to play much, if at all, but that was okay. "Of course, I was happy to get invited and to have a chance to represent my country," he admitted. "I just played it by ear. Harry didn't tell us who'd be playing, so I just wanted to have a good camp and solidify my position on the team. But naturally Tony and Ken were coming off great years. I was extremely happy to be with the Bruins. We had just won the Cup, so everything was pretty good."

There were thirty-eight players invited to camp, a bloated roster, to be sure, but one that was the greatest collection of stars Canada had ever gathered in one place at one time. "Being invited to camp was a big deal for me," Johnston explained. "I had a pretty good idea that Kenny and Tony were going to play, but getting the opportunity to play in Sweden was a very great thing. It made me feel like I was part of the team. I played well. I think I was even the number-one star, and they had about forty-four shots on me. I was feeling pretty optimistic at that point, thinking I might get into one of the games against the Russians, but it worked out fine even though I didn't."

Make no mistake. That Sweden game was no meaningless bone thrown Johnston's way. By that point in the series, Canada had won one of four games, faced a mammoth uphill battle, and was now playing on a rink size almost none of the players had ever experienced before. Sinden had some serious paring to do with his roster to ready the team for Moscow.

"That game in Sweden was important," Johnston explained of his start, "because the next four games were in Moscow, and I wanted to play well so that if they needed me, I had proved myself."

Johnston's experience was invaluable in other ways. He had played for a decade in the NHL with the Bruins, and his role became almost one of goalie coach for Dryden and Tony Esposito, both of whom had plenty to handle adjusting to the Soviet style of play. A fresh set of eyes helped the two starters immensely.

"We talked a lot, especially during the games in Canada," Johnston explained. "In Sweden, we had the opportunity to stay there a week. By that time, we had things figured out mostly. Patience was the big thing. We knew, for instance, that when the Russians got the puck off to the side, they never shot. They'd move the puck back to the other side. So, as a goalie, what you had to do was position yourself at the top of the crease and stay there. You couldn't chase the puck, or they'd have an open net. I talked with Kenny and Tony throughout the series about having more patience because of how they handled the puck in our end. We had meetings every day with the coaches going over strategies about what we should and shouldn't do, both for ourselves and against Tretiak."

One fact of being the backup for six games that didn't faze Johnston was the prospect of being put in during a game. Sinden gave his starters full latitude, and it might have been unfair to put in Johnston cold. "There wasn't really any question about coming in," he agreed. "Whoever started that particular game was going to finish it, barring any injury, but it never came to that."

Like every other player with a significant other, Johnston was only too happy to see the players' wives arrive in Moscow for a little home comfort and morale-boosting – but it wasn't always perfect.

"I think it was very important to have our wives and girlfriends there," he said, "but they weren't treated like us. They never ate with us. They always ate by themselves. We were like dignitaries, but they couldn't eat with us. You talk about Cold War – it was Cold War. Cold War and cold borscht."

The wives' support was bolstered by incredible fan support that had been all but absent during the four-game series in Canada. "Before the last couple of games we got thousands of telegrams from people right across Canada," Johnston said. "We put them all over the dressing room. That was terrific. That gave us such a big boost. Plus, we had a good contingent who came over to watch the games. We finally got some cheers from the stands. It really encouraged us."

Of course, Johnston was part of the celebrations that erupted in the dressing room after game eight, a strange blend of elation, exhaustion, and utter relief.

"When we got to the dressing room, you saw twenty guys who were crying," he noted. "There wasn't a dry eye in that dressing room. It was such an emotional moment, and winning for Canada. Everybody was crying. It's tough to be able to tell people how great we felt. I was on a couple of Stanley Cup teams, but I never in my life had seen emotion like when we were in the dressing room after game eight."

Third goalie Ed Johnston was the backup for all of Canada's games except the first and the last.

#4 BOBBY ORR – HOPE DENIED FOR A TEAM PLAYER

It just wasn't meant to be. After leading his Boston Bruins to their second Stanley Cup in three years in May 1972, Bobby Orr underwent knee surgery less than a month later and was still very much recovering when Team Canada's training camp opened in mid-August.

"He was so far and away better than everybody else that the symbol of him being on the team we thought would be a benefit," coach Harry Sinden said of his extending an invitation to a player who probably wasn't going to play.

Orr arrived at Maple Leaf Gardens a few days after everyone else and immediately settled into a workout routine with the Leafs' physiotherapist, Karl Elieff, after which he'd skate lightly with the rest of the team. It was a given that he wouldn't play any of the games in Canada, but he hoped to be ready for the Moscow half.

The rehabilitation of the knee got to the point that Orr scrimmaged with the team on September 7, in Winnipeg, before the team flew to Vancouver, but he didn't feel well enough to make any predictions afterwards.

Such was his reputation, though, that the Soviets extended him a special courtesy. While the agreement stipulated that Canada could take only thirty players to Moscow, the Soviets agreed to make it thirty-one provided that extra player was Orr. They wanted him to play as much as he did.

The turning point came when Team Canada was training in Stockholm, Sweden. On September 13, he expressed a hope to play in the team's intra-squad game in Stockholm, and if all went well he'd play the weekend exhibitions against Sweden with an eye to getting in shape for the four games in Moscow.

"I want to play very badly," he admitted then. "I just hope I can get the green light to dress right away."

His situation was decided upon the day after his first practice with the team in Sweden, though. His left knee swelled up considerably, and he was unquestionably not going to play in the Summit Series. Still, Orr stayed with the team right through to the end. He watched every game with the other players not dressed that night, came into the dressing room between periods to support those skaters who were playing, and even practised while the team was in Prague, ever hopeful to get in some game experience.

Orr brought along his younger brother, Doug Jr., to Moscow, and young Doug served as the team's stick boy for game five, the first game in Moscow.

But, alas, Bobby never played for Team Canada, forced to the stands because of a knee that had only a precious few years of hockey left in it.

#14 WAYNE CASHMAN – GREAT CORNERMAN SILENCED IN SWEDEN

"Being part of the team was the best," Wayne Cashman said with pride. "Things didn't go well in Canada, and there were some hard feelings when we left for Sweden. We showed Canadian spirit, and the guys never gave up, even in the last game. We were down in the game, down in the series, down in just about everything, but we showed Canadian fighting spirit and won in the end."

Cashman was part of that spirit, especially in game two and again during the exhibition games in Sweden. He came from the Bruins, and his invitation to camp was based largely on his physical play in the corners on a line with Phil Esposito and Ken Hodge.

"I was very, very surprised and very disappointed that Ken wasn't invited," Cashman conceded. "Our line in Boston had set all kinds of scoring records over the last couple of years. It's not for me to question who was there, but I was disappointed. But when you think of it, there were a lot of guys who weren't there."

Team Canada coach Harry Sinden noted that Hodge "just wasn't that calibre of player" as the others in camp, but Cashman made the most of his opportunity. "I played with a bunch of different guys in camp," Cashman said. "I remember playing with Stan Mikita, and also with Gil Perreault, and with Phil, of course."

Sinden moved him around because he knew by default he could put Cashman with Espo and things would work out. After the disastrous result in game one, with Cashman watching from the stands, he got the call for what became a crucial game in Toronto.

"Sitting there watching game one, I understood some of the problems we had against them," Cashman articulated. "One was definitely that they were in better shape than us. They had played a lot of hockey over the last few months. That was their key training time. You could see our timing was off, and they appeared much faster."

More than that, their freewheeling style went unchecked, something Canada couldn't allow to keep happening. "I talked to Fergie before game two, and he asked me what I had seen in the last game. I told him our conditioning wasn't as good, they were a little quicker. He didn't have to say anything. That's why I was going in, to play a bit of a physical role without getting into any trouble, try to help slow them down. Nothing was really ever said."

One reason why Cashman was so good in the corners was that he knew it was his job to go to the "dirty areas" and get the puck to Esposito in the slot. If he could do that, Espo was the best in the world with his

Wayne Cashman brought much-needed tenacity and physicality to the team, but an injury in Stockholm prevented him from playing in the last half of the series in Moscow.

quick release and deadly shot. But few had the true grit needed to fill that role effectively game in, game out, every shift.

"It's a physical game," Cashman said matter-of-factly. "You have to be able to use your strength along the boards, use your body to get the puck into a position where you can pass it, time it with Phil. It's something we worked on a lot. Phil was great at getting into position in the slot so I could get the puck to him. That role was a physical part of the game. It was something that worked very well for us. We knew our roles, and each guy was good at what he did."

Cashman, like most players on the team, had a period of adjustment in training camp because this was the first-time players from various teams banded together as one.

"In those days, teams didn't get together with members of other teams," he explained. "Maybe at a golf tournament, but that was about it. That's how we were trained back then. Given that, I thought everything came together pretty well at training camp."

As well, he was one of many who came from small-town Canada (Kingston, Ontario, in his case) and followed the NHL exclusively. The Soviets and Czechs and international rules were the furthest thing from his conscious growing up and loving the game. "I played with Danny O'Shea in junior with the Oshawa Generals, and he had played with the Olympic team, and that was about all I knew about international hockey. There was little coverage back then."

Although he played well in games two and three (a win and a tie), Cashman was a healthy scratch for game four as Sinden sought to get some new players into the lineup. As fate would have it, Cashman played only in the two Swedish exhibitions, the second resulting in a serious injury that kept him off ice for the rest of the Summit Series.

"That series became quite physical," he said of the two Stockholm games. "At the end of the period of the second game, I was skating off the ice, and a guy came up behind me and speared me in the face. That's all I know. I didn't go to the hospital for a couple of days, but finally I had to go because it got so bad. It should have been stitched, but it never was. I didn't eat for two and a half weeks. I lost eighteen pounds. I had no energy, and we were in a country with different foods and diet. It wasn't like I could go and get a blender and make milkshakes."

Despite his poor health, Cashman, ever the team player, soldiered on, offering his support in street clothes without being able to go into the corners for Espo.

"We were in Russia … I wanted to be part of the team. There were a lot of great players there, but a lot of them didn't get to play. They never got credit for the fact that if we didn't have all these extra guys to practise against, we would have been in trouble. We would have had no one to practise against. We needed each other's competition. The guys who came along were NHL players, and they pushed you."

He watched the games in Moscow close to the players, vocal to the last. "I was sitting on the end of the bench when Paul scored. Right on the bench. Fergie told me to sit there … Everybody ran out when Paul scored. One of the wives ran out there. Harry, everybody went out. The emotion after the game was pure exhaustion, mentally and physically. Some guys had played a lot of hockey."

As for Cashman, he returned home and then went to the Bruins' training camp to work his way back into health and put on many lost pounds. "I was starting to get my energy back then, but I wasn't really ready then to play in Russia. I remember coming back home and for a couple of weeks I stuffed myself trying to get my weight back up."

#32 DALE TALLON – MR. VERSATILITY

W as Dale Tallon a forward who could play defence or a defenceman who could play up? Probably the latter, though even he wasn't so sure.

"I played defence my rookie year in Vancouver," he began. "Then I played different positions my second and third years. At the end of the third year, I played defence, and then I was traded to the Black Hawks. I was a centreman most of my life. In the last half of my last year of junior with the Toronto Marlies, we had numerous injuries, so our coach, Gus Bodnar, asked me if I could play defence. I had played some defence as a kid up in Noranda, so I became an offensive defencemen. And then when I was drafted by Vancouver, there were so many different opinions. Some people there thought I should be a centreman; some thought a left-winger, or defence. The coach asked me where I could play, and I said I'd play anywhere to help the team. I thought I was a better centreman all around. On defence, I was more of an offensive defenceman. I carried the puck and passed it. I had fifty-six points in my rookie year. As a defenceman in Chicago, I had sixty-two points one year."

Harry Sinden considered Tallon a defenceman and gave him a shot to play in the second game of the exhibition series in Stockholm, where he acquitted himself quite well. "I didn't play any of the games in Canada, but I played in Sweden. I went back and played defence. I was excited about my opportunity, and there was a chance I was going to play the first game in Moscow. I had a great time in Sweden and great time in Russia. I was just happy to be there. It would have been nice to play, but I also played in Prague. That was a helluva hockey game. The Czechs had a fantastic team. They were as good as the Russians, I thought. They were big and strong and could pass and skate."

"Sometimes it's not good to be versatile," Tallon added. "It's hard enough to be good at one position, let alone numerous positions. But it was Team Canada – I didn't care. I would have been a stick boy if they had wanted. It was just an honour to be on that team."

It was, of course, Tallon's first time on the bigger European ice, but he adjusted quickly and well and understood the differences. "You had to play more of a zone defence. You couldn't chase. The big ice forced you to play a zone. If you chased, especially given the way the Russians moved the puck, they were good in tight and made short, quick passes. You had to let them come to you because a lot of the play was in the corners and behind the net, and we weren't used to that, especially in the smaller ice surfaces. Every building had a different configuration. The Stadium in Chicago, the Boston Garden, the Aud, all had different dimensions. Pittsburgh was five feet wider than anywhere else."

In some respects, Sweden was the highlight for Tallon. "I learned a lot there," he admitted. "I had more confidence. Bobby Orr went with us on the trip. When I played in Sweden, he told me I should just play defence. 'Just do what you did in Sweden.' I felt good about that. The more I played, the better I felt. I felt I could have played any of those games in Russia, although I wasn't so confident going into game eight."

"At practise, though, the over-and-backs were long. Harry would skate us from one corner of the end of the red line to the other corner of the blue line, to the red line far boards, to the blue line far boards, to the end and back, so I had to get used to that."

Tallon came to training camp through three criteria. First, he was the second overall draft choice by the Canucks in 1970 and was considered one of the top young players in the NHL. Second, Team Canada wanted to have at least two players from each Canadian team, so he and Jocelyn Guèvremont were nominated from Vancouver. And last, he knew the assistant coach very well!

And, as luck would have it, an injury the previous season meant Tallon was in good shape once Canada's training camp started.

"I tore my knee in March, so I spent the summer rehabbing. I was also playing lots of golf that summer. I had a place in Vancouver, but I was playing golf on the Canadian Tour. I was also skating in Montreal on Monday nights in a summer league with [assistant coach] John Ferguson. I had just come off knee surgery at the end of my second season in Vancouver. I told Fergie that I was ready to go and I'd like to be involved, and I was selected to go to training camp in August in Toronto."

Prior to that, his knowledge of the Soviets and hockey overseas was negligible. "My recollections of international hockey were about Father David Bauer and Canada's National Team, guys who were dedicated to that team and travelled around. Age-wise, I was a bit in between. I was nineteen in 1970, but the Olympics was two years earlier and later. And pros weren't allowed to play. I went from junior to pro directly."

For Tallon, getting the invite was like going to a dinner party with all the people you admired in the world. "I was just twenty-one years old. We were there just to impress. It was a tough lineup to crack obviously. I was just elated to be there. I played on a line with Richard Martin and Gilbert Perreault, two great skaters. I was the safety valve. Let them do their thing. Harry told me to make sure I was the third guy and to cover up. It was a pretty good line, actually."

Necessity almost brought Tallon to a date with destiny. Injuries were threatening to force Sinden to make changes to his lineup at a time he wanted to maintain the status quo, and although he did so, there was a tenuous moment when Tallon almost got into the final game.

"Before game eight, Harry approached me and said that both Whitey Stapleton and Bill White were injured, and it was doubtful they'd be able to play. He told me get ready. I dressed for the warm-up. I was a little nervous. But they were both able to play. I got dressed and watched the game from various places. I walked around. Then, in the third period, I sat in Bobby Clarke's seat in the dressing room. He had a rabbit's foot there. I was being superstitious. Stupid stuff that doesn't have any impact on the game. I just waited and listened to the sounds — you know, who scored and who didn't based on the crowd. There were three thousand vociferous Canadians in one corner."

It's too bad Tallon never played game four in Vancouver, his NHL team, but then maybe it wasn't so bad after all given that the expansion Canucks were only two years old and not such a good team.

Dale Tallon (right) trades pins with Muscovite hockey fans.

"The atmosphere in Vancouver was just oppressive," he recalled of Team Canada's visit. "I was used to the booing. They had booed me plenty. By the time we lost game five in Moscow, it was like we had been abandoned. We were the dregs of society. We just pulled together and became really close and stayed close together in spite of what the media was saying. It all just made me stronger."

Ah, memories. Tallon may not have played against the Soviets, but he was a team player and proud of his role. "It was the best time of my career. It feels like it was just yesterday. I always look forward to our next get-together."

#34 MARCEL DIONNE – HALL OF FAMER GETS EARLY HONOUR

One might say that Marcel Dionne got his invitation to Team Canada's training camp as one of the kiddie corps of the NHL. Small but speedy and a superb stickhandler, the twenty-one-year-old had just completed his rookie season in the NHL with the Detroit Red Wings. He recorded twenty-eight goals and seventy-seven points and immediately established himself as one of the best young players in the league.

"In the summer of 1972, I had just finished my first year in the NHL, and after I got the call to come to Toronto to be on the team I started training. I knew exactly what I was up against. We were told that everyone might have an opportunity to play, but you look at all the great players. Looking back, this was the proper way to do it. It was the first time they were doing this kind of format, so players needed a training camp. It would have been tough just to have twenty-four guys practising against each other."

Indeed, the honour of being invited soon gave way to the realization that with thirty-five of the best players in the league, there wasn't much hope of making the team and playing all eight games. Whatever hope there was dwindled after the stunning 7–3 loss in game one.

"For me, I was young and in pretty good condition for training camp. The young guys were probably ahead of the veterans in that respect. And there were conflicting reports about how good the Russians were, but I know for a fact that changed after the first game. I walked into the dressing room and saw Yvan Cournoyer. He just said, 'Oh, my God, they are unbelievably strong.'"

Dionne had little exposure to the international game, save a few highlights the team reviewed during camp. "There wasn't that much international hockey to follow," he explained. "There was only *Hockey Night in Canada*, no sports networks or Internet. When I was playing junior in St. Catharines, I knew about Father Bauer and the National Team and guys like Fran Huck, but once you play in the NHL, you think that's it. The Olympics was for amateurs, but we found out pretty quickly how good our amateurs must have been after game one in Montreal."

The infamous scouting reports were partly to blame, but camp wasn't as focused or as carefully thought out as future teams would be. "Maybe there was a lack of intensity," Dionne suggested, "but it was three weeks of training camp, and everyone wanted to start playing games. We put the team together like it was an All-Star Game."

Without question, the first lesson Team Canada executives learned from the Summit Series was that you can't keep thirty-five players in a series that requires seventeen skaters a night. And those seventeen skaters have to have specific roles.

"It's impossible to have a team of nineteen great players," Dionne emphasized. "It's impossible. Nineteen superstars is impossible. It comes down to ice time. Great players need to play more than a minute or two every few shifts. If they don't, they're not effective, and they're not happy."

Dionne didn't care about these details back then. In 1972, he was getting exposure to the best players in the world, every minute of every day. "I looked at all the players there who were my idols, guys like Phil Esposito and Rod Gilbert, Jean Ratelle. Of course Montreal players like Lapointe and Savard and Cournoyer, whom I had met years ago. I knew Rick Martin really well, and Gil Perreault, Dale Tallon. I felt good about it. Just practising with the Roadrunner [Cournoyer] every day and seeing his speed, seeing how he practises, knowing how many Stanley Cups he's won. You get to understand winners."

Although Dionne didn't play in Canada, he did travel with the team to Stockholm for the two exhibition games. He played in the first of these, the first time he had played overseas on a sheet of ice that was fifteen feet wider (3,000 square feet of additional ice) and a much larger area behind the goals. "Playing on the big ice in Stockholm was a big, big difference," he admitted. "I was really amazed. I said to myself, 'You mean, hockey is played like that?' There's a lot more room to move the puck and play with it. A lot."

The entire team carried on to Moscow for the final four games at Luzhniki Arena, but desperate times called for desperate measures, and Coach Sinden decided to whittle his lineup down to the minimum and leave the other players irrevocably on the sidelines. In the process, four players went home, back to the training camps of their NHL teams, where they were vilified for their flight.

"If there was one problem," Dionne explained, "I think there was a lack of communication. I could have come back home as well — there were pressures back home — and it affected Rick Martin forever. I swear to God he never got over being called a traitor. Somebody should have come in and said to the young guys: 'Listen, this is one of the greatest events that might take place.' I was fortunate because I was with my wife-to-be, and I knew this was going to be a special time. For her, it was probably the best trip she ever had."

Although Dionne was happy he stayed — in part so he wasn't branded a traitor as well, in part because he got to experience the greatest series ever — it wasn't all roses and chocolates in Moscow.

"It was very difficult at the end," he admitted. "We didn't practise. When we got to Russia, the big team was on its own. The pressure was unbelievable, so the rest of us were by ourselves. It's like a horse. You keep that horse in the barn — that horse wants to come out and run! I realized that it wasn't going to happen that I play, but I had my shot later on in the World Championships, and in the Canada Cup in 1976. Sinden and John were under tremendous pressure, and I understand that. But you understand that when you mature in life. But I look back and think, 'Thank God I stuck with it.' If I looked back, I'd have felt really bad if I had left."

Dionne and the others who didn't play became fans, literally. "We were in the stands for the Moscow games," he said. "We walked around with the other guys who weren't playing and chitchatted. We'd see the guys in the dressing room after, but we didn't want to mope around. They had to play. We didn't have to be around for them — they knew we were supporting them."

The day after victory and a long celebration, the team was on another plane and off to "game nine," before coming home. "We got out of Moscow the next day pretty quickly," Dionne said with a chuckle. "The Russians weren't too happy with us, and we still had one more game to play in Czechoslovakia. It was a relief for everybody. And going to Prague was all about the return of Stan Mikita. That's all that mattered. The Czechs were the world champions that year. I remember Stan buying some crystal – about $10,000 worth – and then when he got home everything was broken."

Arriving home a changed man, Dionne picked up where he left off. "For me, going back to training camp in Detroit, I couldn't believe the difference in pace. It was so much slower with the Red Wings! It was just a notch higher skill-wise with Team Canada."

That notch may well have been a contributing factor in Dionne's development, though, one which took him to eight 100-point seasons and a career total of 1,771 points, second only to Gordie Howe at the time.

Marcel Dionne walks the streets of Moscow during an off day.

#37 JOCELYN GUÈVREMONT – EXPERIENCE IS THE KEY

In the 1971–72 NHL season, newcomer defenceman Jocelyn Guèvremont recorded thirteen goals and fifty-one points, impressive numbers given he was also big and strong and solid in his own end. He was one of Team Canada's young players invited to training camp to fill out the roster, even though he didn't except to play in any games.

"The NHL wanted to have two players from every team at training camp," Guèvremont explained, "so that's why Gilbert Perreault and Rick Martin were chosen from Buffalo and me and Dale Tallon from Vancouver. They needed to get thirty-eight players or so to scrimmage because they only had four weeks to get ready. The coaches picked their main team and then completed the roster with players from other teams."

Of course, the twenty-one-year-old accepted the invitation, but it was clear he wasn't there to challenge Brad Park or Pat Stapleton for a spot in the starting lineup. "I don't know about the other guys," Guèvremont said, "but they were very specific when I got there. They shook my hand and told me to enjoy the experience, but the feeling I got was that I wasn't going to play. I can understand that. They didn't want to have an extra sixteen guys floating around everywhere. But for me it was a great experience being on the ice with these guys. I was just a rookie, being out there with the top defencemen in the league."

Like most others in camp, he wasn't in top shape the day he arrived for first workouts at Maple Leaf Gardens. "I got the call only a couple of weeks before. We usually went to training camp to get into shape."

And like most of the others, his knowledge of the international game was almost zero. Being born in Montreal, and playing junior hockey there, his dream was the NHL. "I knew nothing about international hockey at the time," he admitted. "I was playing for the Montreal Junior Canadiens and I had been drafted by Vancouver. That's it."

Nonetheless, the experience was invaluable for Guèvremont, who happily accompanied the team across Canada and then on to Sweden and Moscow. Indeed, he played in both exhibition games in Stockholm. "The deal was that we would all go to Moscow," he explained. "And most of the guys played at least one of the two games in Sweden. I was lucky enough to play both. That was my first time playing overseas, but it's such a sad thing. I was just twenty-one years old and going with the flow, so I didn't realize at the time how special that was and what was happening. Even when we left Canada and we had won only the one game, tied one, and lost two, I didn't realize the importance."

Going from the freedom of Canada to the Iron Curtain was not so easy for him. "Moscow was a big culture shock," he said. "Whenever we stepped outside, someone was following us or escorting us. We went on one sightseeing tour, but that was it."

A significant part of the Moscow experience for the players was having their wives and girlfriends with them. In Guèvremont's case, though, it led to his early departure from the team and Moscow, which was never properly explained.

"The guys who were running the team knew exactly why I was coming home," he began. "My wife came to Russia, but from the first day she was sick. She couldn't eat. She was throwing up. So after three days I tried to get the doctors to help. I went downstairs and saw Alan Eagleson in the hotel lobby and asked him if the team doctors could see my wife. He said the doctors were only there for the players! I said, 'Well, I love you, too, but I think I'm going home.' I didn't know the other guys [Perreault, Martin, Gilbert] were leaving until a couple of hours later. They flew to Toronto, and I was the only one who went to Montreal. That's when I got bombarded by the media. They called me a deserter."

After settling his wife back in Montreal and getting her to full health, Guèvremont travelled west to attend the Canucks' training camp. It was from there that he followed the rest of the series.

"I watched game eight in Vancouver during training camp," he noted. "Actually, it was near the end of camp. A bunch of the players got together – it was an early morning game in Vancouver – and went to the house of André Boudrias or Orland Kurtenbach, I can't remember which. When I was watching the game, all I was thinking was, 'I wish I was there.' If my wife hadn't got sick, I would have stayed. I never would have left. That's not who I am."

Frank Mahovlich goes in alone on Vladislav Tretiak but the goalie makes the save.

#38 BRIAN GLENNIE –
READY, WILLING, ABLE

Dallas Smith's loss was Brian Glennie's gain. The Boston defenceman did not accept an invitation to play in the Summit Series, clearing a spot for Glennie to join Team Canada. Glennie, a bruising defenceman known for his excellent execution of the hip check, was anything but a scoring defenceman. In his first three NHL seasons, all with the Leafs, the twenty-six-year-old had exactly three goals. But he was a fine defenceman in his own end. He also had played for Canada at the 1968 Olympics in Grenoble, so he knew the Soviets, the international rules, the bigger ice, and all the associated elements that made the game so different in Europe from Canada.

"I was one of the last picks and got the phone call from Harry on short notice," Glennie said. "I got a couple of solid weeks of training in before camp. I usually started about a month before, but this was short notice."

"It was a brief training camp, all things considered," Glennie believed of the team's trying to put together a group to beat the best from the Soviet Union in just three weeks, in August no less. "I think their initial plan was to have that many players on the team because they had nobody to play against. We had some intra-squad games, which we called Red-and-White games, and some hard practices. At the start, I think Harry thought he'd get everybody into some games, but that changed in a hurry."

That change was the result of the game-one loss in Montreal, of course, but despite the stunning result, Glennie didn't see any game action in the series. "All we could do was keep working hard and get ready in case of injury," he said. "But Harry's hand was forced early. The more games you played, the better your situation. There's a difference between practice and games, and to put someone into the third or fourth game after missing the first few would have been very difficult. Everyone else was getting up to speed and getting that feeling of games being for real. It was a tough situation. The Soviets trained year-round and were as professional as we were. That was their job in the army – to play hockey."

Glennie's experience in Grenoble stood him well, although players had a tough time separating the warnings from the likes of him and Ken Dryden, who had played in the 1969 World Championship, and those made by coaches and general managers throughout the NHL who predicted an 8–0 rout in games by the Canadians.

"I think that my Olympic experience was part of the reason I was selected," he agreed. "I think also that I always played well at Boston Garden [where Sinden had coached]. I knew the Russians were a lot better than they were being given credit for. That being said, I think we worked as hard as we could in training camp. The hardest thing for us was to become a team, really, because we had been playing against each other for years in the NHL. I'm not saying you don't leave everything on the ice, but there were people you didn't know that well in the beginning of camp or didn't like that much, but we had to work our way through that. I think it took us a while to become a team. There were a lot of great players, and I'm sure there were some who were disappointed they didn't get to start the first game in Montreal."

Scheduling and preparation were the two major factors that kept the series close in Glennie's mind. To try to make a team out of superstars so quickly – and at a time of year when players are generally snoozing away the summer – was unreasonable, to say the least.

"I go back to what Father David Bauer said," Glennie noted. "He said the Canadian team will be fine so long as they don't score a couple of quick goals. And that's exactly what happened. The Russians played such a different style of game. During the Olympics, I'd get very frustrated because they'd come up ice, and then they'd turn around and go back because they didn't like what they saw. They always had great speed. I don't think that by the time game eight of the series was over that they'd ever beat us again if we kept playing. It was an adjustment for us, and we just weren't in the best of shape. And to mould us into a team in a couple of weeks, man, that was tough. In many ways, the deck was stacked against us, and it took some incredible strength and talent from the guys who ended up doing it for us."

Glennie did play in the first exhibition game in Sweden, a game that featured Borje Salming and Inge Hammarstrom on the other side. Those Swedes came to Canada the next year, playing with Glennie and the Leafs and transforming the league into one with true international flavour for the first time.

Because he didn't play in the series, Glennie spent more time walking the streets and was perhaps more aware of the political and cultural differences between East and West, democracy and Communism.

"In Russia one time," he told, "our bus made a wrong turn and we were immediately surrounded by police, who told us to back up. Obviously there was something on that street we weren't supposed to see. This was the Iron Curtain back then."

"I think even when we were in Sweden," he continued, "the Soviet authorities phoned us and said because of various bookings the wives had to stay in one hotel and the husbands in another. It was mind-warping. It was all sorted out, but it was all about disruption away from the rink."

The effect was all positive for him, though. "The Canadian fans all sat in one section, and it was quite humorous to see the soldiers trying to take the cowbells from them. But it was strange seeing soldiers with guns in a hockey arena. It's a whole different world that made you very, very happy to be born where we were born."

Glennie and the other non-playing members of the team were known as the Black Aces, an old term to refer to what today would be called a taxi squad. They practised hard and hoped for a chance to play.

"Harry would post the lineup on game day," Glennie explained. "That's the way he'd do it. That's the way you knew if you were playing or not. The Black Aces, as we called ourselves, worked very hard under John Ferguson. He kept everybody up because you never knew if somebody was going to get hurt. In game eight, two of our defenceman weren't sure they were going to be able to go, so Harry told Dale Tallon to be ready. As it turned out the guys could play. It was just a privilege to be on the team. On game days we'd have our own hard workout, and the boys would go for their pre-game skate, check their equipment."

One little-known story still holds a place in Glennie's memory of Moscow and the final game. "After game eight, Harry was in the dressing room. He told us to forget about everything the Soviets had done to us – the off-ice stuff was ridiculous – just find your bride and get on one of the two buses we have. The wives aren't going on one bus and the husbands on another like they told us. We were supposed to go to this function for both teams at the end of it all. We got there, but the only two Russians who showed up were Tretiak and Yakushev. They were getting an award of some sort. There were some derogatory remarks made toward Canadian management, so Harry told us to get on the bus and go back to the hotel for our own party."

Glennie got into one other game during the tour, the final game in Prague. Again, he was a keen observer of the social qualities of life as much as what happened on ice. "When I was in Prague just before the '68 Olympics, we played an exhibition game there," he related. "The people were so happy because Alexander Dubcek was coming into power, and people were smiling and laughing and happy. And then, going back there to play the exhibition game, seeing how the city had changed was shocking. Russian soldiers on the corners with guns. It was quite disturbing.

"I'll never forget the ovation the fans gave Stan Mikita," he said of the pre-game player introductions. "They started throwing flowers on the ice. They had to be an inch deep all over the ice surface. I had tears in my eyes. Incredible tribute to the man. I've never seen anything like it since or before. It's something I'll always remember."

After coming home, Glennie reported to Leafs training camp right away. That season saw new and special friendships with many former on-ice enemies, but not all. "It was special for a lot of the guys, but not everyone," he admitted. "I think the first exhibition game I played when I got back [Bobby] Clarke high-sticked me and I had to fight Schultz again. When it's over, it's over – in some people's minds. The great thing about keeping this anniversary going is that some friendships have really developed."

And as for returning to Moscow later in life, to where the series ended in triumph? "I really haven't had the urge," he deadpanned.

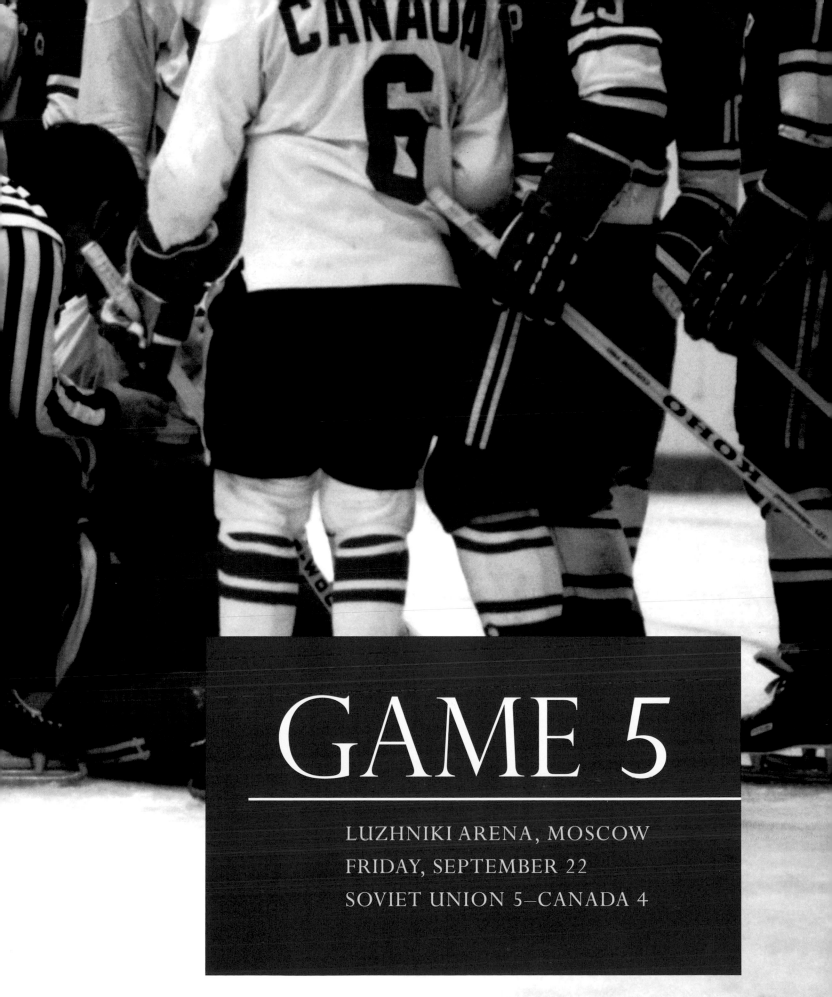

GAME 5

LUZHNIKI ARENA, MOSCOW
FRIDAY, SEPTEMBER 22
SOVIET UNION 5–CANADA 4

"It was a tremendous effort all the way through, and it's almost unbelievable how it ended up after Canada had so much of the play in the first two periods."

—FOSTER HEWITT

The importance of game five was forgotten for a few moments during player introductions when Phil Esposito's pratfall enlivened the sombre atmosphere of Luzhniki Arena.

TURNING A WIN INTO A LOSS

After a two-week break and a trip to Sweden that was crucial to team development, Canada had to cope with the departure of three players the day before game five as Vic Hadfield, Rick Martin, and Jocelyn Guèvremont flew home to their NHL training camps.

And, after a sensational two periods of play, Canada collapsed in the third period and turned what looked like an impressive and critical 4–1 win in game five into a devastating and humbling 5–4 loss. The Soviets scored goals eight seconds apart to key the comeback in a game in which the Clarke-Henderson-Ellis line was dominant.

The first game in Moscow's old Luzhniki Arena began with Olga Barinova presenting assistant captain Jean Ratelle with a loaf of local bread, followed by forty-four figure skaters ranging from ages six to fifteen presenting players from both teams with flowers.

The differences between Canada's arenas and Luzhniki were immediately evident. The Plexiglas was replaced by wire fencing reminiscent of Original Six days in the NHL; centre ice consisted only of a simple circle; and there was only one tier of seating in the arena. The rink was much wider and the goal creases semi-circular, not rectangular. Of course, Canada's red sweaters were white and the Soviets' white sweaters were now red. Rinkboard ads were all in English – Gillette, Catelli, Hitachi TV, CCM Sports, Jockey, Turtle Wax.

Player introductions took a turn for the lighthearted by the pratfall of Phil Esposito, who bowed to the crowd with his butt on the ice after he slipped and fell. On the other side, Vyacheslav Anisin was the only player on either team sporting a blue helmet!

Canada had the better of play in the first period and could have had more than a one-goal lead after twenty minutes. That goal came off a couple of fine plays. First, Rod Gilbert put on the brakes at the Soviet blue line to stay onside, and Gilbert Perreault tore down the right side, using his speed to intimidate the Soviets. Three opponents watched him and Perreault backhanded the puck into the slot, where J-P Parise snapped the first goal of the game.

Canada continued to be the much better team in the middle period, scoring the only two goals. The first came from Bobby Clarke. He won the faceoff to Vladislav Tretiak's right, and Paul Henderson slipped him the puck as Clarke went to the front of the net. He outmuscled Alexander Maltsev and slid the puck between Tretiak's pads, perhaps the first dubious goal the goalie had permitted in the series.

The third goal also came from the Clarke line off a faceoff, this time to Tretiak's left. Clarke won the draw, and a point shot from Guy Lapointe was blocked by the stick of Gennadi Tsygankov. It landed in front of Henderson's stick, and his quick shot beat Tretiak, who was still readjusting after the deflection.

Canada got a scare later in the period when Henderson had a partial breakaway. His shot was stopped by Tretiak, but Henderson fell on the follow-through, tumbled into the boards, and lost consciousness. In the meantime, Canada's goalie, Tony Esposito, made some big saves, but the Soviets got on the board early in the third when defenceman Pat Stapleton was beaten at his blue line and Yuri Blinov went in alone from the left wing. He cut in on goal, and as Tony Esposito raced out to cut him off, Blinov waited and slipped the puck into the empty net.

Canada's fourth goal was a thing of beauty. Clarke got the puck inside his blue line and looked up to see Henderson streaking up the far wing. Clarke lobbed a perfect pass between two Soviets, and Henderson went in alone, beating Tretiak between the pads with a quick shot.

Incredibly, the rest of the game belonged to the Soviets. Canada lost control of the game and tempo, and the home side managed a remarkable rally. It started with a point shot from Yuri Lyapkin that was deftly deflected in front by Anisin. Just eight seconds later, Vladimir Shadrin sprung free and beat Esposito along the ice to the far side. In a breath, a dominant 4–1 lead became a tenuous 4–3 advantage.

Playing four-on-four after the mid-period change of ends, the Soviets tied the game when Alexander Gusev's shot from the top of the circle beat Esposito to the short side over his glove. Canada almost recovered, Jean Ratelle hitting the post on a clear chance in front, but then Vladimir Vikulov got the go-ahead goal. Clarke lost the puck outside his blue line, and Vikulov was first to the loose puck, slipping it between Esposito's pads.

In the final minute, desperate to tie the game, coach Harry Sinden had the Clarke line out with Phil Esposito as one of the defencemen. Yvan Cournoyer had a sensational chance to tie the game, but his slap shot from close in was blocked by Tretiak. Canada now trailed 3–1–1 in the series. Their margin for error was down to zero.

"Harry told us to go for more goals," Clarke said after the game, "and I don't think we were tired. So, how can you explain it? You just tighten up instinctively."

Canada celebrates a goal early on, but by the end of the night the team was reeling from a 5–4 loss, its third in five games.

Tony Esposito reacts in frustration during a third-period blitz in which the Soviets lit the very large goal lamp four times to win game five.

Goalie Tony Esposito and defenceman Guy Lapointe follow the puck as it bounces high in the air in front of Canada's goal.

LINEUPS

SOVIET UNION — Vladislav Tretiak, Viktor Zinger (did not play) — Vladimir Lutchenko, Gennadi Tsygankov, Yuri Blinov, Alexander Maltsev, Boris Mikhailov, Alexander Yakushev, Vladimir Petrov, Valeri Kharlamov, Vladimir Vikulov, Vladimir Shadrin, Vyacheslav Anisin, Viktor Kuzkin, Alexander Ragulin, Alexander Gusev, Yevgeni Mishakov, Alexander Martinyuk, Yuri Lyapkin

CANADA — Tony Esposito, Ed Johnston (did not play) — Brad Park, Yvan Cournoyer, Phil Esposito, Frank Mahovlich, Bobby Clarke, Gary Bergman, Ron Ellis, Paul Henderson, Pat Stapleton, Bill White, Rod Seiling, Rod Gilbert, Gilbert Perreault, Jean Ratelle, Peter Mahovlich, J-P Parise, Guy Lapointe

GAME SUMMARY

FIRST PERIOD

1. Canada, Parise (Perreault, Gilbert) 15:30
Penalties: Ellis (CAN) 3:49, Kharlamov (URS) 12:25

SECOND PERIOD

2. Canada, Clarke (Henderson) 2:36
3. Canada, Henderson (Lapointe, Clarke) 11:58
Penalties: Ellis (CAN) and Kharlamov (URS) 5:38, Bergman (CAN) 8:13, White (CAN) and Blinov (URS) 20:00

THIRD PERIOD

4. Soviet Union, Blinov (Petrov, Kuzkin) 3:34
5. Canada, Henderson (Clarke) 4:56
6. Soviet Union, Anisin (Lyapkin, Yakushev) 9:05
7. Soviet Union, Shadrin (Anisin) 9:13
8. Soviet Union, Gusev (Ragulin, Kharlamov) 11:41
9. Soviet Union, Vikulov (Kharlamov) 14:46
Penalties: Clarke (CAN) and Tsygankov (URS) 10:25, Yakushev (URS) 15:48

SHOTS ON GOAL

Soviet Union:	9	13	11	33
Canada:	12	13	12	37

IN GOAL

Soviet Union:	Tretiak
Canada:	T. Esposito

REFEREES

Uwe Dahlberg (SWE) and Rudy Bata (TCH)

OUTSTANDING PLAYERS

Soviet Union:	Vladimir Petrov and Alexander Yakushev
Canada:	Tony Esposito and Paul Henderson

#16 ROD SEILING – TOUGHING IT OUT

Rod Seiling had been in the NHL for the better part of a decade by the time 1972 rolled around, and he was one of the few players on the team who had international experience outside the professional confines of the NHL.

"I had played them in 1964 at the Olympics as well as a number of individual games in junior with touring Soviet teams," he noted. That Olympic experience in Innsbruck included a 3–2 loss to the Soviets on the final day of the tournament, a result that gave the U.S.S.R. the gold when a win would have meant gold for Canada. That team included the likes of Terry O'Malley, Brian Conacher, Marshall Johnston, and legendary amateur goalie Seth Martin.

"I was working on my farm just outside Waterloo and I got a phone call inviting me to training camp," Seiling said of 1972. "I was delighted. Any time you're asked to represent your country, it's a great honour."

But a training camp with amateurs for an Olympic competition was radically different than one with pros competing for the first time. Seiling understood as well as anyone the word team was a far more complex beast than simply writing nineteen names down on a piece of paper and the coach yelling, "Play!"

"Training camp was somewhat serious because those were the days when the guys on the other teams were your enemies, so you had this group of players used to going at each other, playing at the highest level, all of a sudden playing together," he began. "It's different. There were just certain elements you couldn't nail down but that were part of the fabric of the game. You could draw your pictures and diagrams and say you should be here and I'll be there, and all those other things, but that's only part of it. The team has to be able to work together, know automatically where the other players are going to be, work for one another and stick up for one another, and that doesn't come overnight. When you put this group of players together, it was asking a lot based on how the league was structured. Today is so different where so many of the players are friends. There was the camaraderie of going out to dinners, but we still weren't a team."

Seiling partnered with Don Awrey in training camp, and the tandem acquitted themselves well enough to be in the starting lineup for game one. "I certainly didn't underestimate them," Seiling said, "and I had suggested to the coaching staff prior to the first game that we dress six defencemen that night. We didn't, but we did thereafter."

Indeed, with only five defencemen working their way into shape playing seventeen Soviets in superb condition, it was only a matter of time before trouble started.

"What became clear partway through the game was that we were in no way in condition to play against them," Seiling admitted. "They were in mid-season form, and we were a bunch of NHL players who were used to coming to training camp and playing ourselves into shape. In those days, we played twenty-game exhibition schedules, unlike today when everyone comes to camp ready to go and there's ice anywhere you want it. Today, you can find any rink that has ice in the summer. They were few and far between in 1972 even if you wanted to find ice, but that just wasn't the way NHL players got ready for the season back then."

Coach Sinden made eight changes to his lineup for game two, and Seiling didn't play again until game four in Vancouver after the Montreal duo of Serge Savard and Guy Lapointe both were unable to play because of injuries. Seiling played once in Sweden and was right back in the lineup for game five in Moscow, but he was a healthy scratch for the final three games.

"I was standing behind the bench for the games I didn't play," he said, "but when Henderson scored I went out onto the ice with the whole team. I remember afterwards we were supposed to go to a reception at the hotel with the Soviets, but they never showed up, so we had our own party."

While some players choose to romanticize the experience of travelling to the heart of the Soviet Union in 1972, Seiling tells it as it is – or was. "Moscow was a Third World city in those days. As my wife later said, it wasn't one of our most memorable trips."

And, although he got to socialize with the Soviet players at later reunions – and even at an exhibition in Dubai with four U.S.S.R. players – Seiling has no regrets about a total absence of contact with their opponents in 1972. "You have to realize, it was a war then. We didn't want to talk to them."

Rod Seiling (left) and Peter Mahovlich shake hands with Vyacheslav Anisin (#22) and Vladislav Tretiak.

#33 GILBERT PERREAULT – END-TO-END MASTER

One of the greatest skaters the game has ever seen, Gilbert Perreault was another member of the "kiddie corps" who was invited to attend Canada's training camp but who wasn't likely to be an integral part of the series because of his youth.

"It was a great experience for me as a young player," Perreault said of the invitation. "There were thirty-eight players, and I was lucky to be part of it. Every summer I returned home to Victoriaville, where I was born. After I was invited to training camp, I started to train, but when you're twenty-one, you're in pretty good shape all the time."

A lifetime member of the Buffalo Sabres, he formed the famed French Connection line with Rick Martin and René Robert. The threesome was known for its tremendous speed and ability to be creative off the rush. Perreault had been drafted first overall by Buffalo in 1970 after an outstanding junior career with the Montreal Junior Canadiens, during which time he played an exhibition game against a travelling Soviet team.

"I played them once before when I was with the Junior Canadiens," he explained. "They were touring and playing the top junior teams in Canada. They played their final game against us at the Forum in Montreal. It was pretty much the same team as the one we played in 1972, Tretiak, everybody. I think we beat them about 9–2. We had some great players and great moments in that game."

"During any training camp," he noted, "you don't know if you're going to make the team or not. There were thirty-five players, but if you look at those years, Boston won the Stanley Cup in 1970 and 1972 and Montreal won in 1969 and 1971. They were the powerhouse teams, so we expected that most of their players would make the team. Those were the guys with the most experience as well. I was twenty-one, Marcel Dionne was twenty-one, Dale Tallon was twenty-one. You always hope to make the team when you're in training camp, but you have to go with experience."

Perreault was in the seats for the first three games of the series, but in game four, in Vancouver, Sinden decided to give the youngster a spot in the lineup.

"I didn't get many shifts in game four," he related. But he did score a goal early in the second period and briefly got the Vancouver crowd excited as it cut the Soviet lead to 2–1.

"My son and I watch the tape of it once in a while," Perreault said. "I got the puck in my own end, and

Gilbert Perreault was an electrifying skater, but also one of the younger players, so he didn't see as much ice time as he might have in a less-dramatic series.

I went all the way. That was my style of play, rushing the puck most of the time. I tried to cut in front of the net, and I was trying to make a pass to either Frank Mahovlich or Yvan Cournoyer. One of their defencemen put the puck in his own net as he slid down to try to block the pass. It was not a beautiful goal. It was a nice rush, but the goal wasn't much."

Perreault played one game in Sweden on the big ice and then was back in the lineup for game five in Moscow. "Game five was the same thing. I only got a few shifts. I understand. I was a young player. You have to play your veterans, who were playing great."

The writing was on the proverbial wall for Perreault after game five, another loss. Trailing badly in the series with no margin for error, Sinden went with a veteran lineup the rest of the way, leaving many others watching from the seats.

"You always expect to play every game," Perreault admitted, "but they kept all thirty-seven players. You can only play nineteen players, so that means there are eighteen players who aren't very happy, who want to be a part of it. I asked Harry if he was going to play me again, and he said no. So, I asked him to let me return to Buffalo's training camp to get ready for the season. I had a great start to the season. I had nineteen points in my first seven games. Personally, I think I made the right decision coming home."

Just because he was home didn't mean he had forgotten the team. Perreault watched the remaining three games and was thrilled by the outcome. "Of course, I watched all the games when I got back," he enthused. "It was such a great thrill and honour to be part of that team."

And his cherished Team Canada sweater? "I gave my jersey away to a kid who was a big fan of Team Canada who was in a wheelchair. I signed it and gave it to him. This was 1973."

Perreault went on to play seventeen seasons in the NHL, all with the Sabres, scoring 512 goals and 1,326 points in a career that took him to the Hockey Hall of Fame.

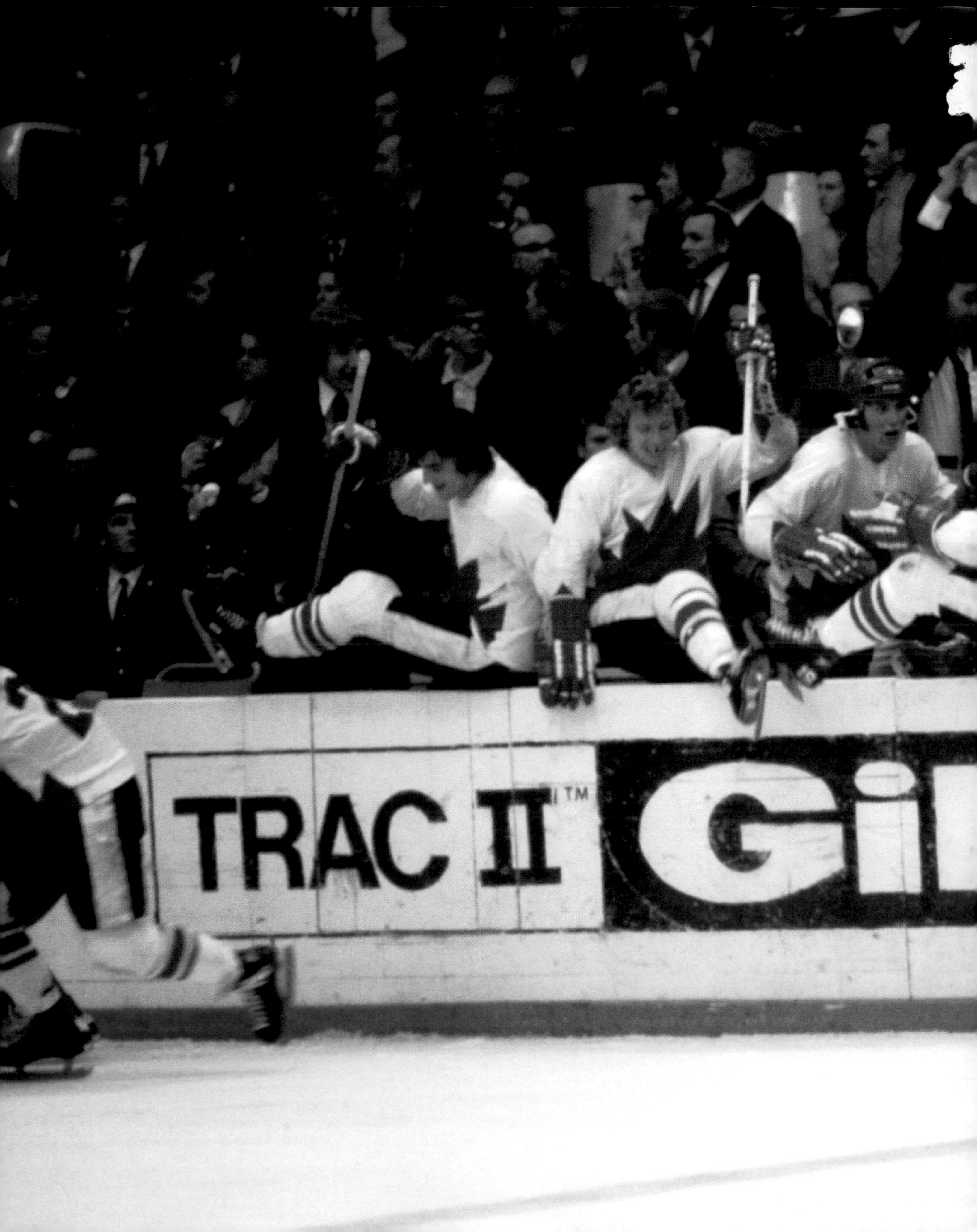
TRAC II™
Gi

GAME 6

LUZHNIKI ARENA, MOSCOW
SUNDAY, SEPTEMBER 24
CANADA 3–SOVIET UNION 2

"The Canadian players are in a frenzy, as well as the fans. They're grabbing each other, hugging each other, while the cooled-out Soviets are standing by."

——FOSTER HEWITT

Defenceman Guy Lapointe makes a lunging check to sweep the puck away from a Soviet player during game six, the first of three successive must-win games for Canada.

A PERFECT ENDING

Canada did in game six what it failed to do two days earlier, though only by the skin of its collective teeth. The team gained the lead and held on for the win, scoring three times in eighty-three seconds in the second period and then checking the Soviets, often ferociously, into the ice in the final, scoreless period for a 3–2 win.

But while the team's performance was overall the most complete and impressive, a new enemy emerged – the officials. A pair of West Germans had the whistle on this night, though soon after Canada would discover that one of them, Josef Kompalla, was East German (i.e., Communist, and biased toward the Soviets by political necessity).

The first five games were fairly refereed by international officials who had the daunting tasks of merging NHL sensibilities with international ones. It may have been different, but it was certainly not unfair for either team. Indeed, if anything the *modus operandi* for the games was "let them play," as many fouls both ways went uncalled, and the fouls that were called were pretty obvious. That all changed in game six.

By the end of the night, Canada had accrued thirty-one penalty minutes to just four for the Soviets. More significant, those numbers translated to 15:09 of power-play time for the Soviets to only two minutes for Canada. And in that power-play time for the Soviets was a two-player advantage for the full two minutes.

More indicative were two offside calls whistled against the Canadians in the second period when they were mounting odd-man rushes that surely would have created good scoring chances. Replays showed clearly these plays were onside, so whether by dint of ineptness or worse, the officials made terrible calls on two potentially important plays.

The controversy began when Gary Bergman got a tripping penalty halfway through the opening period, and as he was whistled off he threw his arms up to dramatic effect in protest. Then, moments after Bergman returned, Esposito earned a double minor deep in the Soviet end, and while he skated off he gave a throat-slashing gesture to Yuri Shatalov in frustration.

These were the only penalties of a physical and goalless first period, all of which were called by Kompalla. Although Canada was short-handed for six full minutes, the team survived the test and developed a greater pack mentality against their opponents and officials both. The vocal three thousand Canadian fans who had made the trek to Moscow, meanwhile, rallied around their heroes with shouts of "Go, Canada, Go!" that easily drowned out local cheers for the Soviets.

Ken Dryden was in top form in the opening period, making the best save of the series for Canada when he dove back to stop a Vladimir Vikulov shot with his stick that was headed for the empty net. Indeed, after two middling performances, he was excellent this night, and he credited his improvement to a radical change in style.

"I've always been a goalie who slid out toward the play to cut down the angles," he noted after the game. "I realized the Russians were getting behind me with quick passes, so I consciously began to drop back into the goal and stay there… It seemed to work out quite satisfactorily."

The second period was a veritable array of event and drama. It began with an early goal by Yuri Lyapkin, whose low-point shot beat Dryden cleanly. Dennis Hull tied the game soon after, though, lifting a rebound off a Rod Gilbert shot over the fallen Tretiak.

This was the first of three goals in just eighty-three seconds for the Canadians. The go-ahead goal was a succession of three rapid plays. Pat Stapleton took a shot that went just wide, but Red Berenson behind the net quickly passed out in front, and Yvan Cournoyer wasted no time in making his quick shot count.

Just seconds later, Paul Henderson skated over the blue line and took a quick slap shot that caught Tretiak off guard, giving Canada a 3–1 lead. Midway through the period, Bobby Clarke was given two minutes and a misconduct for a slash to the ankle of Valeri Kharlamov. The chop didn't look like much — and the Soviet played on the ensuing power play — but it kept Kharlamov out of game seven and rendered him ineffective in the grand finale.

Later in the period, Canadian assistant coach John Ferguson incurred a bench minor for vociferous complaining of the officiating, and at the same time Phil Esposito clipped Alexander Ragulin with a highstick that drew blood, resulting in a five-minute major. In all, Espo accounted for nine short-handed minutes on his own.

The Canadian penalty killing on the two-man disadvantage and combined major to Esposito was nothing short of sensational, and in the third period the Canadians were relentless. There was to be one final test, however, when Ron Ellis drew a late holding call. The penalty killers continued to be the star of the night, and Canada clawed its way back into the series with a tenacious victory.

Some 3,000 Canadian fans made the trip to Moscow for the final four games. Several Team Canada players are visible, including Dale Tallon (right of the man with the glasses, foreground), Stan Mikita (right of Tallon), and Marcel Dionne (in front of Mikita).

Alexander Yakushev lets go a shot as Bobby Clarke tries to distract him.

LINEUPS

SOVIET UNION — Vladislav Tretiak, Alexander Pashkov (did not play) — Vladimir Lutchenko, Gennadi Tsygankov, Alexander Maltsev, Boris Mikhailov, Alexander Yakushev, Vladimir Petrov, Valeri Kharlamov, Vladimir Vikulov, Vladimir Shadrin, Vyacheslav Anisin, Alexander Ragulin, Yuri Lyapkin, Valeri Vasiliev, Yuri Shatalov, Yuri Lebedev, Alexander Bodunov, Alexander Volchkov

CANADA — Ken Dryden, Ed Johnston (did not play) — Brad Park, Yvan Cournoyer, Phil Esposito, Bobby Clarke, Gary Bergman, Ron Ellis, Paul Henderson, Pat Stapleton, Bill White, Rod Gilbert, Jean Ratelle, Peter Mahovlich, J-P Parise, Guy Lapointe, Dennis Hull, Red Berenson, Serge Savard

GAME SUMMARY

FIRST PERIOD

No scoring

Penalties: Bergman (CAN) 10:21, P. Esposito (CAN – double minor) 13:11

SECOND PERIOD

1. Soviet Union, Lyapkin (Yakushev, Shadrin) 1:12
2. Canada, Hull (Gilbert) 5:13
3. Canada, Cournoyer (Berenson) 6:21
4. Canada, Henderson (unassisted) 6:36
5. Soviet Union, Yakushev (Shadrin, Lyapkin) 17:11 (pp)

Penalties: Ragulin (URS) 2:09, Lapointe (CAN) and Vasiliev (URS) 8:29, Clarke (CAN – minor, misconduct) 10:12, Hull (CAN) 17:02, P. Esposito (CAN – major) and CAN bench (served by Cournoyer) 17:46

THIRD PERIOD

No scoring

Penalties: Ellis (CAN) 17:39

SHOTS ON GOAL

Soviet Union:	12	8	9	29
Canada:	7	8	7	22

IN GOAL

Soviet Union:	Tretiak
Canada:	Dryden

REFEREES

Franz Bader (FRG) and Josef Kompalla (FRG)

OUTSTANDING PLAYERS

Soviet Union:	Alexander Yakushev and Vladimir Lutchenko
Canada:	Gary Bergman and Ken Dryden

#10 DENNIS HULL –
A FUNNY LOCK ON LEFT WING

I f Dennis Hull never played an NHL game, he still would have had a great career as an after-dinner speaker. Few are as irreverent and downright funny as the "third best Hull," as he later called himself.

But the Summit Series wasn't about yucks, and Hull could be as competitive as occasion called for, which is why his recollections of the 1972 series are both serious and funny.

"I had a hockey school in Chicago that I was running in a rink there," he explained of his life in the summer of '72. "I got a call from Harry inviting me to training camp."

So far, so good, but things went bad pretty quickly when Dennis realized that his brother, Bobby, wasn't going to be playing because he had just signed a huge contract to play for the Winnipeg Jets in the pirate World Hockey Association. "Maybe a week later, they made the announcement that players from the WHA weren't going to be allowed to play," Dennis related, "so I called Harry back and told him if Bobby isn't going to be allowed to play, I don't want to play. He said, 'I understand.' I talked to Bobby a day or two later, but he convinced me to represent the family and not worry about him. Fortunately, I called Harry back and he let me back on the team."

Dennis had been in the NHL with Chicago for eight years and was a top scorer, notching seventy goals with the Hawks over the previous two seasons. He was talented, but he knew the difficulties of putting a group together comprising players from around the league.

"It was very different because unlike today when players play against each other in different games and series and everyone knows each other well, and with free agency they're always moving from team to team, in those days the other guys were enemies. So it was different to meet them as teammates and find out what they were like."

The adjustment was more keenly felt for Hull as well because he had played under one coach and with two linemates for much of his career. "It was very different playing for someone besides Billy Reay as coach," he admitted. "He had been the only coach I'd ever had, and playing without my two linemates, Jim Pappin and Pit Martin, was also a difficult adjustment. The problem with training camp was that we were all promised a chance to play and we were going to win easily, but it obviously didn't work out that way. With all the great players, I thought I was going to get a chance to play sometime, but I certainly wasn't surprised I didn't play the first game."

In fact, Hull didn't get a chance to play until game four in Vancouver, and because that game went poorly he wasn't dressed for game five. He did play in the final three games, though, all victories.

"Harry never talked too much about who was going to play or not," Hull noted of the coach's methods for making rosters. "In Winnipeg, I was told I was going to play, but I came down for the game and found I wasn't playing. I was surprised about that, but I guess they wanted to keep the winning team from Toronto. They switched it up in Vancouver by playing me and Bill Goldsworthy, and I got a chance to play with the great Jean Ratelle, which was a real thrill."

Hull scored the final goal of that game, in Vancouver, but it only served to make the score a little less embarrassing. "I remember Phil Esposito giving me a perfect pass for a breakaway and I fired it past that sieve," Hull joked four decades later of beating Vladislav Tretiak. "The way to beat him was shooting because he stayed back in the net. He wasn't like our goalies who came out and cut off angles."

Like all other players on Team Canada, Hull found the larger ice surfaces in Stockholm and Moscow unfamiliar. "I'd never been on Olympic-sized ice before, so it was very different. I told Harry we needed a

Dennis Hull goes one-on-one against Soviet defenceman Viktor Kuzkin.

snowmobile if he wanted to change goalies, the net was so far away. But it's very hard to play a physical game on the big ice, which makes it better for the skilled players."

The ice must have suited him because he scored a big goal in the second period of game six to tie the score 2–2. "I was in front and the puck came across to Gilbert who passed it to me, and I put it up in the top shelf."

Then, the trademark humour. "That tied the game and then Henderson scored later. I set the game up for him," he said, trying (desperately) to take some credit for Henderson's heroics in the series.

Hull went on to joke that the only reason he played the final three games was that he was the last one standing on the left wing. "There was only one reason I played. Attrition. Two of the guys who went back to Canada were left-wingers, Richard Martin and Vic Hadfield. I was the only one left, so I played the last three games, thankfully."

Hull took over Hadfield's place on the Rangers' line with centre Jean Ratelle and right-winger Gilbert, "which was quite a thrill," he said.

More than being a thrill, the line changed focus and played a starring role in the come-from-behind series win. "I was proud of the way we played as a line," Hull said. "I was Vic Hadfield's fill-in, and to play a regular shift with Gilbert and Ratelle and hold our own against a fabulous Russian team, I thought we did a good job. I'm not sure we were ever scored on in those final three games. I don't think we were. I played my position well. I went up and down the wing and took direction from Ratelle. He was very helpful. I think we played very well as a line."

Hull had a stall next to Yvan Cournoyer in Moscow, and it was this proximity that led to a lifelong friendship – and a final Summit Series jab. Hull never won a Stanley Cup during his lengthy NHL career while Cournoyer won ten times with the Canadiens.

"My greatest memory was right after the final game," Hull started. "I was sitting next to Yvan Cournoyer, and I asked him if this what it was like to win the Stanley Cup. And he said to me, 'You don't know!?' Pretty mean, right?"

After a pause, Hull furnished a postscript. "Yvan said this is ten times better than the Cup, so I always figured I won ten Stanley Cups."

Hull played two nights later in Prague but not necessarily because he had made the team full-time by now. "We'd been up all night," he related, "and when we got to Prague, Harry Sinden picked the team this way. The bags were coming out, so he lined everybody up along a wall and walked down the line and he said, 'You look like you can play. You don't look like you can play.' That's how he picked the team."

On a serious note, one of the few on Hull's guffaw-filled register, he noted what most players felt. "Things changed for sure after the series. Billy Reay, one of the cleverest guys I ever met and my mentor, said to me that it's never going to be the same playing against these guys because you've gone through something like that. And he was right."

#15 RED BERENSON – WORLD CHAMPIONSHIP GOLD

Few men in hockey have had a career to compare to Red Berenson's. Born in tiny Regina, Saskatchewan, in 1939, he was one of the first Canadians recruited for an American university. After playing three years with the Michigan Wolverines in the early 1960s, he embarked on an NHL career that lasted seventeen years and nearly one thousand games, and then he returned to University of Michigan in 1984, where he has been coaching ever since.

Berenson told the story of how he went from Canada's west to the centre of American hockey. "I was playing junior hockey in Regina and the coach there was Murray Armstrong. The previous year, before I was on the junior team, I used to practise with him, so I was one of the young prospects coming up through the system. He went to the University of Denver to coach, and he tried to recruit every player out of Regina to play in Denver. And he did. All kinds of players went down. He had played in the NHL, and he was a big-name coach. In the meantime, I got the message that education is important, that you want to have something to fall back on because you don't know if you're going to play in the NHL. There were only six teams. Careers are short. I made up my mind that's what I was going to do, and when I started looking at different schools, we came up with Michigan as being a big-time school with a great hockey history, and it's right next to Detroit, where Gordie Howe played, so it appealed to me. This was a huge step, and five of us from the Regina Pats team made the decision to come down here. Bill Hay also made the NHL through college, but we were among the first ones to come straight from college to the NHL. I really liked Murray, but it just didn't work out that I went to Denver."

Berenson started his pro career with the Canadiens at the end of the 1961–62 season and went on to play for the Rangers, St. Louis, and Detroit, the team he was with in 1972 when he was recruited for the Summit Series by coach Harry Sinden.

"I went to Alaska that summer," he recalled. "I took my family there. We took our trailer and spent the summer up there. We came back in time for the training camp. I think we left in June and got back in late July. In my passport photo, I had a thick beard because I had been in Alaska all summer and hadn't shaved. When they called me, I had to have my picture taken for my passport, and I had this ugly beard. It was the only time in my life I had a major beard."

Beard or no, the helmeted Berenson happily showed up for camp in Toronto in August. "Like everybody else, I was honoured to be part of the team trying out. At that time, no one knew who was going to play.

There were no guarantees. I think we were promised to play in at least one game. In those days, it was an honour to be chosen to play in an All-Star Game, and this was sort of like that at the start. We had no idea it was going to become the series it became. But it was also a compromise because we had to report in August, which meant we were giving up a nice chunk of our summer."

Two other factors separated him from the others. First, he had played for Canada at the 1959 World Championship, winning gold in Czechoslovakia with teammates such as J-P Lamirande, Al Dewsbury, and Pete Conacher. As well, he was president of the NHL Players' Association, and as such was on good terms with one of the Summit Series organizers, Alan Eagleson.

"I was one of the players who had had some overseas experience playing on the big rinks and against the top teams there," Berenson concurred. "But we didn't know who was going to be on the Soviet team in 1972. I played with the Belleville McFarlands in 1959, which was thirteen years previous. Still, I had a lot of respect for those players because they were the best. No one was in the pros yet, so I knew they were good, but nobody knew how good."

Based on his play at training camp, Berenson played in game one in Montreal. As (bad) luck would have it, he didn't play again until game six. "I played with Mickey Redmond and Peter Mahovlich," he recalled of the series opener. "We were together in training camp, and we had a pretty good camp, so we were in the start-ing lineup. It was a pretty big deal. We played hard and played pretty well, but when you look at the result, the coach had to make some changes. Nevertheless, Peter was the most prominent player of the three of us as the tournament wore on. I'll never forget that game in Montreal. Kharlamov was just flying. That's when we realized they're not only in better shape, but they're really good players. They looked like high-school players with shoddy uniforms. They looked like second-rate team – until the puck dropped."

"When we got into that first game, we were all pumped up, and Espo scored right away, so we took the lead and started to think, 'Well, they're good, just not as good as we are. It was only a matter of the score,' we thought. By the end of the second period, we were just whipped, and they were just starting to come on. It was all conditioning, and they were in much better shape than we were. They were used to playing tour-naments like this, and they probably had skated all summer. They were in mid-season form while we were in pre-season form. It was a shock to everyone in Montreal that by the end they were much the better team, but I can tell you, a big part of it was game condition."

Red Berenson is checked closely by Vladimir Petrov of the Soviet Union.

One of the central problems for the team as it travelled across Canada was Sinden's being pulled in two directions. He had promised thirty-five players that they'd get into at least one game, but it became immediately clear he had to go with his best because the Soviets were much better than expected.

"Harry and Fergie did a great job of keeping the players in the right mental state and sticking together, working together, having some fun," Berenson explained. "We had all these extra players. Our top line was probably expected to be Ratelle, Gilbert, and Vic Hadfield. They had a fantastic year the last year. Frank Mahovlich, Cournoyer, Marcel Dionne, we had a lot of good players. You could have put together probably seven good lines. The coaches had to change the look of our team and play them on a regular basis. By the time we got to Vancouver, we had lost, won, and tied. Losing in Vancouver was the back-breaker."

Berenson played in the second exhibition game in Sweden, and that bode well for his chances to play again once the series resumed in Moscow. "We went to Sweden, and I played well in one of the two games there, so I was an option. But Sinden realized he had to go with the players who were getting into game shape and keep going with them because they're getting better every game. We can't keep changing the lineup every night and expect players to come in and catch up with the game speed."

Although he didn't play in game five, the first in Luzhniki Arena, he was in the lineup two days later because of the monumental collapse at the end of that first game. "I remember game one in Moscow. We had a three-goal lead, but the Russians came back and took over and won the game. But I remember going into the dressing room after and telling the guys, 'We can beat this team. The way we played tonight is the way we have to play,' outside of the last ten minutes when they caught fire. We started to play our game and had success. That was the building block for the rest of the series. I played the second game, but I never got my nose out of joint that I didn't play again."

In looking back, Berenson recalled how the country's and team's approach to the series changed so quickly and so dramatically. An "exhibition" became a "war," and an easy eight games became a fight to the death for pride and nation. "We wanted to win. We did not appreciate the monumental-type series that this was becoming. We just wanted to save face and win some games over there, show that we could beat them and be the better team. We had the momentum at the end. We had them on their heels. It wasn't a surprise to me that we won. It wasn't a big overachievement. We expected to win, maybe not the way it happened, but our expectations started growing in game six. It finally happened in game eight. We finally proved that we were the better team. It wasn't just one player. Henderson had a terrific and heroic role, but it was so many players. It was our defence and it was our goalies and penalty killers, and it was Esposito and his leadership, so many unsung heroes on that team, and even the coaching staff for keeping it together. It was a great team effort."

True to the team and its meaning to the players and to all of Canada, Berenson has remained an active member of Team Canada '72 – and he wouldn't have it any other way. "The hockey part doesn't change as much, but the reputation of the event has endured," he said with surprise. "This group gets together every year for a golf outing in Toronto. And there are always things that come up that I didn't know about at the time. Stories keep adding to what you remember or read. It's unbelievable some of the stuff. It's too bad we didn't all keep a diary. The Russians helped us a lot. They helped us focus more on conditioning, on playing the off wing and one-timing the puck. And look at how things have evolved. Forty years later look at all the Russians and Europeans in the NHL, and look at the skill level."

#23 SERGE SAVARD – MR. UNDEFEATED

"I don't think it's possible to elevate yourself emotionally any higher than we did in 1972. We were so proud. The country stood still for that last game. Everyone remembers where they were that day. I was a proud man."

Proud yes, and for good reason. Serge Savard is the only player on either team who didn't play in a losing game. By virtue of playing in games two, three, six, seven, and eight, he can boast something pretty special.

"It just happened that way," he said with a laugh. "Every time you play, you want to win, and it just happened that way. It's something I'm proud of, but I don't take credit for it. If I played in the first game, I don't think I'd have that record."

Indeed, fate and circumstance help him post that unbeaten record. Savard was invited to camp perhaps with little expectation, but he shone when given the chance. Yes, he's a Hall of Famer, but in 1972 he had missed most of the last two seasons with serious breaks of the same leg. Who knew of his determination and powers of recovery?

"I was very happy to be invited to the training camp," he acknowledged. "I wasn't sure if I was going to be invited because of my injury the year before, but then a few guys didn't come to camp, like Jacques Laperrière and Dallas Smith, so it made room for a guy like me. I went to the camp in Toronto. I don't think they expected me to make the team at the start, but it was a challenge for me."

On the positive side, Savard knew first-hand about the Soviets from his junior career in the Montreal system. "I was pretty aware of them because I played against the Russians with the Junior Canadiens and with the Toronto Marlies in Toronto. The Marlies played against the Russians, and they took four players from other teams, including me and Bobby Orr. We lost at the Gardens 4–3, and the next night in the Forum we beat the Russians 2–1 with Jacques Plante in the net. He came out of retirement, and he played one of the best games of his career. In 1965, we played against them as well, winning 2–1 again, I think."

Despite the odds, Savard was impressive at Canada's training camp in 1972, and it was clear he had recovered from his injuries. "I was ready every day to work hard and I had a very good training camp," he admitted. "I think I played well enough in camp and in the exhibition games to start the first game in Montreal. I thought I should, and I was a little disappointed that I wasn't dressed."

It was a blessing in disguise for him. He got to watch the Soviets from the seats and was able to make

Serge Savard was arguably the best and most poised defenceman on Canada's roster.

some adjustments from the comfort of the press box rather than game situations on the bench. He was more than ready for game two.

"The team was expected to win all the games, but I wasn't expected to be a starter. If Canada had won the first game, I don't know that I would have played at all. That's the way it is. We lost badly, so they made changes for the second game. We won that, and I played the rest of the series."

Well, not every game. Savard was a calm and cool presence on the blue line in the big win in Toronto and played in the 4–4 tie in Winnipeg. Then, more bad luck befell him.

"After game three in Winnipeg," he related, "we had a practice the next morning. I took a slap shot from Red Berenson off my right ankle. I had a hairline fracture. I flew to Vancouver with the team, but when we landed I needed a wheelchair because I couldn't walk. I went to the hospital and then flew home the next day. Actually, I was on the plane flying to Montreal when the game was being played, so the pilot would come on the intercom all the time to give us the score. We had a week off and then flew to Sweden. I didn't play the two exhibition games, but I practised."

Savard thrived on the wider European ice despite his injury. A puck-carrying defenceman who controlled the pace of play with masterful success, he was a general on the blue line whenever he was out. "The big ice was an advantage for defencemen who were more mobile, and I looked at myself as a mobile defenceman. I was fairly successful on the bigger rink."

Although Savard was ready for game five, Sinden opted to rest him. Plans changed quickly, though, as in game one in Montreal, after Canada let a dominating 4–1 lead slip away in a 5–4 loss. Savard was back for game six.

Team Canada's hotel was also host to some big names in Montreal, and Savard remembers the circumstances well. "The Rocket was there, and I spoke to Jean Béliveau at the hotel several times, and our manager, Irving Grundman, was also there. This was the number-one sports event of the time."

Savard had won the Stanley Cup three times before the Summit Series and won again five times after, but nothing can challenge the place in his memory of those twenty-eight days in September 1972.

"It was a great feeling when Paul scored and an even greater feeling when the game was over. We went through so many emotions. It's the greatest thrill of my career. I don't think you can compare this to the Stanley Cup. Hockey was so different in those days. Hockey was Canada and Russia, and today hockey is so international. The Americans didn't produce many players, but today they have about 20 per cent of the players in the NHL. We have players from many countries now and the NHL is international now, and '72 is one of the main reasons."

Despite his highly competitive streak, Savard was always a gentleman on ice and off. As a result, he appreciated the players as teammates and opponents, and socially as well.

"I had more friends than I had before," he said with a laugh forty years after some of his toughest adversaries became united for a common cause. "The funny thing is, it's the guys you really don't like whom you become friends with, like Bobby Clarke and Phil Esposito. Those are the guys you don't like to play against, but then you're on the same team with them and you say, 'Well, they're not that bad.' And then they become friends!"

#29 KEN DRYDEN – SUMMIT SERIES DIARIST

Does the goalie make the man or the man make the goalie? Is Ken Dryden who he is because he's a goalie, or is he a goalie because he has a singular perspective?

Who else has such a story to tell about simply receiving a phone call inviting him to Canada's training camp?

"I was in Vienna, Austria, when I got the call," Dryden explained. "The U.S. ambassador's son, who was about twelve, really loved hockey but didn't have much opportunity to play, so the U.S. Embassy was looking to set up a hockey school for four or five days that would involve kids from across the international community living in Vienna. They asked if I would be a part of that. As well, they arranged for a couple of soldiers who played on the Canadian Forces Base team in Lahr, Germany, to come down, so the three of us ran this hockey clinic. Then, through the Canadian Embassy, I got word that Harry Sinden was trying to find me and would be calling."

And almost from that moment on, Dryden started taking notes for a book he'd collaborate on, his first full-length project that would fascinate him to the point of writing again and again. It was an itch first scratched through Hockey Canada three years earlier.

"The first article that I ever remember doing was for a magazine that lasted about five issues called *Sport Canada*," he related. "When I finished at Cornell, we had played at the NCAA finals in Colorado Springs and then I flew to Stockholm as an add-on for the Canadian National Team for the 1969 World Championship. And *Sport Canada* asked me after that World Championship to write a story about that, which I found really fun to do. And then I had gotten to know Mark Mulvoy because he used to cover college hockey – to the extent that *Sports Illustrated* covered it – and he was doing a story on my coach at Cornell, Ned Harkness, so he was with our team for two or three games. By the time I was with the Canadiens, Mark was the hockey writer for *Sports Illustrated*, and I got to know him that much more. And then in the summer of '72 he came to me with the idea of doing a book together on the series, and I said sure. Mark was the one who did the writing. We did lots of interviews and I would keep notes, so there's a lot of me in it that way, but it's the only book that I've been involved with that I didn't really write."

Writing and goaltending go hand in hand, so to speak. After all, a goalie needs to observe and understand what is happening in front of him in order to play sound positionally and make a save. To that end, Dryden had

175

two significant adjustments to make for the Summit Series. They weren't easy and they weren't natural, but they needed to be done.

First, being an NHL goalie, he liked to come out of his net to cut down the angle of the shooter. Second, he played with a rectangular crease, so he got his bearings that way. Neither of these was going to work against the Russians.

"Starting in the early to mid-1960s, the slap shot was the big offensive weapon, so if you're a goalie, you had something coming at you faster than you were used to facing and you had less time to react than you were used to," he started. "So you had to position yourself in a way that you may not need to move far or not at all. So the style for a goalie was to come out and cut down the angle. So when you move out, you need reference points or else you lose where your net is. You've moved far enough out that you can't even touch it. Goalies are used to using the shaft of their goalie stick almost like an antenna and whack the post with it so you know where you are. So, when you move from the rectangular crease to something that is both a different shape and is an arc, which has a continuous lip to it, it's hard to tell where you are. That, in combination with the way the Soviets played – they didn't play vertically back to front, they played more side to side – made it impossible to move out as far as you're used to. If you do, you have the angle covered, but if he makes a pass to the side, the receiving player has nothing but an open net. You had to make the two adjustments together. You had to take control of your game, and some of the things you'd normally do spontaneously you had to hold yourself back. But it was an absolute necessity. You couldn't play that Soviet team any other way."

Making things a little trickier as well was establishing a rhythm. Both Dryden and Tony Esposito were their NHL teams' main goalie, used to playing every game. But neither was exceptional enough against this new opponent to play every game, and coach Harry Sinden alternated them with some unpredictability.

"As a goalie, you like to play," Dryden acknowledged, "but you also know the other goalie is really good. It may have been natural for me to play in Montreal, but certainly the next two games were obvious that Tony would play. We tied in Winnipeg, 4–4. If you looked at that with the perspective after game five, a tie was a pretty good result, but they came from behind to win. So it was much less obvious that he would play the fourth game. But after I played the fourth game, Tony was going to play the fifth game. And then they came back to win. It was after that game that I recall Harry telling me that I was going to play the next game, then Tony would play the seventh game, and then I would play the eighth game. The first five followed an obvious pattern, but then for whatever reason Harry decided, instead of going game by game, he wanted to play it out for the last three games that way."

Dryden also expounded on the concept of heart and desire overcoming the skill of the Soviets. Today, if Hockey Canada wanted to inspire its World Junior team to great things, it could show highlights of Henderson's goal in 1972, the Gretzky-to-Lemieux goal at the 1987 Canada Cup, Sidney Crosby's golden goal at the Vancouver Olympics. But in 1972, what did Team Canada do for inspiration? How could it go to the arena for game six, and then game seven, and then game eight, knowing it had to win each time – and then do just that?

"What you draw on are your own life experiences," Dryden theorized. "When I was with the Leafs in 1999, we decided to create a century-ending/century-beginning retrospective on hockey. That became

Dryden's height and pensive gaze make this one of the most famous and iconic poses in hockey.

Open Ice, and it was very interesting and proved to be useful, but one of the points of that – and one that had come out over the course of the previous twenty-five years as well – was that clearly in terms of the style of approach for the Soviets and for us, we played a lot more games and they practised a lot more. That was a very obvious difference between us. And we always had a kind of understanding that you developed your skills in a game, and if you had a chance to play a game, you played a game. Why practise? If you had an hour of ice time, why not play a game? That's what we had done right from the time we were kids, and that's what everyone before us had always done. If you practised, you did that on your own time. You did it on the streets or driveways or a patch of ice somewhere. What was very much a part of the focus of that Open Ice conference was that at that time most of the NHL awards were going to Europeans. That's what had developed at the end of the century, now how do we make the next century different? The concept evolved that we're good in closed ice and we're not good in open ice. Part of it was a different balance between numbers of games and numbers of practices. That's a long preamble to asking what are the special skills of the Soviets. They had skills associated with practices. Five-man play, passing, lines that never changed, year after year the same players playing together. What were our skills? We played games. We were so much more experienced in games than they were. They were so much more experienced in practice. What do you learn in a game? You learn how to compete. You may think you have an answer going into a game, but if you don't, you know how to find one. And you know there is an answer. And you know you have up until the final buzzer to find that answer. And it's there. You may not find it in time, but that doesn't mean it wasn't there. It's there. It's up to you to find it. For us, that was our life experience, and the life experience of those who came before us in Canadian hockey. We knew how to compete. We knew the lessons of competition. We knew that there was always a way to win. We knew there was always a way to lose. We knew that even if there's five minutes to go and you're down four goals, there's a way. As unlikely as it is – you're down 4–0 and you haven't even scored one goal in fifty-five minutes – there is a way of scoring four in the last five minutes to tie the game and find a way to winning it in overtime. That's what you draw on. It's not one specific memory. Every one of those players in our dressing room had thirty of them in their lives where they had the game won, and they lost, and in forty other games they had the game lost – and they won."

The series was full of unique situations and crazy moments. Think Esposito falling during the player introductions in game five, Alan Eagleson being escorted across the ice, Parise swinging his stick at a referee, Henderson's winners in games seven and eight, to list just a few. And after Henderson's final goal, there was Dryden skating the length of the ice to join teammates, coaches, and even a couple of the wives on the ice to celebrate.

"It was just the most natural thing in the world to do at a moment like that where, after all that had gone before, and all of the disasters and then building everything slowly, one piece at a time, and then finally putting that final piece into place, then that incredible combination of huge euphoria and huge relief, I suppose that's what made my legs move. And I suppose just as some people say they don't have any kind of "mind memory" but have an oral memory or memory based on smell. Well, the oral memory I have – and it's absolutely clear – is in that skating up the ice with goalie skates that were big and really awkward, and trying to skate as quickly as I could, but skating *clonk clonk clonk*, and that sound in my head and the *clonk clonk clonk*. And then, as if it's coming from somebody else, is hearing my own whoop, screaming, 'Yay!' as I moved up the ice. And what I absolutely remember in the middle of that pile of celebration is thinking, 'Oh, my God, there's still thirty-four seconds to play! I have to get a hold of myself. I can't blow it now!'"

Dryden's best effort was game six. This was the game when he clearly changed his style of play, staying in the net more and taking away the backside pass the Soviets used to such great effect. He made many big saves in that game, and although it wasn't a classic in many ways, the team won to live another day.

"I probably got the most personal satisfaction out of game six. It wasn't that I was that good in it, but I hung in there and that was kind of nice given that things had gone kind of badly the first two games I played. I was absolutely uncertain if I would get another chance, but being told I had another chance, and feeling the series might have been lost by that point, we all hung in there. We found a way to win that night. We did what we had to do."

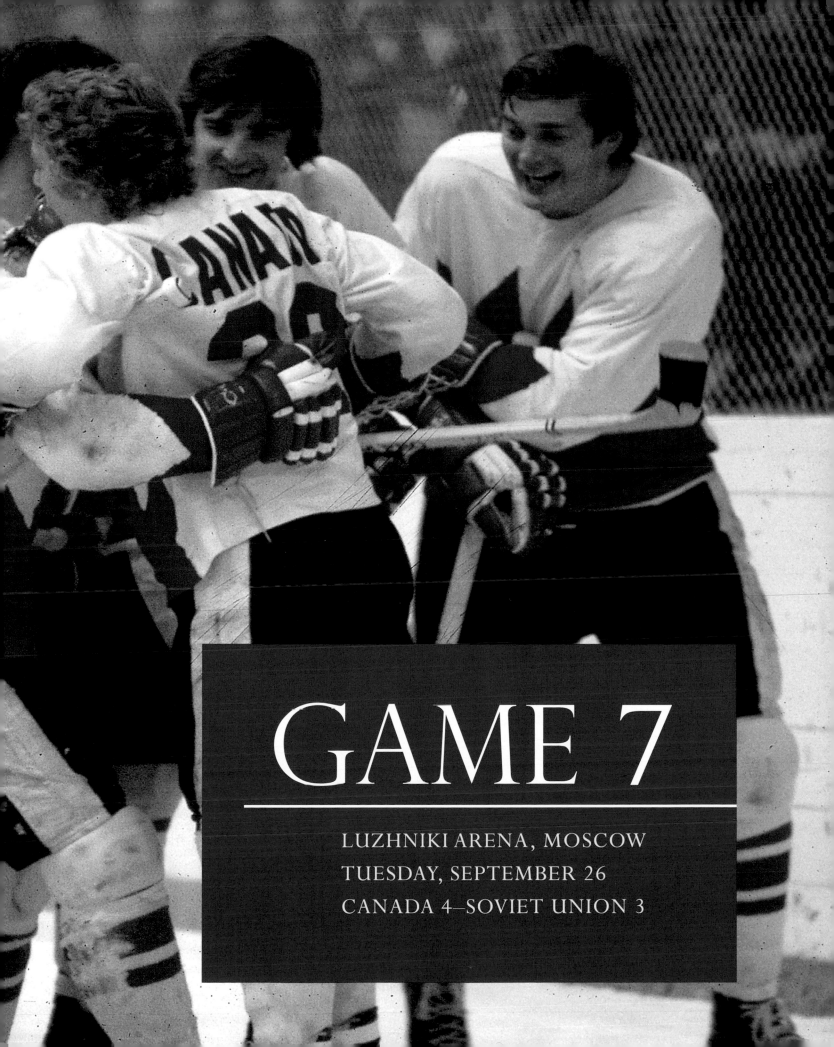

GAME 7

LUZHNIKI ARENA, MOSCOW
TUESDAY, SEPTEMBER 26
CANADA 4–SOVIET UNION 3

"Henderson going down ... got through the defence, goes right in on goal, he scores! Henderson! Right through to score for Canada! A beautiful goal by Paul Henderson!"

—FOSTER HEWITT

Bobby Clarke carries the puck into the Soviet end surrounded by opponents.

HENDERSON'S CAREER GOAL

Another must-win game for Canada ended in dramatic fashion as Paul Henderson scored the go-ahead goal with just 2:06 left in the game on one of the greatest plays in hockey history. It began with the ever-calm Serge Savard flipping the puck out to centre ice while teams were playing four-on-four.

Henderson collected the puck, and he was alone against two Soviet defencemen in front of him and two Soviet forwards backchecking to catch him. Henderson flipped the puck between the defence tandem of Valeri Vasiliev and Gennadi Tsygankov and then skated to the outside around Vasiliev.

Henderson caught up with the puck, but he was falling as he let go a shot over the blocker of Vladislav Tretiak that stunned the goalie and the entire Soviet team. Canada had now tied the series and made game eight the most anticipated hockey game in history.

"It was the greatest goal of my life," Henderson said of his dramatic game winner. "I can remember thinking I'd have to get the puck upstairs – up high, you know – because the goalie was sliding out in a crouch."

Henderson also made a key play on the opening goal as he was covering at the point. He sent the puck deep along the boards to linemate Ron Ellis, and Ellis quickly centred the puck for Phil Esposito. Espo beat his man by turning and fired in one motion low to Tretiak's stick side for a 1–0 Canada lead early in the game.

The Soviets got the next two goals, however. On the first, Alexander Yakushev's long blast down the left wing beat Tony Esposito through the legs, and then Vladimir Vikulov made a sensational pass up the middle to Vladimir Petrov. He outwaited a sprawling Tony O and slid the puck into the open net.

Phil Esposito tied the game a minute later when Savard made a nice spin-a-rama play at the blue line to draw a penalty, but he immediately got the puck to Espo in the slot again, and Esposito's quick shot beat Tretiak.

The second period was notable for its rough play as the pressure of the series reached a climax. Tony Esposito played terrifically well in goal for Canada, and teams headed to the dressing room after forty minutes locked in a fierce 2–2 tie.

The third saw two early goals. First, Boris Mikhailov made a terrible pass from one corner behind his net to the other. Rod Gilbert picked off the weak pass and snuck out in front, beating a surprised Tretiak with a quick backhand.

Yakushev drew a penalty soon after when he beat Gary Bergman to the outside and the Canadian defenceman was forced to haul him down. On the ensuing power play, Yakushev took a great cross-crease pass from

Alexander Maltsev and his one-timer tied the game 3–3. The rest of the period was tense and hard hitting, and tempers boiled over behind the net with three and a half minutes to go.

Bergman and Mikhailov were involved in a harsh pushing and shoving match, earning off-setting major penalties. But that forced teams to play four-on-four, setting the table for Henderson's winning goal. It all started with a key faceoff win in Canada's end by Bobby Clarke, and then Guy Lapointe got the puck to the other side for Savard, who quickly moved the puck out as he was being checked by Maltsev and Vikulov.

The Soviets were without Valeri Kharlamov for the game, sidelined by a sore ankle after a wicked slash from Clarke the previous game that had rendered the star forward ineffective the rest of that game as well.

Tony Esposito keeps a close watch on the puck as teammate Guy Lapointe gains possession.

LINEUPS

SOVIET UNION — Vladislav Tretiak, Alexander Sidelnikov (did not play) — Vladimir Lutchenko, Gennadi Tsygankov, Alexander Maltsev, Boris Mikhailov, Alexander Yakushev, Vladimir Petrov, Vladimir Vikulov, Vladimir Shadrin, Vyacheslav Anisin, Alexander Ragulin, Yuri Lyapkin, Valeri Vasiliev, Alexander Volchkov, Alexander Gusev, Viktor Kuzkin, Yuri Blinov, Yevgeni Mishakov

CANADA — Tony Esposito, Ed Johnston (did not play) — Brad Park, Yvan Cournoyer, Phil Esposito, Bobby Clarke, Gary Bergman, Ron Ellis, Paul Henderson, Pat Stapleton, Bill White, Rod Gilbert, Jean Ratelle, Peter Mahovlich, J-P Parise, Guy Lapointe, Dennis Hull, Serge Savard, Bill Goldsworthy

GAME SUMMARY

FIRST PERIOD

1. Canada, P. Esposito (Ellis, Henderson) 4:09
2. Soviet Union, Yakushev (Shadrin, Lyapkin) 10:17
3. Soviet Union, Petrov (Vikulov, Tsygankov) 16:27 (pp)
4. Canada, P. Esposito (Savard, Parise) 17:34

Penalties: Mikhailov (URS) 2:00, P. Mahovlich (CAN) and Mishakov (URS) 5:16, Mishakov (URS) 11:09, P. Esposito (CAN) 12.39, White (CAN) 15:45

SECOND PERIOD

No scoring

Penalties: Gilbert (CAN) 0:59, Parise (CAN) 6:04, Anisin (URS) 6:11, P. Esposito (CAN) and Kuzkin (URS) 12:44, Parise (CAN) and Kuzkin (URS) 15:14, Stapleton (CAN) 15:24

THIRD PERIOD

5. Canada, Gilbert (Ratelle, Hull) 2:13
6. Soviet Union, Yakushev (Maltsev, Lutchenko) 5:15 (pp)
7. Canada, Henderson (Savard) 17:54

Penalties: Bergman (CAN) 3:26, Gilbert (CAN) 7:25, Bergman (CAN – major) and Mikhailov (URS – major) 16:26

SHOTS ON GOAL

Soviet Union:	6	13	12	31
Canada:	9	7	9	25

IN GOAL

Soviet Union:	Tretiak
Canada:	T. Esposito

REFEREES

Uwe Dahlberg (SWE) and Rudy Bata (TCH)

OUTSTANDING PLAYERS

Soviet Union:	Alexander Yakushev and Boris Mikhailov
Canada:	Phil Esposito and Bill White

#28 BOBBY CLARKE – TWENTY-THREE AND SIMPLY SENSATIONAL

In another life or another time, Bobby Clarke might well have had the most international experience of any player to represent Canada in 1972. But, it was not to be.

"The National Team was based in Winnipeg, run by Father David Bauer," the Flin Flon, Manitoba, native explained. "Both Reggie Leach and myself dominated junior hockey the two years we played there, and then the third year we asked if we could play for the National Team. But Reggie had quit school after the sixth grade, and I had quit after the tenth, and the team was all college kids, so Bauer wouldn't take us. We wanted to play because we felt the level of competition was going to be higher than junior hockey, but everybody on those teams was going to college. Reggie and I had quit school and were working in the mines."

Clarke did get some consolation that season all the same. "We did play an exhibition game against the Russians in Brandon that year, an all-star team from the juniors, and beat them about 10–2. We had some really good players."

A Hall of Famer, Clarke later got the last laugh, but the rejection still smarts. "Of all of those players from the National Team, only a few of them ever made the NHL, and they were just fringe NHL players."

Clarke was never a fringe player, not before the Summit Series and certainly not after. He had just finished his third season with Philadelphia, and in that time he had gone from forty-six to sixty-three to eighty-one points and fifteen to twenty-seven to thirty-five goals. He was about to become one of the top, all-round centres in the game, and playing for Team Canada was an important part of his development.

"It really advanced my career," he acknowledged. "Like most players, I was getting better with experience, but I think that really took me to the next level, for my own play. I might never have got there had I not played that series. Who knows? But that series really helped me as a player."

His invite to Team Canada was anything but a gimme, yet he was likely the third-best player for Canada in the series after Henderson and Esposito. "Walter Tkaczuk turned them down because of a hockey school, so I got the call," he noted. "I wasn't expecting to play on a team like that. I'd had a little success, but nothing close to what most of the other players had had in the league. I was living in Flin Flon. I was married, but I was young, and we went to Flin Flon in the summer. I was a runner, so I trained all the time in the summer. I didn't work hockey schools or anything. There was no ice up there in those days. They never kept the ice in the rinks in the summer up there."

At training camp, he had success right from the time he skated out on Maple Leaf Gardens ice, but make no mistake – that success was created by his own ambitions.

"They put Ellis and Henderson and myself together right off the bat, and all three of us felt that if we all didn't work at training camp, that we wouldn't be playing very much. And, of course, all of us wanted to play. Fortunately for us, a lot of players didn't work that hard at camp, so we stood out."

As a result of their great camp, the threesome were in the lineup for game one, and even though the team stammered to a 7–3 loss, the Clarke line could take solace in its own decent play that night.

"We weren't nearly ready to play that level of competition, and we weren't expecting that level of competition, but I can guarantee you if you were on the bench after the first ten minutes, you knew we were in trouble. We couldn't keep up. We couldn't pass like them, shoot like them, or skate like them. We had had no real games until that time. We had played against each other, but we were not even close to being ready for that level of competition. Even though Ellis and Henderson and I and some others worked really hard in training camp, we still weren't prepared for that level of competition. You only get to that level by playing games."

While many players looked to game five as a turning point, Clarke didn't share their optimism at the time. "That should never happen to any team of professional players, let alone a team that's supposed to be as good as we became. I don't know how we ever let that get away," he said of the team's massive letdown in the third period to turn a 4–1 lead into a 5–4 loss.

"The one thing that really hurt our team in that game when we had the 4–1 lead was that we were without Serge Savard. He missed that game because he cracked his ankle. Savard was by far the best defenceman in that series. Even though we had other players who were pretty good to replace him, it's hard to replace a guy who is so good defensively, such a good passer. He could really control our end of the ice. I think that hurt us a lot not having him for that game."

Clarke wasn't happy about playing on the big ice – it didn't suit his game. "The style of game that I liked to play was closer checking, more contact, but when you get on that big ice, it's hard to hit guys. There's so much room for players to go. You're always chasing them and never catching them."

As well, he didn't have a single point in the last three games, all victories, but that didn't matter. Clarke's contributions were massive all the same. He may have started training camp as a long shot to make the team, but by game two and for the rest of the series coach Harry Sinden used him on virtually every critical faceoff in Canada's end. If Phil Esposito didn't take the draw, it was Clarke. He won an overwhelming majority of those draws – he became known for his faceoff skills with the Flyers – and as a result Canada could confidently know any stoppage in play would likely result in puck possession after Clarke did his thing.

Clarke is oddly out of tune with his status. He has the ability to pull back and analyze from afar even when he was in the thick of things. Part humility, part hockey smarts, he revealed several clues about the nature of Canada's win.

For instance: "I don't know about other countries, but I think it's unique for Canadian teams that when Canadian players get together, they become a team really quickly. I think it's why the Canadian juniors who play in international competitions can bring players together and they come together as a team quickly. I think we didn't come together on ice as quickly as we would have liked, but off ice and socially we got along really well."

On the Stockholm exhibition games: "That time in Sweden was really good for us, but it also proved the Swedes were as good as the Russians or as good as we were."

On team chemistry: "The majority of the credit should go to Harry Sinden and John Ferguson. They had to deal with lots of big egos and lots of issues, but they pulled through for us in the end."

On Phil Esposito's play: "Those four games that Esposito played in Moscow were the best four games he ever played in his life. He was the guy who played differently over there than he played in the NHL in a lot of ways, but he still scored. He scored a million goals in the NHL, but we needed those goals out of him, and we got them, but we also got body-work and stick-work and all the other things that we needed from him. I thought he was the most impressive player. Not taking anything away from Paul."

Clarke shed light on perhaps the most elusive element of the Summit Series – the comeback. Canada was expected to win all eight games, but after game five it had won only once and could not afford a loss or even a tie. Yet the players showed incredible determination and heart, producing a comeback unlike any other. How did that happen? Where did that heart come from?

"You learn the important things about the sport and the challenges when you're younger," Clarke explained. "When you go through the Canadian junior programs, you learn what it takes. You learn whether you have the commitment or not. Some players have great talent, but they're not willing to commit to what it takes to be a good player. It's done on a daily basis, every practice, every game. I've seen guys like that. And in '72 there were stars in the league who came to work every day, and that helped. But I'd seen the other side, too, guys who didn't work very hard and then had trouble in the series."

And what were the highlights of the series in Clarke's opinion?

"The one thing, as far as the on-ice play, that sticks out to me is the short-handed goal that Peter Mahovlich got in the second game in Toronto. It was absolutely a spectacular one-man show that you don't see that often at that level, when one guy can do something like that. And, of course, Paul's three goals. But even though Paul's goals were so important, it was only because someone else had scored before. Someone else had to get us to the tie in game eight. Those goals were important because we won, but as important as those goals were, it still comes down to the team. It's always the team, never the individual."

Bobby Clarke wasn't assured of a place on the team at training camp, but through hard work and dedication he earned a prominent role in the series' history.

#35 TONY ESPOSITO – OUTPLAYED TRETIAK WHEN IT MATTERED

"We had to win," said the goalie they called "Tony Zero" because of the high number of shutouts he accumulated. "That's how Canadians are with hockey. It's our game, and nobody's better."

There's truth and meaning in those words, but the degree of swagger was certainly greatly reduced after the Summit Series. In fact, at the start the series seemed so insignificant that Tony and his brother, Phil, were more than a little put out by having to cut their hockey camp short to play the Soviets!

"Phil and I were in Sault Ste. Marie running our hockey school, but we had to leave for training camp," Tony explained. "They had talked about the series, but we didn't really know if it would come to fruition. When it did, it didn't seem like it would be a tough series. In a sense, we didn't have a choice. We were going to play for our country and play against the Russians. It was the time of the Cold War."

Esposito was like many players in that he knew little of international hockey, but the appropriate thing is that this ignorance was the reason why the team took its opponents so lightly.

"International hockey in those days was much different than today," he acknowledged. "Canada was represented by senior hockey players then. There were no pros allowed. Basically, it was like Tier II Canadians, but the Russians were like pros."

It was clear at training camp that Esposito and Ken Dryden were going to be the two goalies in the series, but as coach Harry Sinden said, neither played so well as to assume clear number-one status. The result was that both goalies played four games, although the order or rationale was a little haphazard.

"We worked hard at camp, but we didn't know who would play when, although I assumed Ken would play in Montreal. That seemed like a no-brainer," Esposito suggested. "I didn't really worry about it. Whoever was going to play was going to play."

Of course, Dryden did play in his NHL team's home for game one, giving Esposito time to analyze the Soviets from the comfort and safety of the seats.

"I knew that we were in for a battle after game one, but I didn't think we were ready for a battle. Goaltending is different, though. We didn't have to go out and skate all over the ice. In practice, we had no choice to work hard because everyone is peppering us with shots. But the skaters probably didn't train as hard as they should have because we didn't expect that kind of a series. We weren't ready, physically."

Esposito played very well in game two, a crucial 4–1 win in Toronto, and as a result he got the call for the next game as well. His style was equipped to handle the Soviets' style, so he had less of an adjustment to make than the taller, more strategic Dryden.

"They didn't shoot as much," Esposito explained. "They preferred to work the puck in. My style of goaltending was more of a reflex style, quickness, going from side to side, whereas Ken was more of an angle goalie, the old school, who came out more and played the angles. But with the Russians, when you come out like that, they score a lot of open-net goals. You just can't play like that. I knew they weren't going to shoot from far out, so as they were coming in, I was looking to see where the other guys were without the puck. I knew they'd try to draw me over and then pass it back across the ice. They liked those open-net goals. They try to get you out of position. I never came way out anyway. I didn't have that much of an adjustment."

Esposito didn't start game four, Sinden wanting to get Dryden into another game and Tony part of the team that blew a two-goal lead in the third game, in Winnipeg. Dryden, as it turned out, got the short straw for Vancouver, when the team played its worst game and was booed off the ice.

"It was embarrassing, to tell the truth," Esposito said. "Everyone was up in arms, all the Canadians. It's not like we were trying to lose. But that's how it goes. We were down in a hole, and we had to get out of that hole. But I could see in practice guys were getting sharper. They were playing better and skating faster. It's easier to see when you're in net. Then we played a couple of exhibition games in Sweden, and that helped. We played a bit better, got our legs going, played harder, were better conditioned."

Once the team arrived in Moscow, Esposito was struck by the cultural and societal differences between home and the Soviet Union.

"I never realized until we got over there that it was such a second-rate country," he said. "The lifestyle, the clothing, the cars were all abysmal, black and brown, nothing flashy. The clothes were all the same dull tone. A lot of the people had screwed-up teeth. They had no money. They were poor. A lot of body odour. They ate cured food all the time because they didn't have good refrigeration. They weren't clean."

Just like after game one, Esposito started game five after the poor team showing in game four. But that first game in Moscow was a devastating loss. Leading 4–1 after two periods and in total control, the Soviets scored four unanswered goals in the final twenty minutes and skated off 5–4 victors. Needless to say, Dryden started game six.

"We lost control," Esposito admitted. "We took some stupid penalties, lost our composure. It all adds up. You have to bite the bullet. You can't retaliate because that's what they want you to do. We did, and it cost us."

But the loss, at least from his perspective, had nothing to do with the international rink. "I had no problem on the bigger ice. The only thing was that you had to be patient. You can't challenge them and force the play. You have to wait for them, let them take their time. Let them come in and set up, and watch as they try to make the nice play."

After game five, Sinden planned the goaltending for the rest of the series, giving Dryden games six and eight and Esposito seven. As it turned out, Dryden's best game of the series was game six, and Esposito's best game was seven.

"Ken was a different cat," Tony described in 1970s' lingo. "His idea of fun was reading a book. But he wasn't a hermit. We all talked about the team and players. We didn't care who was in net, so long as we won."

Of course, after such a series where emotion is high and the speed and skill of the game another level altogether, readjusting to NHL life was difficult.

"The main thing I noticed was that the game was slower," Esposito said of his return to the Hawks. "That series, by the end, was very fast. The competition was the best of the best. When you come back to the NHL, every team has three or four great players, not ten or twelve. It took me a few weeks to get playing back to normal. It was a different game, more shooting and less passing."

Goalie Tony Esposito caught with his right hand and positioned himself with knees together and feet apart, a unique and effective stance that often puzzled shooters.

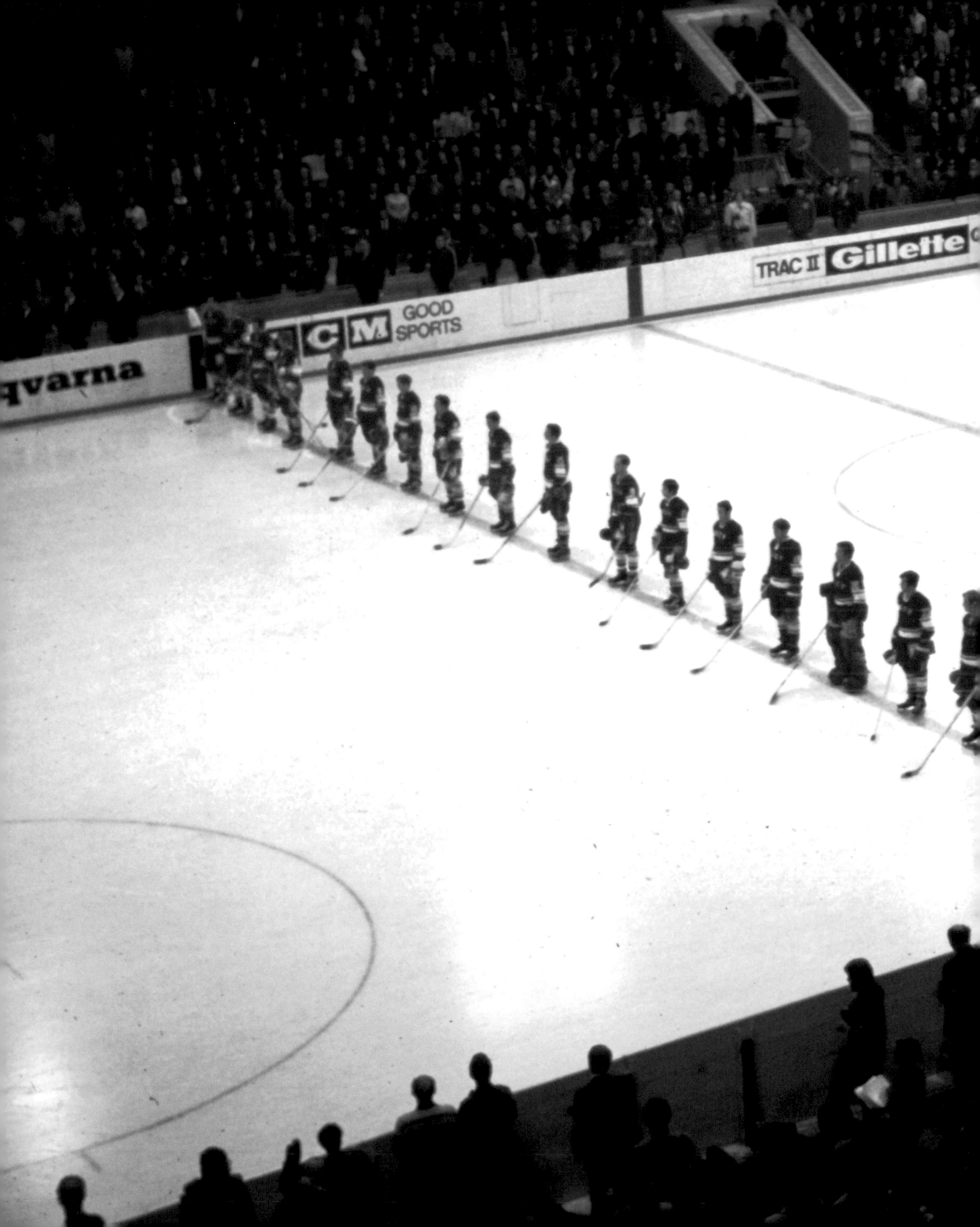

qvarna
CCM
GOOD SPORTS
TRAC II
Gillette

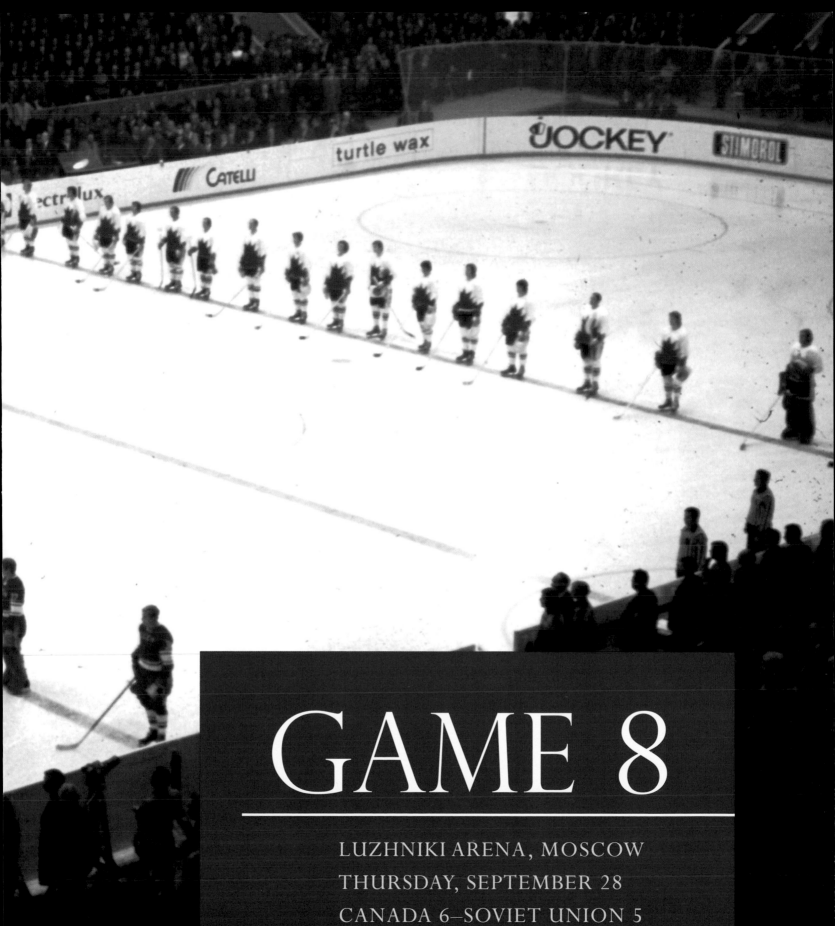

GAME 8

LUZHNIKI ARENA, MOSCOW

THURSDAY, SEPTEMBER 28

CANADA 6–SOVIET UNION 5

"Henderson made a wild stab for it and fell. Here's another shot ... right in front! They score! Henderson has scored for Canada!"

—FOSTER HEWITT

Phil Esposito is all business as he scores early in the third to make it a 5–4 game for the Soviets, starting Canada's miraculous and final comeback.

HENDERSON THE HERO

The greatest hockey series ever played came down not just to the final game but to the final minute. It was a game soaked in pressure and tension from the moment the players came on the ice, heightened by the presence of the two referees Canada campaigned against until noon of game day. But in the end, the Soviets got their man, Josef Kompalla, and the result was a first-period fraught with controversy.

Gary Bergman enlivened the player introductions by waving a "V" for victory to the crowd, but victory looked anything but assured for most of the sixty minutes. Indeed, Alexander Yakushev scored on a rebound early on to give the Soviets the jump, but it came with two Canadians in the penalty box.

All hell broke loose just a couple of minutes later when J-P Parise was called for another penalty. He went berserk, swinging his stick at Kompalla and earning a game misconduct for the threatening gesture. The game was delayed several minutes as Phil Esposito and other Canadians crowded the referees looking for answers.

Despite this early series of penalties, Canada tied the game on its own power play, Phil Esposito pouncing on a rebound in front of Vladislav Tretiak. But Vladimir Lutchenko put the Soviets up on another power play later in the period when his point shot found its way past Ken Dryden through a maze of players.

The Soviets had an excellent chance to make it 3–1 when they had a two-on-one, but Yuri Blinov tried to make a difficult pass to Boris Mikhailov rather than shoot from a good position. As Foster Hewitt observed, "Sometimes you can pass too often."

Canada seized the chance to tie the game on a great give-and-go between two New York Rangers teammates. Defenceman Brad Park carried the puck up the ice and passed off to Jean Ratelle, but Park, a rushing defenceman, continued in on goal, got the puck back from Ratelle, who knew Park would keep going, and the defenceman beat Tretiak with a nice shot under the blocker to tie the game 2–2.

The Soviets pulled ahead again, though, thanks to a rare miscue from Paul Henderson. He lost the puck at his blue line, and Vladimir Shadrin took a quick shot after Yakushev's initial shot ricocheted off the end netting, past a surprised Dryden, and back into the slot.

Another Canadian defenceman, Bill White, tied the game for a third time when he redirected a nice pass from Rod Gilbert in close, but just a minute later Phil Esposito was outsmarted on a faceoff in his own end. Although he won the draw, Shadrin reached in behind his opposing centre and swept the puck to Yakushev, who was alone against Dryden when Park committed to going after the puck behind Esposito.

Phil atoned soon after, though, when Blinov had deked Dryden down and out, but his shot into the open net was cleared by Esposito before it crossed the line. Nonetheless, the Soviets took a two-goal lead late in the period on another power play, and teams headed to their dressing rooms with twenty minutes left in the series and the Soviets with a commanding 5—3 lead.

Canadian heart came to the fore in that final period, thanks largely to perhaps the greatest period of hockey one player has ever played in a game of this magnitude. Phil Esposito was at the very height of his power at this moment, and he got a quick goal to get Canada right back in the game. Peter Mahovlich did the heavy lifting, outmuscling two Soviets in the corner to send a perfect pass to Espo in the slot. He had to catch the bouncing puck before smacking it home.

Midway through the period, Park hit Espo down the right wing with a pass reminiscent of the Park-Cournoyer combination in game two. Tretiak stopped the shot, but Esposito got to the rebound and centred the puck where Yvan Cournoyer banged it home to tie the game. In truth, replays seem to show Esposito knocking the puck down with a high-stick and then being the first player to touch it thereafter, meaning play should have been blown dead. Perhaps this was one instance of poor refereeing helping Canada?

All hell broke loose at this point. Alan Eagleson, sitting opposite the players bench by the penalty box, was incensed that the goal light didn't come on immediately after Cournoyer's goal and began making a ruckus. State police corralled him, and many players from Canada's bench came over, notably Peter Mahovlich, who climbed into the seating area and threatened the guards, who let Eagleson go. The players escorted him across the ice, and play eventually resumed.

Canada almost scored the go-ahead goal with less than four minutes to go when Park hit Gary Bergman with a great pass on a three-on-two rush, but Tretiak made the save. Then, with 1:48 left in the game, the final sequence played out. With a faceoff in Canada's end, Sinden replaced the Clarke line with Esposito, Cournoyer, and Mahovlich. Espo, in a rare move, huddled the players together, and then won the draw!

Eventually, Henderson screamed at Mahovlich to come off, and he tore down the left wing when he came on. Cournoyer missed him with a long pass, but Esposito got to the puck, flicked it in front, and Henderson, on the second whack, knocked the puck in for the victory.

"I found myself in front of the net," Henderson described to a massive group of reporters after his heroics, "and Tretiak made one stop, but the puck came right back to me. There was some room under him, so I poked the puck through. When I saw it go in, I just went bonkers."

J-P Parise threatens referee Josef Kompalla with his stick in the first period of game eight.

Henderson (helmeted) celebrates the greatest goal ever scored with Yvan Cournoyer and Phil Esposito (left).

LINEUPS

SOVIET UNION — Vladislav Tretiak, Alexander Sidelnikov (did not play) — Vladimir Lutchenko, Gennadi Tsygankov, Alexander Maltsev, Boris Mikhailov, Alexander Yakushev, Vladimir Petrov, Vladimir Vikulov, Vladimir Shadrin, Vyacheslav Anisin, Yuri Lyapkin, Valeri Vasiliev, Alexander Volchkov, Alexander Gusev, Yuri Blinov, Yevgeni Mishakov, Viktor Kuzkin, Valeri Kharlamov

CANADA — Ken Dryden, Tony Esposito (did not play) — Brad Park, Yvan Cournoyer, Phil Esposito, Bobby Clarke, Gary Bergman, Ron Ellis, Paul Henderson, Pat Stapleton, Bill White, Rod Gilbert, Jean Ratelle, Peter Mahovlich, J-P Parise, Guy Lapointe, Dennis Hull, Serge Savard, Frank Mahovlich

GAME SUMMARY

FIRST PERIOD

1. Soviet Union, Yakushev (Maltsev, Lyapkin) 3:34 (pp)
2. Canada, P. Esposito (Park) 6:45 (pp)
3. Soviet Union, Lutchenko (Kharlamov) 13:10 (pp)
4. Canada, Park (Ratelle, Hull) 16:59

Penalties: White (CAN) 2:25, P. Mahovlich (CAN) 3:01, Petrov (URS) 3:44, Parise (CAN – minor, misconduct, game misconduct) 4:10, Tsygankov (URS) 6:28, Ellis (CAN) 9:27, Petrov (URS) 9:46, Cournoyer (CAN) 12:51

SECOND PERIOD

5. Soviet Union, Shadrin (unassisted) 0:21
6. Canada, White (Gilbert, Ratelle) 10:32
7. Soviet Union, Yakushev (unassisted) 11:43
8. Soviet Union, Vasiliev (unassisted) 16:44 (pp)

Penalties: Stapleton (CAN) 14:58, Kuzkin (URS) 18:06

THIRD PERIOD

9. Canada, P. Esposito (P. Mahovlich) 2:27
10. Canada, Cournoyer (P. Esposito, Park) 12:56
11. Canada, Henderson (P. Esposito) 19:26

Penalties: Gilbert (CAN – major) and Mishakov (URS – major) 3:41, Vasiliev (URS) 4:27, Hull (CAN) and Petrov (URS) 15:24

SHOTS ON GOAL

Soviet Union:	12	10	5	27
Canada:	14	8	14	36

IN GOAL

Soviet Union:	Tretiak
Canada:	Dryden

REFEREES

Rudy Bata (TCH) and Josef Kompalla (FRG)

OUTSTANDING PLAYERS

Soviet Union:	Alexander Yakushev and Vladimir Shadrin
Canada:	Paul Henderson and Brad Park

#3 PAT STAPLETON – WHITEY ON THE BLUE LINE

Two moments from the television broadcast at the end of game eight shed light on one of the most important questions the Summit Series has left us with: what happened to Paul Henderson's puck?

After the goal, amid the wild Canadian celebrations to the left of Tretiak, the Soviet goalie swipes the puck into that left corner as Ken Dryden arrives on the scene to celebrate with teammates. Referee Rudy Bata, number 15, clearly picks it up and starts to skate to centre ice, but the camera, of course, stays with the Canadian players and then cuts to the bench.

When we next see Bata, he is standing at centre ice ready to drop the puck. The final thirty-four seconds of the game are played, and just as the game ends the puck slides through the left faceoff circle in the Canadian end. Without question Pat Stapleton skates hard to retrieve the puck, though we don't actually see him pick it up.

"I have the puck that was played with for the last thirty-four seconds of the game," he admitted in Moscow, in February 2012, where many players attended a celebration of that series. "I have the puck that ended the game. Now, was that the puck that was scored for the winning goal? I can't swear to that. But no one seemed to worry about the puck after the goal. The referees took it back to centre ice, and we played thirty-four seconds, and the game was over. I had the puck at the end, stuck it in my glove, and that's it. At that time, pucks were pucks. They weren't collected for memorabilia and sold. After the series was over, we talked to the Hall of Fame. Lefty Reid was in charge, but he said, 'It's just a puck.' So I put it in my pocket and went home."

Several times during the game another bit of evidence provided by Stapleton is substantiated by the TV coverage. The puck is just black and unadorned, unlike the pucks used during the Canada games of the series on which many times during the broadcasts we can see a logo on at least one side.

"At that time," Stapleton went on, "pucks had no logos on them. This puck is just black. I've picked up many black pucks along the way, but I have a pretty good idea which one it is. When Scotty Morrison was head of the Hall of Fame, he asked me about it a lot. But I think it's bigger than the one puck. I think it's for children to dream upon this puck in their own imagination. Let your imagination run with it."

Stapleton was one of eight players who didn't dress for the series opener but who was in the lineup for game two. On the one hand, it might have been an advantage to measure his opponent from the seats; on the other, he now entered the series at its first critical stage, no mean task.

"Game two was the most tension-filled game for me personally," he admitted. "I joked with Peter Mahovlich later that I had to take a penalty to make sure he scored one of the greatest goals ever. What a wonderful goal."

Indeed, Mahovlich's short-handed goal early in the third period remains a highlight of the series, and Stapleton carried on to play the remainder of the series, paired with his Chicago Black Hawks defence partner Bill White. They were a force on the blue line for their composed play in their own end.

"For me, the higher the level of play, the more peaceful and more calm I become inside," Stapleton suggested. "I became quieter, and I didn't allow my emotions to get the better of me. By controlling your emotions, you controlled the game. That was me. I'm sure everyone is a little different."

Stapleton offered one unique observation about the Moscow half of the series that perhaps explains a positive from having so many players on the team, even though many didn't see game action.

"I think our practices were better at the end than the beginning because when you have thirty-five guys on the team who all want to play, those practices became pretty intense. It wasn't that way at the start of training camp. So even the players who didn't dress contributed to the victory in the end because they raised our battle level in practice. Everyone accepted his role."

Like all of the players, he grew in confidence as the series went on, to the point that trailing by two goals with one period left was not a devastating predicament.

"Our focus in the second intermission was not about being down 5–3 but about who was going to score the goals," he said. "We just felt we were going to score. I don't know if the Soviets were thinking, 'Hey, we're up 5–3 and we have to play just twenty minutes to win,' but we never discussed that."

Several players and coach Harry Sinden all referred to one critical element that is echoed by Stapleton – the ability of Canada's players to change their game, their approach, their attitude, anything and everything to turn losing into winning.

"I think one thing the Soviets took from that series was that they could see how we made more adjustments," he explained. "All of us made adjustments. I don't think they made adjustments when they had us down and could have squashed us because with us, each individual brought his own adjustments to the next game. This is a part of the game you can't coach or draw on a board. It can be such an individual-thinking game, when you see players do certain things with the puck."

Stapleton, as much as any player in 1972, was aware of the WHA and its effect on the NHL game – and salaries. In fact, he played one more year with the Hawks and left for greener pastures to a game that was far more international than the NHL at the time.

"The series raised the competitive level of each player," he started. "The Canadians felt we were the only ones who played the game, and we all got a rude awakening – everyone can compete if they have the proper training. Hockey has expanded immensely since 1972. After '72, the WHA started, which allowed more Europeans into the North American game. I think of Anders Hedberg, and Leif Holmqvist, a goalie I played with, Ulf Nilsson, Lars-Erik Sjoberg, wonderful players. I spoke to Anders, and he said when we played those exhibition games in Sweden, he realized he could play against us. And that's the thing. Once the Russians realized they could play against us, they were a different team."

Note: *The quotes from this interview were provided by Szymon Szemberg of the IIHF, who interviewed Stapleton in February 2012 in Moscow.*

Stapleton and Bill White formed an impressive defensive tandem for Canada.

#7 PHIL ESPOSITO – CAPITAL "C"

In the beginning, he didn't even want to be there. In the end, he was the leader and superstar, the man who made it all possible.

"I was in the Soo doing a hockey school with my brother," Phil Esposito explained, looking back on the summer of 1972, "and Alan Eagleson called. I said I wasn't interested. Then, maybe five or six days later, Bobby Orr called me and said, 'Phil, I can't play. I'm having surgery on my knee. We need you to play. The team needs you.' I said, 'Bob, for you, I'll do it.' Then I asked him about getting paid. I'm a professional, after all. He said, 'No, the money was going to the pension fund and older players who were in need.' So I said, 'Okay, I'll still do it.' And I remember we left the Soo on August 14 because that was my oldest daughter's birthday. Tony and I had to give all the money back to the kids who had registered in our hockey school, and they weren't too happy about that. Neither were we, actually. But we had to do what we had to do. That's how it happened."

Like his Boston Bruins linemate Wayne Cashman, Phil Esposito was also displeased that the third member of their line wasn't there. "I was very surprised Ken Hodge wasn't invited. We were the best line in hockey. No doubt about it. And when Gilbert, Hadfield, and Ratelle were invited, I thought, 'What the hell, we three should have been as well.' But maybe Harry didn't think Kenny could do the job. He was wrong. Kenny scored fifty goals. A hundred points."

Although Team Canada preferred to appoint four assistant captains rather than hand the "C" to one man, it became evident quickly and with frequency that Esposito was the leader. One early example was his stance on the team's name, which he mentioned in training camp.

"I thought it was a travesty we were called Team Canada," he said with typical animation even forty years later. "We never should have been. We should have been called Team NHL, and I brought it up at a meeting. I said, 'Gordie Howe isn't playing. Bobby Hull isn't playing. Gerry Cheevers isn't playing.' And a bunch of other guys who were in the WHA and were good, good players weren't playing."

Of course, a greater example of Espo's leadership occurred after game four when the team was booed off the ice by fans in Vancouver. Esposito skated to one end of the rink to do an interview with Johnny Esaw, and what spontaneously sprung forth has become a defining moment in Canadian history: "the speech."

"It just came out," Esposito explained. "There were these three guys in their late twenties standing just above me in the seats above the Zamboni entrance when I was talking to Johnny, and they were yelling obscenities and screaming that Communism was the best and we should be Commies. I'll never forget those three guys. Johnny asked me a question, and I just went off. I don't remember what I said. I never saw it until ten years later. The first time I did see it, I was embarrassed. I couldn't believe that I was that emotional and that intense."

Esposito started the series with a laugh and ended with tears. He started as a citizen and ended as a soldier. It was he who scored the first goal of the series after just thirty seconds, and as he skated back to centre ice for the faceoff, he was all smiles, figuring this was going to be as easy as everyone had said it was going to be.

But by the time game four was over and he had given his speech, he knew he was in a do-or-die hockey battle. "One thing above all else that series proved to me," he said. "You cannot win unless you're a team. One guy, two guys, three guys can't do it. It has to be a team. It takes everybody. And you have to become a team, and you have to care for one another and be willing to go through a wall for your

Esposito did it all in 1972 — scored, passed, led by example, and inspired the team to victory.

teammates, or you don't win. It happened for us in Sweden. It happened because by that point nobody else cared about us. Quite frankly, by that time we weren't playing for our country or the NHL – we were playing for ourselves."

Indeed, after his speech in Vancouver and the team's flight to Sweden a few days later, the Canadian players felt isolated and desperate. They then had several practices and two violent games against a Swedish all-star team to unite, and by the time they got to Moscow for game five, they were a different group that had assembled in the comfort of a sweltering mid-August day in Toronto.

And yet, amid the incredible pressure and intensity, Esposito produced another spontaneous moment that was the height of humour. Prior to the player introductions for game five, a small Soviet girl skated onto the ice with a bouquet of flowers. A petal fell off, and moments later when Esposito was introduced, he took one step forward, slipped on the petal, and fell to the ice.

"That girl must have dropped a little flower, and I didn't see it," he said with a hearty laugh. "I went on my ass and took a bow – what the hell was I supposed to do? I decided, the hell with it. I made perfect eye contact with [Communist Party general secretary Leonid] Brezhnev. That was the best part of it. And then I blew him a kiss. And the guy next to him started to laugh, but Brezhnev looked at him and the guy turned stone-faced. And the funny thing – I remember this in particular – were his eyebrows. I always had the impression that if he combed them back, he wouldn't have a forehead."

Esposito added to the story by recounting a follow-up anecdote.

"The next game, I skated by [assistant coach Boris] Kulagin – I called him "Chuckles" – the Soviet coach. I grabbed the boards along the bench at the introduction, and I held on to it. Guys are laughing, but he isn't. I said to him, 'Hey, Chuckles, I'm not going to fall today.' He didn't look at me."

Esposito's focus and concentration were remarkable. Here was a player in the most desperate situation of his hockey career, able to make the transition from serious to comical to serious again in a matter of moments. The player who arrived at Maple Leaf Gardens just a few weeks earlier was now leading the greatest comeback in hockey history – and doing so with flair!

With each passing day, with each passing game, Esposito's demeanour became more and more focused to the point that by the time game eight had arrived, he was at the very apex of his hockey career. Yet even still, he was able to combine a bit of wit with the seriousness of the moment.

"I wanted to get that last game over with, and I wanted to win, no matter what. I couldn't wait for the game to start. You know why? Because as soon as it was over, we were getting the hell out of that country!"

Game eight was close to being a nightmare for two periods. Canada headed to the dressing room with twenty minutes to play and trailing 5–3, but that didn't faze Espo.

"In that dressing room – and I wasn't the only one – I said, 'We will not lose this game!' I don't know if it was divine providence, but I believed in my heart of hearts that this was our society against their society, and we couldn't lose. We just couldn't."

Only one player from either team in the series had four points in a game or three points in a period. That was Esposito in game eight, in the third period, almost without question the finest twenty minutes of hockey a player has ever played given the situation.

"I've said for many years that at least in my career, I've never seen another player have a period where there was so much so pressure and was still able to accomplish what he did," said Ron Ellis, who witnessed Esposito's heroics first-hand. "It was amazing. He had such stamina. He could go forever."

"I didn't want to come off [in the third]," Esposito confessed. "Harry knew it. I remember telling him, 'Harry, I have to play. I have to play a lot.' And I asked him during the second intermission to put me with Cournoyer and Peter Mahovlich. I don't know what it was, but Peter was chomping at the bit, and he made some great plays in the third period. He was unbelievable. But everybody was. Those guys will always be special for me."

After a moment to reflect, Esposito added, "There was no stopping me. And I think some of the guys got a little angry with me. If we had lost, I would have been the goat. But we didn't lose. I just had enough faith in myself that I was going to get it done, one way or another."

"That was his finest hour," Coach Sinden acknowledged with Churchillian exactness.

After game eight, the team flew to Prague the next day and played a day after that. Even the 3–3 tie was eventful for Espo. "We went to Prague, and I got a stick in the nose and broke my nose. If you look at photos when we came back, I had a big scar on my nose. But I played. I don't know how. I don't know how any of us played. But we did – and we didn't lose."

Esposito made his living in the slot, that area of the ice between the hash marks directly in front of the net. If Cashman or Hodge, or Peter Mahovlich or Cournoyer, could put the puck on Espo's stick in the slot, it was as good as in the net. Never before had a player used that area of the ice so effectively, but it was not by luck that Esposito discovered its value.

"When I got traded from Chicago to Boston," he began, "Harry Sinden was coaching. He said he was going to make me a scorer by playing me with two guys who could get me the puck. I could snap the puck. I didn't slap the puck a lot, but I did snap it. Bobby Hull taught me that. He was very prominent as a teacher for me like that. My feeling ever since I was a kid was that the pucks just seemed to go between the hash marks in the slot a lot. So I decided from dot to dot at the hash marks, that's where I was going to score. I'd move from side to side depending on where the puck was. I used a big stick so that the guys would have a target to pass to. I told them to look for me, and if I got the puck, I'd score. A big stick took away from my shot a bit, but it didn't matter. If you hit your spot with the shot, the goalie couldn't get to it in time. That was my thing, to hit the spots. I started doing that when I was a kid, shooting at targets against my dad's garage. I started with a bushel, then down to a basket, and then to one end of the basket. I never quit shooting. Then later, if I missed a goal from the slot, I'd work from that spot at the start of next practice."

It was that shot that gave him most of his goals in the Summit Series, and that determination that gave the team an historic win.

"I talked to Petrov a lot on ice," Esposito said, "because he played against me all the time. One time, I said to 'Petty' – that's what I called him – 'I'm sorry, but you're not gonna stop me.' I did things over there I never, ever did in the NHL. Ever. Not before or after. It was supposed to be a fun time, but it was a war over there. It's amazing how quickly a fun time can change."

#12 YVAN COURNOYER – THE GREATEST HUG OF ALL

Like many outstanding players of his era, Yvan Cournoyer ran a hockey school in the summer. In his case, it was with Jacques Lemaire and other Montreal players, and his lasted some thirteen years. It was at this time that he got a phone call that changed his life. "We knew there was going to be a series with the Russians, and I thought maybe with my speed and the way I was playing, I hoped to be invited, and I was."

"The way I was playing" referred to a 1971–72 season in which he had a career-high forty-seven goals. In his nine years in the league, all with the Canadiens, he had won the Stanley Cup five times. Still, all the skill and experience in the world couldn't prepare him for what was about to unfold.

"We knew the Russians were winning a lot of international tournaments, but they were playing against our non-professional players, guys who were strictly amateur," he said. "But I told Frank Mahovlich before the first game that I was pretty scared. I didn't know anything about the team. If we had had a video of their team, it would have helped. The only report we had was that they didn't have a good goalie. We weren't sharp enough to play against them at first. They had a different style. They kept the puck a lot and passed around the net. The key was to block the front of the net and let them go around the outside, but we didn't know anything about it at first."

As metaphors go, Cournoyer provided the best in describing Canada's shocking 7–3 loss in game one, in Montreal. "We went in with guns and they had cannons," he said. "We had to retreat to get some better guns and go back again. For us, the biggest game was the second one in Toronto. If we were to lose that game, it would have been two losses out of eight total games, and we wouldn't know if we could beat them. But winning the second game, we knew we could beat them. We had the guns, and we could play them again."

Indeed, "the Roadrunner" provided one of the cannons in that crucial second game, scoring one of the most electrifying goals of the series. "It was a beautiful pass from Park," he said, starting his description." I told him before the game to look for me, if possible. It's really rare in hockey that you can have a set play in hockey. You can talk about it, but it's rare that it happens the way you talk about it. As soon as he got the puck on this play, though, I knew his intention was to give it to me. So I prepared to gain speed at the perfect time for him, and I went around the defenceman, Alexander Ragulin, and was lucky enough to beat

Tretiak on the shot. I was a right wing shooting left. When you get around a defenceman, you don't have time for a slap shot, but I always had a good wrist shot, so I took my best one and beat him."

Although Peter Mahovlich's third-period short-handed goal was perhaps even more sensational, Cournoyer's highlight-reel marker stood as the game winner. Canada, however, blew a two-goal lead in game three and struggled badly in game four, but Cournoyer wasn't as down as others might have been, and he had good reason.

"I was glad that the games were over in Canada because it's like when a team plays four or five games in a row at home, and sometimes it's tough. You're nervous; you're tight. I had more confidence knowing we were going away. We can build a team. If we can play together for a few games, I thought we could win. The important thing was that we went to Sweden to play those two games. That helped us adapt to the rink. I think it's more difficult to adapt from a small rink to a big rink than from a big rink to a small rink. If we went directly from Canada to Russia, and went straight from a small rink to a big rink, I think we would have lost. But in Sweden we had time to get in shape, get the right guns, and adjust to the size of the ice."

Of course, skating being his strong suit, Cournoyer excelled on the huge ice of Luzhniki Arena, but like most everyone, the problem was with the roster, not the ice. "I played on a line with Phil Esposito and Peter Mahovlich, but we changed lines a lot. That was one of our problems. Everybody was promised to have at least one game, so we were changing our lineup all the time. I was fortunate enough to play all the games, but if you change the lineup all the time, you don't become a team. You have to have a team to beat the Russians."

A terrific forty minutes to start game five gave way to a horrible letdown in the final period and a potentially crushing defeat. "Game five was like the first game," Cournoyer explained. "We started big, but then we lost our guns. We were all professionals. I remember in the finals we were down to Detroit 2–0 and we came back and won four in a row. Guys in the NHL don't quit. They always find a way to win. After game five, we went game by game. We were ahead, and we knew we could score, so if our goalies could play well, we knew we could come back and win game six. After winning that game, we knew we could win again, and then we all know what happened in the last game."

Cournoyer was front and centre in that climactic finale. "I scored the tying goal in the eighth game," he said of his goal midway through the third period. "If the series ended in a tie, we knew they were going to claim victory because they scored more goals. I didn't think so, but they did. My goal was a rebound in front of the net. That's where you score goals. If you don't go to the front of the net, you'll have a hard time scoring. I got to the rebound and put it in, and I said, 'Okay, now we have a chance to win.' There was still lots of time."

It was the Roadrunner who started the play that led to the series-winning goal from Paul Henderson. "On the winning goal, I was right wing and Phil was centre. Pete Mahovlich was the left wing. I was really far away from the bench, which was on the left-wing side, and I was exhausted. The puck went behind their net, and I thought I should come off for a change, but I changed my mind and stayed on the ice. I always say it's like when you like your job, you always want to give more. If you give more, you're going to have more. So if I had gone to the bench, I would have been finished, but the bench was so far away, I changed my mind. The Russians tried to clear the puck out along my side, but I stopped it. I saw Paul coming in the middle. I tried to get him the puck, but somebody tripped him and the puck went in the corner. By the time the puck went back in front of the net, I was right behind Paul. If I had a camera with me when he scored, I could have taken the best picture of the goal. When he scored, I hugged him and shouted, 'We did it! We did it! We did it!' The relief was unbelievable."

Some players remember what happened the next morning on the plane to Prague, others were too tired or were sleeping, but Cournoyer remembers clear as a bell. "When we got on the plane to fly to Czechoslovakia, as soon as it took off, we stood up and sang 'O Canada!' That was very nice. And if you ever stand up right after takeoff, it's a hell of a thrill. We all stood up. That was something very special."

The Summit Series had tremendous impact on Cournoyer on ice and off. "I had my best year in 1972–73," he noted. "I was on Team Canada at the start. Montreal won the Stanley Cup, and I won the Conn Smythe Trophy. For me, it was the greatest year. When you win the '72 Summit Series and the Cup in the same season, it's incredible. I was very lucky to be there for both wins."

Yvan Cournoyer won the Stanley Cup ten times with Montreal, but these victories paled in comparison to the importance of winning the Summit Series.

#19 PAUL HENDERSON –
A LIFE SAVED, A HERO MADE

It takes only two or three degrees of separation to connect CCM to the Summit Series winning goal, for without a helmet Paul Henderson might not have been invited to Team Canada's training camp, and if he had, he would absolutely have been scraped off the ice on a stretcher in game five and been in a coma or coffin when game eight was played.

Who can tell the sequence of events better than Henderson himself?

"Goldsworthy, Mikita, and Red Berenson also wore helmets. I was forced to put one on. I got a concussion in my first game of Junior B, but didn't put a helmet on. Got a concussion in my first game of Junior A – didn't put a helmet on. Then, I got a really bad concussion with Detroit, and the doctors told me that I could not play without a helmet. It happened in late February, so they put a CCM helmet on me. At the end of the season, CCM approached me and offered me an endorsement deal if I would continue to wear their helmets. It was a nice chunk of money. And my wife had really been bugging me and said I should just leave it on. By this time, I had gotten used to it, but I went to training camp with it and Sid Abel, the coach, said we don't want our players wearing helmets. I told Sid what CCM was paying me to play with it, so I told him that if he thought I wasn't playing well, I'd take it off. But as long as I'm playing well, I think I should be allowed to keep it on. He said okay. About ten games into the season, I scored four goals in a game and was leading the league in goals with Bobby Hull. After that game Sid told me he had no problem with me wearing the helmet! I probably would have taken it off if CCM hadn't come along with the endorsement. Thank goodness I wore it because I got another concussion in the first game in Moscow. In game five, I beat a guy to the outside and skated around him, but he cut me down, tripped me. I was going so fast that he spun me around and I went into the boards backwards so hard that my skates almost stuck into the boards above my head. I hit the back of my head. Jim Murray, the doctor, examined me and told me I had a slight concussion and told me I couldn't play. I said, 'Jim, don't do this to me.' Harry came in and asked what was going on, and Jim said, 'He has a small concussion; he can't play.' I told Harry I'm playing. I said, 'Don't do this to me. I want to play.' I even promised him that I'd be careful, but I said please, please don't take me out. Harry said, 'Well, if you want to play, I'm not going to stop you.' I had a pounding headache, but I did score in the third period. There's no question I would have had a fractured skull without the helmet. I mean, I had it on and I was still knocked unconscious. It might have even killed me – who knows?"

Despite scoring a career-best thirty-eight goals with the Leafs in 1971–72, Henderson had other plans for August 1972 when he started the summer. "I was working with a company called AP Parts," he told. "They were in the automotive aftermarket business, and I had put together a two-week trip down the Rhein River for some of their key customers. We were really looking forward to going on this, and it was to take place the first two weeks of August. My wife was not a happy camper when I got the call from Harry, but we decided this would probably be the only chance I'd ever get to represent Canada."

Henderson had two bits of good luck drop into his lap on the first day of training camp. First, he had teammate Ron Ellis at camp, and second, the two Leafs were paired with another eager young talent wanting to prove he could play at this level – Bobby Clarke. "Ronnie and I played with Normie Ullman for four years as a line, so we knew they'd put us together," Henderson explained. "We thought they might give us Mikita as a centre, but we really just weren't sure. They were just experimenting on the first day to see who might work together or not, but it worked out well with Clarke because we were all underdogs to make the team. All of us wanted to prove to ourselves and everyone else that we could play hockey. We got very serious about it very quickly."

The line had a great training camp and had absolutely played their way into the starting lineup for game one. And while everyone else around them could call the game an unmitigated failure, the Clarke line had its measure of success.

"Our line scored two goals and we had only one goal against in the first game," Henderson extolled. "We were certainly the only 'pluses' in the game [in the plus-minus stat], but it was only our first game. I knew we were going to play better, but I think we were happy with the way we played."

Henderson scored once on a nice passing play with his linemates, and he and Ellis set Clarke up for a second goal for the line. "My goal was Clarke over to Ellis back to me, and I scored. And on the other one, I went into the corner to get the puck to Ronnie, and his shot was tipped in by Clarkie. We had worked hard. We were in better shape than most of the other guys, I think. We knew we were going to play in the first game. It was obvious to everyone we were playing well, and we could play defensively. We weren't going to be a liability."

In all, the line accounted for nine goals and nineteen scoring points in the series, their only off night coming in Vancouver, an off night for everyone. And when the team got to Moscow, and the bigger ice, Henderson thrived.

"I was confident playing on the bigger ice surface," he agreed. "My biggest assets were definitely my speed and my shot. The better hockey players you play with, they're going to get you the puck when you want it, and I felt I would play well in Moscow. It suited my game."

Henderson scored the game-winning goal in game six, but this lacked the dramatics of his later exploits. It came late in the second period, a slap shot from long range that beat Tretiak to make it 3–1 Canada. The Soviets made it 3–2, and Henderson's stood up as the winner.

Game seven, however, was another matter. Late in that game he scored the most beautiful goal of the series, a stunning play in which he was surrounded, literally, by four Soviets from centre ice and in, yet managed to get around the defence and beat Tretiak with a shot while he was falling.

"The best goal I ever scored in my life," Henderson said with a simplicity that belied the beauty and skill of the play, the series-saving importance, and late-game heroics. "There was only two and a half minutes left in that game. I remember going out thinking this could be my last shift of the game. Man, I had to do something. You couldn't write a script better than that one. I said to Eleanor, my wife, after the game, I can die a happy man because I'm probably never going to score a bigger goal in my life. If I don't score at the end of game seven, it's all over. Two days later, I score what I call a garbage goal but what became known as the goal of the century. I'll take it."

But, of course, history and fate had bigger plans for number 19. Canada and the Soviets battled tooth and nail in game eight, and with the score tied 5–5 and the clock winding down, a tie seemed inevitable. A voice within told Henderson different.

On his second last shift, Henderson delivered perhaps the hardest hit of the series. A Soviet player moved inside the blue line and took a slap shot with his head down, not realizing his position. Henderson stepped into him and delivered a ferocious – and clean – shoulder check that left the Soviet stunned.

"He'd jabbed me at the other end," Henderson recalled vividly. "I shook him up, I'll tell you. I nailed him with my shoulder, and he didn't know where he was. I had his number. They were so bad with their sticks. That was the thing about European hockey back then. They'd stick you all the time. That's what drove our guys crazy, the spearing and all that."

Ellis recalled what happened in the final minute of play. "When our line came off the ice with about two minutes left, Harry Sinden told us we were going right back out after Phil. That's why Paul was standing up, and why he was able to call Pete off. Cournoyer was on the far side. Our bench was on the left-wing side. Peter fortunately was right next to our bench. If Paul was yelling at him across the ice, it would never have happened. And Cournoyer couldn't come that far. I was ready and watching for him. But he was on the far side."

Indeed, for one player to call another player off the ice is illogical and counter to everything hockey players are taught. Teammates aren't selfish with ice time. Players wait their turn on the bench until told to go out. Line changes are planned. Yet none of this concerned Henderson as he got up and shouted at Peter Mahovlich to get off, which he did with unconscious obeisance.

"I never thought about scoring the winning goals or anything like that," Henderson rationalized, "but as the last game wound down – it still boggles my mind why I did it; it was so unpremeditated – I was sitting there thinking, 'Geez, I've got to get out on the ice.' Maybe because I scored the winning goal in game seven, I don't know. But I just found myself standing there yelling at Peter Mahovlich. Players don't do that. I never did it before, and I never did it again. Never once, ever called a player off the ice. But I just had a sense that I needed to get out there. Thank goodness I listened to my inner thoughts."

Coach Sinden had some romantic notion that because Henderson had scored the winner he deserved to finish the game. Now, for a second time within a minute, Henderson called his own play, as it were.

"After I scored the goal I went back to the bench and Harry told our line to finish it up. I said, 'Harry, I'm done.' I would have been petrified to be out there the last thirty-four seconds. The tank was absolutely empty. I was physically, emotionally, mentally done. I told Harry I wouldn't trust myself out there. I am done!"

One of the strangest aspects of that winning goal is that while Henderson celebrated with his teammates after the game, the country celebrated from coast to coast as they watched Foster Hewitt with his famous call of, "Henderson has scored for Canada!" And yet, it was many years before Henderson actually heard Hewitt's immortal call of the goal!

"One television station did a program on the series, and I came in and commented on it," Henderson told. "As they showed the goals I would comment on them. It was probably a couple of years after the series. But that was the first time I heard Foster's call. After that, every time I heard it I'd get tingles up my back. That went on for about six or seven years. Every time I saw it. It was unbelievable."

"I never once thought about scoring the goal or being the hero. That just never entered my mind. It was just winning."

Henderson tries to make a point with controversial referee Josef Kompalla.

#22 J-P (JEAN-PAUL) PARISE – PASSION AND RAGE

The second-most famous photo from the Summit Series is part humour, part horror. The situation was game eight, early in the first period. Canada had taken two early penalties, and after the Soviets got another, J-P Parise took a third for his team in the first five minutes of the game. It was a marginal call, but worse it was assessed by Josef Kompalla, the East German referee who had made life miserable for Canada in game six. In fact, Canadian officials threatened to pull out of game eight if Kompalla had the whistle, and it was only on noon of game day that a resolution to the dispute was settled. Each team chose one referee, so Canada took Rudy Bata and the Soviets, as expected, took Kompalla.

But here was Canada, in the biggest game in history, seemingly being singled out by the referee again. Parise could take no more, and after circling the referee several times in a rage, he approached him and swung his stick at him, stopping just short of clubbing him. Kompalla raised a leg and covered himself in fear. Parise got a game misconduct to go with his minor penalty.

As the player explained forty years later: "When we heard that Kompalla was officiating, we went back to game six when he did everything to make sure the Russians won. The penalties were like 11–3. Against a good team like that, we couldn't play like that the whole game. So when we heard he was back for game eight, we just thought we're screwed. We were determined to win, determined to beat Communism. We're fat-cats, but we're going to win using our system. But Kompalla was not supposed to be officiating that game. There was nothing we could do. The Soviets wanted him in to make sure everything was FAIR! So, sure enough, we start the game and right away we get a penalty. That penalty expires and bang, we get another one. Then, I was killing that penalty with Phil and this guy made a sweep in his own end. I kind of hit him, so Kompalla says to me, 'Two minutes for interference.' I said, 'He's carrying the puck!' He says, 'You've got ten more!' That's how it went. I said, 'Well, if I've got ten, you're dying right here.' That's how I got kicked out."

Parise played a central role in Canada's win in 1972, but today he is the second- or third-most famous player with that name. He has two sons, one in turn more famous than the other. Zach is an NHLer who has been with New Jersey while Jordan has been playing in Europe, most recently in the German Ice Hockey League (DEL) with Augsburg.

"I lived in Minnesota," Parise began. "I spent my summers there. We were just starting to make good

J-P Parise tries to screen goalie Vladislav Tretiak during game two at Maple Leaf Gardens.

enough money that we didn't have to work. I was making about $29,000 a year. Today, Zach makes that in about an hour."

As he points out, he might not have been invited to training camp had the team not barred WHA players from participating, but that was his gain, and he was happy for it. "I always felt like I had a guardian angel looking over me. That summer, the WHA started, so players like Bobby Hull and Derek Sanderson went there, so they couldn't play against the Soviets. I thought I'd be one of those guys who helped the team in practice, help the players train, give them some competition. I swear, that was my thinking. All I asked Harry was that I play one of the games in Sweden or Czechoslovakia. I had no thoughts that I'd be playing against the Russians. With all the great players we had, I had no reason to think I'd play."

Parise came to camp and was pleasantly surprised by the easy way he was welcomed, a hard-working, checking forward now among the best players in the country.

"In those days, the league was pretty nasty. I mean, you just didn't have friends on other teams. But when I got to Toronto, I checked into the hotel. In the lobby sitting there was Stan Mikita. He said, 'Hi, J-P.' And in those days, you just didn't talk to those guys. He said, 'Why don't you go put your stuff upstairs and we'll go for a beer?' This was Stan Mikita, the superstar! He took me to a place where the rest of the guys were just sitting and having a beer. I was just an average player compared to those guys."

Parise didn't get into the lineup for game one, but he was front and centre in game two, and he knew it. "I didn't know anything about international hockey. I knew they were good, but I mean, who could be better than our pros? I couldn't imagine how good those guys were. When you look at the team the Russians had, all that speed and skill, it was clear after game one we couldn't try to match them skill against skill. Those guys were in such good shape and much better prepared than our skill guys. So Harry and Ferguson decided to use different players for game two to try to take away the centre of the ice and try to play a game more along the walls. So Wayne Cashman and I played on a line with Phil. We'd do the dirty work and get him the puck. I was just thrilled to be asked to play."

Canada won that game, of course, so Parise played in game three as well, where he had a goal and an assist in a 4–4 tie. His goal came early and staked Canada to a 1–0 lead at 1:54 of the first period. "I was standing in front of the net, and the puck came in front and I just smacked the rebound in. That didn't take much skill."

He then set up linemate Phil Esposito early in the third to give Canada what seemed to be a solid 3–1 lead. "It was a play in the corner, and I got the puck to Phil in front. He scored, as he always does."

Parise sat in the press box for the fourth game, the disaster in Vancouver when the home fans booed the Canadians. He understood the rationale, but was disheartened, to say the least, by the fans.

"Those really skilled guys needed to play, and the thought was that by this time they were in better shape," he hypothesized. "I didn't care. I wasn't supposed to be there, so for me just to play a couple of games, my goal had already been accomplished. And the guys who came in were great guys, like Jean Ratelle and Vic Hadfield. I've never gone through anything like that, where my own team was booed by the fans. This is where I realized how big this series was. This where it became not just a hockey game, but it was system against system, Communism against democracy. I think that's when it was no longer fun, no longer a friendly hockey game. It was politics. We were always prepared to play hockey and not have to worry about anything else. The

Russians did a wonderful way of promoting how good our system was and we were spoiled fat-cats, indicating how much better their system was. They had all of OUR country believing it!"

More than anything, Parise had always been a team player, just skilled enough to be among the best, but not so skilled that he didn't have to work hard every night, every shift, to earn his keep.

"I never questioned Harry," he said emphatically. "I was brought up to believe that you didn't question the coach. You didn't question who was replacing whom. That was not being a good team guy because if you ask why he's playing one guy, it means you feel there's a fault with the coach's decision. I was brought up with the Bruins and Hap Emms and knowing the coach was always right, and that's it. Your job is to go out and play and do whatever the coach tells you to do to help the team win. If you play first line or fourth line, your job is to help the team."

Not surprisingly, Parise had tremendous praise for Sinden and Ferguson, the two coaches who operated under incredible pressure from fans and media and, more importantly, the thirty-five players who all wanted to play. "The coaching staff had us believe that they couldn't play without us, that we had a role to play and our job was to fill that role. We couldn't be replaced."

The team faced another crisis of sorts in Moscow, prior to its first game. Sinden posted the starting lineups, and those whose names weren't on the list were likely not going to play again. Four players flew home to much controversy, although those who soldiered on bore no resentment, then or now.

"I don't blame them," Parise said. "Their club teams had training camp going on, so if they weren't playing they might as well go. To me, it would never have crossed my mind to do that because I accepted my role, and it wasn't being a superstar. There were many better players. The guys who remained chose to remain and accept the situation. Take a look at Frank Mahovlich. He had all kinds of reason to leave, but he didn't."

Parise got the opening goal – and the only goal – of the first period in game five, the recipient of a nice pass from Gilbert Perreault in the slot after a great rush. But it was his tenacious play and ability to adapt to the bigger ice that continued to endear him to Sinden.

"That was the first time I saw ice so big," Parise said, still in awe of his first games on the international ice. "It was tremendous because it's a different game altogether. There's a lot more space behind the net and the corners are wider. When it came to forechecking, you had to angle things a different way. In Sweden we realized quickly how different it was. The defencemen had to make a lot of adjustments, especially when the Russians play at high speed. It wasn't just one or two; it was a whole bunch of their players. Our defencemen did a tremendous job. They adjusted to the atmosphere and the speed and the ice."

Parise also recalled the finer points of the cultural differences as well. "This was my first exposure to Communism. When we landed in Moscow, it was as if it was a surprise to them that we had arrived. I don't know how long we sat in that plane, but it was a long time. We waited and waited. We certainly weren't treated like royalty. They put us in this Intourist hotel, and every time we left we had to leave our key with this big Russian woman at the elevator. They were just like crows. If you leave anything in your room that shines, it's gone. And we played every second day, so we had a day off in between. We'd try to see some of the culture of the city, but everywhere we went we had KGB following us, even if we went only a couple of blocks."

Parise played in all four games in Moscow, but, of course, it was the last that remains the strongest in his mind's eye and memory.

"When we were leaving the hotel on the way to the arena for game eight, we get on the bus, and at the back of the bus we saw two or three KGB agents sitting there. And this is before the game – it's time for hockey talk! We asked them very nicely to get off the bus. It was incredible. They tried everything to get under our skin. All it did was motivate us."

Parise saw game eight differently from any other player. He started as a player and finished as a spectator, but he was with the team the whole time. "Frank Mahovlich took my place in game eight after I was ejected. I had been playing with Esposito and Cournoyer. I was sent off the ice to the dressing room, but I got dressed and went behind the Canada bench with Wayne Cashman. I certainly regret the penalty. It was an awful feeling, especially as we went to the third period trailing by two goals."

One story from right after the final game that hasn't made the rounds much since 1972 is well remembered by Parise: "As we were all going back to our dressing room after the game, we didn't want anyone else there. We wanted to celebrate among ourselves, no one else. The players, the coaching staff, the trainers, that's it. So we're standing in line waiting for them to open the door. And in our line was a Russian reporter who insisted he was going to come into our dressing room with us. All of a sudden, Bill Goldsworthy hauls off and pops him one, knocks him out cold, and looks as though nothing happened. We just walked by him and into the room."

And, despite being tossed by Kompalla early in the first period of game eight, this was not to be Parise's final meeting with the referee. "The next morning," Parise starts with a mischievous tone, "we got on a plane to go to Czechoslovakia. We're still buzzing, we're so happy. So one of the players comes over to me and says, 'You're never going to believe who's on the plane with us – Kompalla!' He was sitting at the front. I got up and sat down right behind him and grabbed him by the cheek and squeezed until his whole face was white. I told him I just wanted him to know I was here!"

"You never know how you are under certain circumstances until you're there. But I played fourteen years in the NHL and never won the Stanley Cup, so this series was like my Stanley Cup."

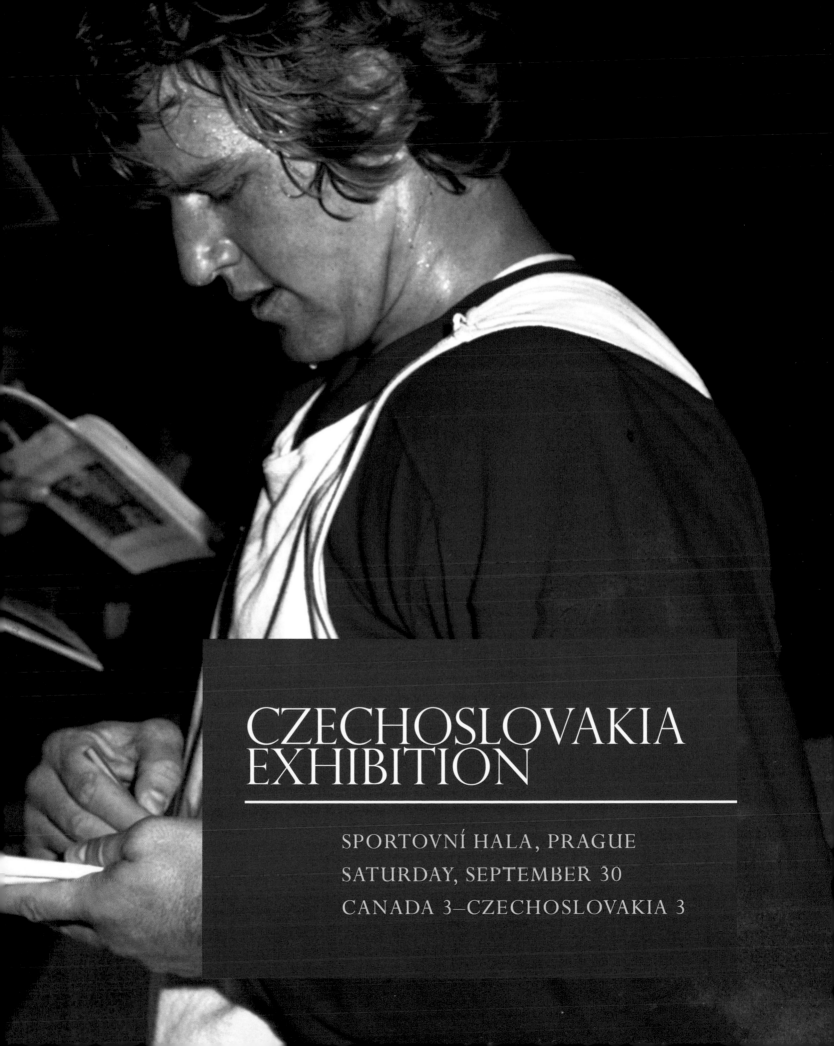

CZECHOSLOVAKIA EXHIBITION

SPORTOVNÍ HALA, PRAGUE

SATURDAY, SEPTEMBER 30

CANADA 3–CZECHOSLOVAKIA 3

A NIGHT FOR STAN

Team Canada's players stayed up most of the night of September 28 and were groggy at best when they left their Moscow hotel at 6 a.m. the next day to catch a flight to Prague. The players' wives flew back to Canada, and coach Harry Sinden tried to find the healthiest players to dress for one more game.

Of course, one thing he didn't have to worry about was his team captain. Everyone knew that Stan Mikita had that honour for this game, a homecoming of sorts for the Czech-born NHLer who had been "adopted" by his uncle in Ontario so that Mikita could legally return to Czechoslovakia to see his parents again.

While Canada put up a good fight given the circumstances, the Czechs proved to be a world-class team that could hold its own against the NHL's best, just as the Soviets had done. Incredibly, Canada tied the game on a goal from defenceman Serge Savard with only four seconds left in the third period, more late-game heroics from the team.

Centre Bobby Clarke played in every game for Canada including the finale, in Prague, on September 30.

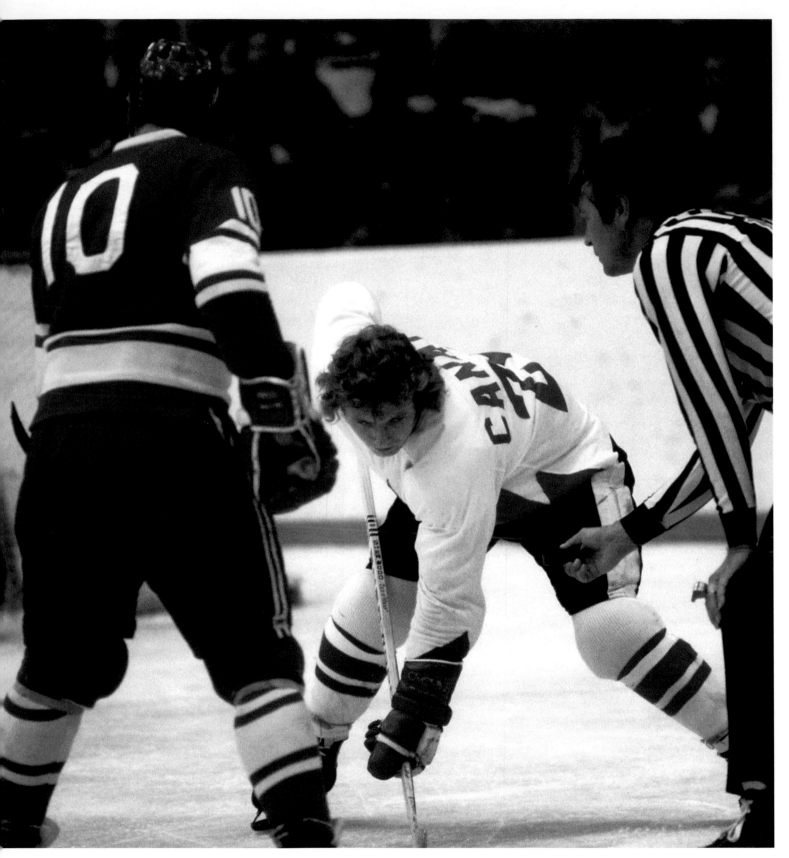

Bobby Clarke's skill in the face-off circle led directly to several key goals for Canada, not the least of which was the winning goal in game seven.

LINEUPS

CZECHOSLOVAKIA — Jiri Holecek — Oldrich Machac, Frantisek Pospisil, Josef Horesovsky, Jiri Bubla, Milan Kuzela, Vladimir Bednar, Jan Klapac, Jaroslav Holik, Jiri Holik, Vaclav Nedomansky, Jiri Kochta, Josef Palecek, Vladislav Martinec, Richard Farda, Bohuslav Stastny, Ivan Hlinka, Bedrich Brunclik, Bohuslav Ebermann

CANADA — Ken Dryden – Dale Tallon, Brad Park, Don Awrey, Rod Seiling, Serge Savard, Brian Glennie, Yvan Cournoyer, Phil Esposito, Wayne Cashman, Bill Goldsworthy, Dennis Hull, J-P Parise, Stan Mikita, Frank Mahovlich, Bobby Clarke, Marcel Dionne, Mickey Redmond, Peter Mahovlich

GAME SUMMARY

FIRST PERIOD

1. Canada, Savard (Park) 8:19
2. Canada, P. Mahovlich (Tallon) 13:55
Penalties: Stastny (TCH) and Awrey (CAN) 7:12, Bubla (TCH) 8:09, Goldsworthy (CAN) 9:26

SECOND PERIOD

3. Czechoslovakia, Stastny (Bubla) 9:02
4. Czechoslovakia, Stastny (unassisted) 15:22
Penalties: Hull (CAN) 3:58, Redmond (CAN) 9:34, Tallon (CAN) 13:43, Mikita (CAN) and Ja. Holik (TCH) 16:57, Clarke (CAN – major), Pospisil (TCH)20:00

THIRD PERIOD

5. Czechoslovakia, Kochta (Holecek) 2:28
6. Canada, Savard (Clarke, Park) 19:56
Penalties: Hlinka (TCH) 4:42

SHOTS ON GOAL

Czechoslovakia: 33
Canada: 24

IN GOAL

Czechoslovakia: Holecek
Canada: Dryden

REFEREES

Rudy Bata (TCH) and Ivo Filip (TCH)

#21 STAN MIKITA – SLOVAKIAN HERO

For everyone else on the team, playing in the Summit Series was about representing Canada and playing hockey. For Stanley Guoth, it was much more.

"My situation was different from the other guys because I had escaped – well, not escaped per se – left a Communist country to come to Canada. In fact, the only way I could ever leave Czechoslovakia and come back later was if I was adopted, so that's how my uncle worked it to get me out of there when I was eight years old. He became my new father." And so Stanley Guoth of Sokolce became Stan Mikita of St. Catharines, Ontario.

Indeed, he left his family behind, and for the next twelve years he wasn't able to go home, but he did develop into a sensational hockey player. "In 1959, when Czechoslovakia hosted the World Championship, the Belleville McFarlands wanted me for their team," Mikita revealed. "I asked Rudy Pilous, who was part-owner of the Teepees junior team, and who later coached the Black Hawks, if I could go, and he said he couldn't afford to send me there because I meant a lot to the Black Hawks. He asked what would happen if I broke my leg or something over there? I was a little bitter, but I understood."

Nevertheless, Mikita made it home a year later and was able to visit periodically after that. He had made his debut with the Hawks at the end of the 1958–59 season and made the team full time in the fall of 1959, never playing anywhere else for the next twenty-one seasons of his Hall-of-Fame career.

"It was a great trip back," he said of his sojourn in 1960. "I even brought my skates and played a couple of games in Kosice. We stayed about two weeks, and then a couple of years later the National Film Board of Canada made a documentary called *24 Hours in Czechoslovakia*, so I went home for that as well. It featured three people for eight hours each. I was there as the sportsman; another person who worked in a glass factory had eight hours; and the third was a young girl talking about what she wanted to do with eight hours. I got married in 1963 and we started going back every two or three years after that. We had four children, and we usually took them with us. We're going to try to have everyone go back in 2013 for our fiftieth anniversary."

When the Summit Series was being organized, it seemed a good idea to end the Moscow half of the trip with a game in Prague, Czechoslovakia, to spread the gospel of the NHL and its talented players. Mikita was thrilled, of course, but the Summit Series became so intense and important that "game nine" got lost in the shuffle, as it were.

"It was one of the great thrills of my life to play in Prague in front of my mother and sister and brother," Mikita said of that game. "I remember I had at least half-a-dozen good scoring chances, but I didn't score. It wasn't much of a game for me."

Despite leaving the Communist country in 1948 and playing exclusively in the NHL, Mikita was nonetheless a hero in his birthland. "They knew of me. Through the black market they could get scores of who was doing what in the National Hockey League. They knew the standings, goals, and assists, and sometimes they'd get a film brought in."

Mikita didn't play in the stunning game-one defeat, but as a result he dressed for game two. "Harry told me after the Montreal game to be ready for Toronto," he told. "So, we had a meeting that night when we arrived in Toronto, and sure enough my name was on the list of players for the game. I thought, 'Oh, geez, I hope I don't make an ass of myself.' I was really happy, but I also thought, 'Now I can get back at those bastards who took over my country.' That's how I felt. My thoughts weren't on hockey then — they were about getting the Soviets. The hammer didn't hit the bell until the next day when it was time for the warm-up. Luckily we won and Peter Mahovlich played a hell of a game, and I was fortunate enough to play with him. I asked Harry if Yvan Cournoyer was playing and he said yes. I asked him who he was playing with, and Harry said, 'You.' I said, 'Okay, great.' So we had two little guys, one of whom could fly and the other thinks he could fly — me — and Peter scored a short-handed goal and we won 4–1."

Mikita played in game three but then not again in the Summit part of the series. That was okay by him because he still had the Prague game to look forward to. And the lead-up to that game couldn't have gone any better for him.

"Harry told me I wasn't going to play in Moscow, so I became a cheerleader. But he did tell me that not only was I playing in game nine, the final game in Prague, Czechoslovakia, but I was going to be our team captain for that game. Then, I found out through Canadian radio and television that they had guys going to Prague early to scout for broadcasting the game. I asked Harry if my wife and I could go with them because it would mean getting an extra twenty-four hours in Prague with my family — my mother, brother, and sister. He said sure, so I got an extra day."

The story only gets better as Mikita and family reunited in time to watch the final game in Moscow.

"We watched game eight in the hotel we were staying at," he began. "There was only one TV there, and we had the manager set it up in the lobby. We had our dinner there, and about halfway through the game a Soviet businessman came in and asked what we were watching. I told him we were watching his team get its ass kicked! He wanted to bet me a bottle of champagne that the Soviets would win. I said, 'Sure, fine.' We were down 5–3 at the time, and he's smiling ear to ear. Then the third period happens, and we make it 5–4, then lo and behold we make it 5–5, and then Mr. Henderson does his thing and we win 6–5. So the Soviet orders a bottle of champagne, and I said, 'No, no — I said *everybody* gets champagne!' He panicked and said, 'Oh, no, how can this be? There are a hundred people here!' I asked the waiter how many bottles of champagne he had. He said he had twenty bottles. The Soviet is sweating, wondering how he's going to pay for it. But he says, 'Okay, twenty bottles.' But after about ten, I told the waiter to stop; the poor guy has been through enough."

Stan Mikita gets a great scoring chance on Tretiak in game two.

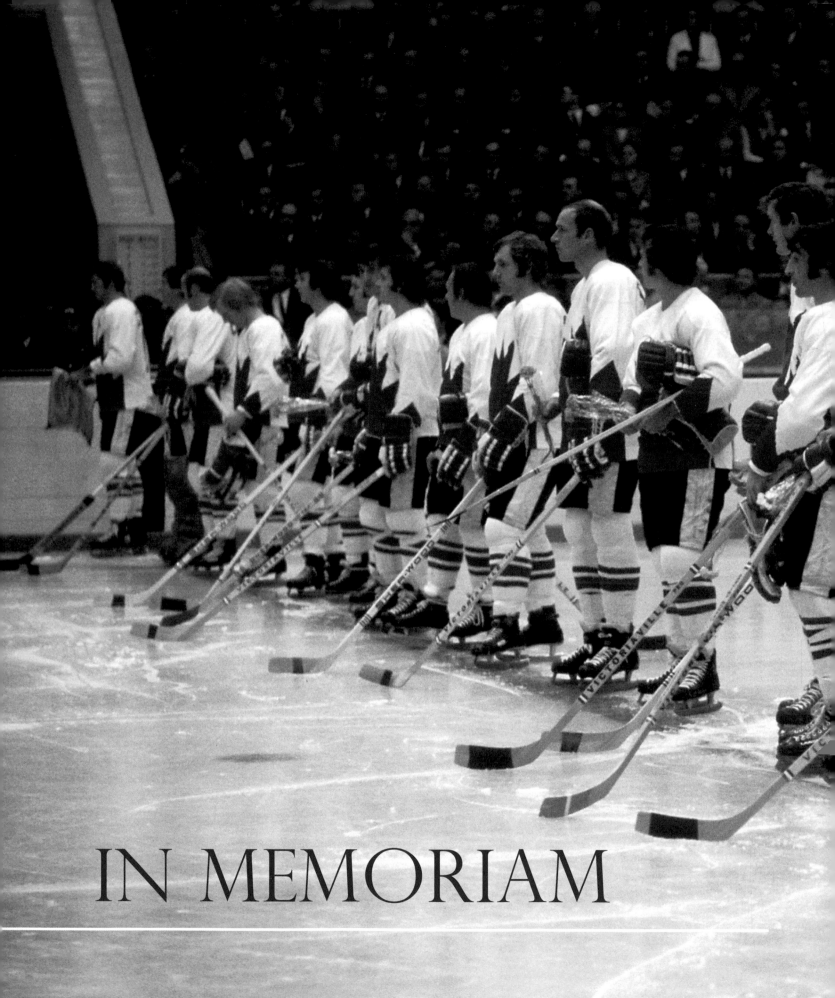

IN MEMORIAM

#2 GARY BERGMAN – SERIES OF A LIFETIME

"Bergman has scored for Canada"? Almost. With less than three minutes left in game eight, defenceman Brad Park led a three-on-two rush into the Soviet end and made a sensational backhand pass to Gary Bergman on the left side. Bergman got off a great shot, but Vladislav Tretiak uncharacteristically came well out of his net and made an even better save. It was that close to being the decisive moment in the series.

Bergman was tough as nails and backed down from no one. In Sweden, he admitted, "You know, I always thought I wanted to win the Stanley Cup very badly, but that is nothing at all compared to the way I want to beat the Russians."

The thirty-three-year-old defenceman was one of the oldest players on Team Canada. By this point in his career he had played all eight of his NHL seasons with the Detroit Red Wings and had established himself as a premier defensive blueliner. Coach Harry Sinden didn't name him to the team for goals or to quarterback the power play; he wanted Bergman to play defence, in his own end, taking care of business in front of the goalies and in the corners. And Sinden heard nary a bad word about the defenceman when he was doing his research with assistant coach John Ferguson prior to training camp.

Bergman was also openly critical of the scheduling of the Summit Series, which demanded the players be in peak condition in September, a time for NHL training camp after a summer off. "NHL players are accustomed to approaching a seven-month, seventy-eight-game schedule, with an important playoff series at the end, and pacing themselves accordingly," he reasoned at the time. "Knowing what's ahead, they work themselves into peak condition by about mid-December. Now, we were suddenly asked to get ourselves into that kind of condition or better – because this is just like playing for the Stanley Cup, only tougher – by the first few days of September! And we had only three weeks of training camp to do it."

Coach Sinden paired Bergman with Park, a clever strategy given Park's offensive ability that could be supported by Bergman's defensive prowess. Bergman had one of the *bon mots* of the series. After game two, a 4–1 Canada win in Toronto keyed by Peter Mahovlich's sensational short-handed goal when he beat Soviet defenceman Yuri Lyapkin with a beautiful move, Bergman said, "That thing hanging from the clock is Lyapkin's jockstrap."

But Bergman was also in the middle of one of the central contretemps in the series. Late in game seven, soon after Henderson had scored his magnificent goal that proved to be the winner, Bergman was involved in a scrap with Boris Mikhailov behind the Canada net that resulted in all players on ice pushing and shoving in a wild scrum that threatened to get out of hand. Bergman and Mikhailov received five-minute majors, although few real punches were thrown. Bergman said his Soviet opponent kicked him in the shins, trying to injure him with the blades of his skates.

"I never thought I'd see the day when another hockey player in any part of the world would kick me," Bergman said after the game. "That is sick conduct. Hockey is a tough sport, but that is something you just can't accept."

By the end of the series, Bergman had become one of the team's unsung heroes and true stars. Among his many and new-found admirers from the series was Ron Ellis, who said, "If I had to pick one guy who I was very happy for, that I think got a lot of respect from all the players, it would have to be Gary Bergman."

Bergman had a malignant melanoma removed from his back in 1994, but six years later it returned with greater ferocity and six months later he was dead. But in the minds of his teammates from 1972, he was one of the reasons Canada prevailed in the series.

Gary Bergman takes a breather during practice in Moscow.

#9 BILL GOLDSWORTHY – FRUSTRATION AND RETRIBUTION

Although he played for the Minnesota North Stars, hardly one of the NHL's glamour teams, Bill Goldsworthy earned his invitation to training camp honestly. He had finished his third straight season of thirty goals or more on a mediocre team, and coach Harry Sinden considered him one of the team's "finesse players." He also happened to be one of the few players to wear a helmet for Canada (the most prominent being Paul Henderson, of course), although Goldsworthy sometimes played without a lid as well.

In camp he played on a line with Marcel Dionne and Dennis Hull, but he had to take a couple days off and miss an intra-squad game after suffering a broken nose thanks to an accidental high-stick from Jean Ratelle during practice.

Goldsworthy didn't play in the first game, in Montreal, but he was in the lineup for game two, a critical win, in place of Ratelle. Sinden elected to swap the two again for game three, despite his admission that "my superstitious side says that I shouldn't make changes in a winning roster," but he believed Ratelle was the better centreman and could be more useful on the power play.

"Goldie" was back in the lineup game four, his low point. He played on a line with centre Phil Esposito and left-winger Dennis Hull, but Goldsworthy took two minor penalties early in the game, both leading to Soviet power-play goals and a 2–0 lead by the 7:29 mark of the opening period. Canada never recovered, and worse, it was the start of the booing of Team Canada by fans in Vancouver.

After the game, Goldsworthy confessed, "I was almost ashamed to be a Canadian when I heard those boos." Teammates came to his defence. Said Brad Park, "Maybe the team would have responded a little to a 'Go, Canada, Go!' cheer with the fans behind us." Bobby Clarke added, "It's one thing to be booed when you're playing for your individual team. It's something else to be booed when you're playing for your country."

Goldsworthy didn't dress again until game seven, when he formed a combination with Esposito and Peter Mahovlich. This was the team's fourth line, though, and Goldsworthy didn't see much ice time. (Esposito also played on the top line with Yvan Cournoyer and J-P Parise.) For game eight, Sinden put Frank Mahovlich in Goldsworthy's place.

Goldsworthy was diagnosed with AIDS in late 1994 and died a year and a half later, the first hockey player known to have succumbed to the disease.

#36 RICK MARTIN – YOUNG AMBITION DOES NOT A TRAITOR MAKE

How odd is life that twenty-one-year-old Rick Martin, the youngest player on Team Canada's roster, is no longer alive to celebrate the team's fortieth anniversary, having died in a single-car crash in Clarence, New York, on March 13, 2011?

In 1972, Martin was a star of the future. He had just completed his first NHL season, with Buffalo, setting a league record for rookies with forty-four goals in seventy-three games. He went on to play many great seasons in the league, but his career was cut short by a knee injury.

Martin was invited to camp mostly to watch and learn and gain valuable experience. His invitation was symbolic of the general preparation and lead-up to the series. Since everyone expected Canada to win all eight games, Sinden decided to invite some young players – such as Martin, Marcel Dionne, Gilbert Perreault, and Jocelyn Guèvremont – to get them some game action.

But immediately after Canada's shocking and decisive loss in game one, when it became clear this was going to be a fight to the death, the youngsters were forced to take a back seat to the veterans and proven leaders. Understandable, to be sure, but disappointing to the young guys all the same.

Martin travelled with the team through Canada and then to Sweden – playing in the second game in Stockholm – and then on to Moscow. But when he wasn't listed in the lineup for game five, and it seemed increasingly clear he wasn't going to play at all, he asked to leave the team and return to the NHL training camp of the Sabres to ready himself for the coming NHL season. Sinden agreed. Joining Martin were Vancouver's Guèvremont and Vic Hadfield, captain of the New York Rangers.

Although it didn't seem like a big deal at the time, the departure of the three was quickly labelled a traitorous act, the reaction of which was over the top. Martin had a tough time dealing with this branding for many years, although the players quickly exonerated him of any wrongdoing. Perhaps the final word on the matter is to say that looking back on the importance of the series, the players regretted not being part of hockey history. But traitors? That's a bit strong.

#41 MICHEL "BUNNY" LAROCQUE – SUPERSTAR JUNIOR PUCKSTOPPER

In order for Team Canada to have two full teams at training camp, four goalies were necessary. The two who were clearly vying for top position on the team were Tony Esposito and Ken Dryden, and Ed Johnston of the Bruins was brought in as the third goalie. Twenty-year-old Michel "Bunny" Larocque was named the fourth goalie, in large part because he was a client of Alan Eagleson, one of the tournament organizers (as were other pre-NHL players Billy Harris and John Van Boxmeer).

Larocque had just finished his fourth and final year with the Ottawa 67's of the OHL and been drafted sixth overall by the Canadiens in the 1972 Amateur Draft. Ironically, after playing in the AHL the following year in the Canadiens' system, Larocque became the back-up for Dryden for most of the rest of the 1970s, playing in the shadow of the Hall of Famer and winning the Vézina Trophy three times with him in the process. As well, he was part of the dynasty that saw the Habs win the Stanley Cup four years in a row (1976–79).

But in August and September 1972, Larocque was merely a youngster only too happy to be fourth goalie on a team that really needed only two.

"Bunny was the target at training camp," Guy Lapointe said with a laugh. "The players would take it easy on Dryden and Esposito, but when Bunny was in goal they were shooting for the top of the net, shooting everywhere. And he was just so happy to be there. He didn't care!"

Dryden has fond memories of Larocque, in part because of their joint participation in the Summit Series, in larger part because of their longer and stronger relationship with the Habs.

"With Bunny, I knew we would be meeting again at training camp afterwards," Dryden reminisced, "and I knew he had been a really outstanding goalie with Ottawa. He was drafted in the first round by the Canadiens, so I was watching him and getting to know him in that way at training camp. He was really a conscientious and hard-working guy. He just loved to stop pucks."

Larocque passed away at age forty on July 29, 1992, in Hull, Quebec, the result of brain cancer.

JOHN FERGUSON – FROM PLAYER TO COACH IN ONE BREATH

Assistant coach John Ferguson had retired the previous year after winning the Stanley Cup five times during his eight-year career with the Montreal Canadiens. He was a tough guy who could also score, a team player as they say, and coach Harry Sinden had even asked him to play in the series. As Sinden noted during training camp: "I got this job on June 7 [1972], and the very next day I hired John Ferguson as my assistant."

Sinden's reasoning was simple. "The main reason I chose him," he explained at the time, "is that my personal record against the Canadiens, when he was playing for them and I was coach of the Bruins, was not good. The Canadiens kept beating us … I figured it was Fergie who was to blame as much as anyone."

Sinden worked closely with Ferguson to select the team. Both men wrote down their choices for ten defencemen and twenty forwards, and then they compared notes and discussed their opinions. It wasn't until July 11 that the team was announced to the public, the coaches having reached consensus only the day before.

"I knew him very well as a player, but not as a person at the time," Sinden recalled forty years later. "He seemed to me the right fit because he had played in the NHL within the last year and was familiar with many of the players and was current on players' thinking and their attitudes. I thought he would be a heck of a benefit to the team, which he was."

Ferguson's most notorious moment came in game six when he talked to Bobby Clarke on the bench, saying something to the effect that, "that guy is killing us," in reference to Valeri Kharlamov. Clarke knew what the message was and went out and slashed at the Soviet forward's ankle, rendering the player ineffective for the rest of game six, forcing him to miss game seven and assume a much-reduced role in the final game.

International rules at the time forbade more than one coach from standing behind the bench, but Ferguson was always in a seat right beside the bench or behind it. He spent much of the game strategizing with Sinden or encouraging the players during a series that was an uphill battle for pretty much its entire duration.

Ferguson was also the victim of a prank from former teammate Serge Savard at the end of the series. The coach had had a stick signed by all players from both teams, a treasured memento from the series. But when the players alighted from their plane in Montreal at the end of the series, where they were greeted by Prime Minister Pierre Trudeau, Savard grabbed the stick and gave it to Trudeau as a present!

Furious, there was nothing Fergie could do, of course, but Trudeau later returned the stick when he learned of the prank. Fergie then gave it to the PM a second time in a more meaningful and genuinely magnanimous gesture in response to Trudeau's returning of it!

Ferguson died of prostate cancer in the summer of 2007.

Assistant coach Ferguson watches Team Canada practice at Luzhniki Arena.

APPENDIX 1

SERIES PLAYER STATISTICS – CANADA

DON AWREY

BOSTON BRUINS
b. Kitchener, Ontario, July 18, 1943 | 29 years old | #26 Defence | 6' 190 lbs.

		G	A	P	PIM
Game 1		0	0	0	0
Game 2		DNP			
Game 3		DNP			
Game 4		0	0	0	0
Sweden 1		DNP			
Sweden 2		1	0	1	0
Game 5		DNP			
Game 6		DNP			
Game 7		DNP			
Game 8		DNP			
Prague		0	0	0	2
SS Totals	2	0	0	0	0

RED BERENSON

DETROIT RED WINGS

b. Regina, Saskatchewan, December 8, 1939 | 32 years old | #15 Forward | 6' 190 lbs.

		G	A	P	PIM
Game 1		0	0	0	0
Game 2		DNP			
Game 3		DNP			
Game 4		DNP			
Sweden 1		DNP			
Sweden 2		0	0	0	0
Game 5		DNP			
Game 6		0	1	1	0
Game 7		DNP			
Game 8		DNP			
Prague		0	0	0	0
SS Totals	2	0	1	1	0

GARY BERGMAN

DETROIT RED WINGS

b. Kenora, Ontario, October 7, 1938 | d. December 9, 2000 | 33 years old | #2 Defence | 5'11" 185 lbs.

		G	A	P	PIM
Game 1		0	1	1	0
Game 2		0	0	0	2
Game 3		0	1	1	0
Game 4		0	1	1	0
Sweden 1		0	0	0	2
Sweden 2		DNP			
Game 5		0	0	0	2
Game 6		0	0	0	2
Game 7		0	0	0	7
Game 8		0	0	0	0
Prague		DNP			
SS Totals	8	0	3	3	13

WAYNE CASHMAN

BOSTON BRUINS

b. Kingston, Ontario, June 24, 1945 | 27 years old | #14 Forward | 6'1" 180 lbs.

		G	A	P	PIM
Game 1		DNP			
Game 2		**0**	**1**	**1**	**0**
Game 3		**0**	**1**	**1**	**14**
Game 4		DNP			
Sweden 1		1	0	1	2
Sweden 2		0	0	0	0
Game 5		DNP			
Game 6		DNP			
Game 7		DNP			
Game 8		DNP			
Prague		0	0	0	0
SS Totals	**2**	**0**	**2**	**2**	**14**

BOBBY CLARKE

PHILADELPHIA FLYERS

b. Flin Flon, Manitoba, August 13, 1949 | 23 years old | #28 Forward | 5'10" 176 lbs.

		G	A	P	PIM
Game 1		**1**	**1**	**2**	**2**
Game 2		**0**	**0**	**0**	**2**
Game 3		**0**	**1**	**1**	**0**
Game 4		**0**	**0**	**0**	**0**
Sweden 1		1	0	1	2
Sweden 2		DNP			
Game 5		**1**	**2**	**3**	**2**
Game 6		**0**	**0**	**0**	**12**
Game 7		**0**	**0**	**0**	**0**
Game 8		**0**	**0**	**0**	**0**
Prague		0	1	0	5
SS Totals	**8**	**2**	**4**	**6**	**18**

YVAN COURNOYER

MONTREAL CANADIENS

b. Drummondville, Quebec, November 22, 1943 | 28 years old | #12 Forward | 5'7" 165 lbs.

	G	A	P	PIM
Game 1	0	0	0	0
Game 2	1	1	2	0
Game 3	0	1	1	0
Game 4	0	0	0	0
Sweden 1	0	0	0	0
Sweden 2	0	0	0	0
Game 5	0	0	0	0
Game 6	1	0	1	0
Game 7	0	0	0	0
Game 8	1	0	1	2
Prague	0	0	0	0
SS Totals	8	3	2	5	2

MARCEL DIONNE

DETROIT RED WINGS

b. Drummondville, Quebec, August 3, 1951 | 21 years old | #34 Forward | 5'9" 170 lbs.

	G	A	P	PIM
Game 1	DNP			
Game 2	DNP			
Game 3	DNP			
Game 4	DNP			
Sweden 1	0	0	0	0
Sweden 2	DNP			
Game 5	DNP			
Game 6	DNP			
Game 7	DNP			
Game 8	DNP			
Prague	0	0	0	0
SS Totals	**DNP**			

KEN DRYDEN

MONTREAL CANADIENS

b. Hamilton, Ontario, August 8, 1947 | 25 years old | #29 Goalie | 6'4" 215 lbs.

		MIN	W–L–T	GA	SO	GAA
Game 1		60	L	7		
Game 2		DNP				
Game 3		DNP				
Game 4		60	L	5		
Sweden 1		DNP				
Sweden 2		DNP				
Game 5		DNP				
Game 6		60	W	2		
Game 7		DNP				
Game 8		60	W	5		
Prague		59:30	T	3		
SS Totals	4	240	2–2–0	19	0	4.75

RON ELLIS

TORONTO MAPLE LEAFS

b. Lindsay, Ontario, January 8, 1945 | 27 years old | #6 Forward | 5'9" 175 lbs.

		G	A	P	PIM
Game 1		0	1	1	0
Game 2		0	0	0	0
Game 3		0	1	1	0
Game 4		0	0	0	0
Sweden 1		0	2	2	0
Sweden 2		DNP			
Game 5		0	0	0	4
Game 6		0	0	0	2
Game 7		0	1	1	0
Game 8		0	0	0	2
Prague		DNP			
SS Totals	8	0	3	3	8

PHIL ESPOSITO

BOSTON BRUINS

b. Sault Ste. Marie, Ontario, February 20, 1942 | 30 years old | #7 Forward | 6'1" 195 lbs.

		G	A	P	PIM
Game 1		**1**	**0**	**1**	**0**
Game 2		**1**	**1**	**2**	**0**
Game 3		**1**	**1**	**2**	**0**
Game 4		**0**	**2**	**2**	**2**
Sweden 1		0	0	0	17
Sweden 2		1	0	1	2
Game 5		**0**	**0**	**0**	**0**
Game 6		**0**	**0**	**0**	**9**
Game 7		**2**	**0**	**2**	**4**
Game 8		**2**	**2**	**4**	**0**
Prague		0	0	1	0
SS Totals	**8**	**7**	**6**	**13**	**15**

TONY ESPOSITO

CHICAGO BLACK HAWKS

b. Sault Ste. Marie, Ontario, April 23, 1943 | 29 years old | #35 Goalie | 5'11" 185 lbs.

		MIN	W–L–T	GA	SO	GAA
Game 1		DNP				
Game 2		**60**	**W**	**1**		
Game 3		**60**	**T**	**4**		
Game 4		DNP				
Sweden 1		60	W	1		
Sweden 2		DNP				
Game 5		**60**	**L**	**5**		
Game 6		DNP				
Game 7		**60**	**W**	**3**		
Game 8		DNP				
Prague		DNP				
SS Totals	**4**	**240**	**2–1–1**	**13**	**0**	**3.25**

ROD GILBERT

NEW YORK RANGERS

b. Montreal, Quebec, July 1, 1941 | 31 years old | #8 Forward | 5'10" 180 lbs.

		G	A	P	PIM
Game 1		0	0	0	0
Game 2		DNP			
Game 3		DNP			
Game 4		0	0	0	0
Sweden 1		0	0	0	0
Sweden 2		0	1	1	0
Game 5		0	1	1	0
Game 6		0	1	1	0
Game 7		1	0	1	4
Game 8		0	1	1	5
Prague		DNP			
SS Totals	6	1	3	4	9

BRIAN GLENNIE

TORONTO MAPLE LEAFS

b. Toronto, Ontario, August 29, 1946 | 26 years old | #38 Defence | 6'1" 197 lbs.

	G	A	P	PIM
Game 1	DNP			
Game 2	DNP			
Game 3	DNP			
Game 4	DNP			
Sweden 1	0	0	0	0
Sweden 2	DNP			
Game 5	DNP			
Game 6	DNP			
Game 7	DNP			
Game 8	DNP			
Prague	0	0	0	0
SS Totals	**DNP**			

BILL GOLDSWORTHY

MINNESOTA NORTH STARS

b. Waterloo, Ontario, August 24, 1944 | d. March 29, 1996 | 28 years old | #9 Forward | 6' 195 lbs.

		G	A	P	PIM
Game 1		DNP			
Game 2		**0**	**0**	**0**	**0**
Game 3		DNP			
Game 4		**1**	**1**	**2**	**4**
Sweden 1		DNP			
Sweden 2		0	0	0	7
Game 5		DNP			
Game 6		DNP			
Game 7		**0**	**0**	**0**	**0**
Game 8		DNP			
Prague		0	0	0	2
SS Totals	**3**	**1**	**1**	**2**	**4**

JOCELYN GUÈVREMONT

VANCOUVER CANUCKS

b. Montreal, Quebec, March 1, 1951 | 21 years old | #37 Defence | 6'1" 180 lbs.

		G	A	P	PIM
Game 1		DNP			
Game 2		DNP			
Game 3		DNP			
Game 4		DNP			
Sweden 1		0	0	0	0
Sweden 2		0	0	0	0
Game 5		DNP			
Game 6		DNP			
Game 7		DNP			
Game 8		DNP			
Prague		DNP			
SS Totals		**DNP**			

VIC HADFIELD

NEW YORK RANGERS

b. Oakville, Ontario, October 4, 1940 | 31 years old | #11 Forward | 6' 185 lbs.

		G	A	P	PIM
Game 1		0	0	0	0
Game 2		DNP			
Game 3		DNP			
Game 4		0	0	0	0
Sweden 1		0	0	0	2
Sweden 2		1	0	1	5
Game 5		DNP			
Game 6		DNP			
Game 7		DNP			
Game 8		DNP			
Prague		DNP			
SS Totals	2	0	0	0	0

PAUL HENDERSON

TORONTO MAPLE LEAFS

b. Kincardine, Ontario, January 28, 1943 | 29 years old | #19 Forward | 5'11" 180 lbs.

		G	A	P	PIM
Game 1		1	1	2	2
Game 2		0	0	0	2
Game 3		1	0	1	0
Game 4		0	0	0	0
Sweden 1		1	0	1	0
Sweden 2		DNP			
Game 5		2	1	3	0
Game 6		1	0	1	0
Game 7		1	1	2	0
Game 8		1	0	1	0
Prague		DNP			
SS Totals	8	7	3	10	4

DENNIS HULL

CHICAGO BLACK HAWKS

b. Pointe Anne, Ontario, November 19, 1944 | 27 years old | #10 Forward | 5'11" 194 lbs.

	G	A	P	PIM
Game 1	DNP			
Game 2	DNP			
Game 3	DNP			
Game 4	**1**	**0**	**1**	**0**
Sweden 1	DNP			
Sweden 2	0	0	0	0
Game 5	DNP			
Game 6	**1**	**0**	**1**	**2**
Game 7	**0**	**1**	**1**	**0**
Game 8	**0**	**1**	**1**	**2**
Prague	0	0	0	2
SS Totals	4	2	2	4	4

ED JOHNSTON

BOSTON BRUINS

b. Montreal, Quebec, November 23, 1935 | 36 years old | #1 Goalie | 6' 190 lbs.

Min	W–L–T	GA	SO	GAA
Game 1	DNP			
Game 2	DNP			
Game 3	DNP			
Game 4	DNP			
Sweden 1	DNP			
Sweden 2	60	T		4
Game 5	DNP			
Game 6	DNP			
Game 7	DNP			
Game 8	DNP			
Prague	DNP			
SS Totals	**DNP**			

GUY LAPOINTE

MONTREAL CANADIENS

b. Montreal, Quebec, March 18, 1948 | 24 years old | #25 Defence | 6' 185 lbs.

		G	A	P	PIM
Game 1		0	0	0	4
Game 2		0	0	0	0
Game 3		0	0	0	0
Game 4		DNP			
Sweden 1		DNP			
Sweden 2		DNP			
Game 5		0	1	1	0
Game 6		0	0	0	2
Game 7		0	0	0	0
Game 8		0	0	0	0
Prague		DNP			
SS Totals	7	0	1	1	6

FRANK MAHOVLICH

MONTREAL CANADIENS

b. Timmins, Ontario, January 10, 1938 | 34 years old | #27 Forward | 6' 205 lbs.

		G	A	P	PIM
Game 1		0	1	1	0
Game 2		1	0	1	0
Game 3		0	0	0	0
Game 4		0	0	0	0
Sweden 1		DNP			
Sweden 2		DNP			
Game 5		0	0	0	0
Game 6		DNP			
Game 7		DNP			
Game 8		0	0	0	0
Prague		0	0	0	0
SS Totals	6	1	1	2	0

PETER MAHOVLICH

MONTREAL CANADIENS

b. Timmins, Ontario, October 10, 1946 | 25 years old | #20 Forward | 6'4" 210 lbs.

	G	A	P	PIM
Game 1	0	0	0	0
Game 2	1	0	1	0
Game 3	0	0	0	0
Game 4	DNP			
Sweden 1	0	0	0	2
Sweden 2	DNP			
Game 5	0	0	0	0
Game 6	0	0	0	0
Game 7	0	0	0	2
Game 8	0	1	1	2
Prague	1	0	1	0
SS Totals	7	1	1	2	4

RICK MARTIN

BUFFALO SABRES

b. Verdun, Quebec, July 26, 1951 | d. Buffalo, New York, March 13, 2011 | 21 years old | #36 Forward | 5'11" 167 lbs.

	G	A	P	PIM
Game 1	DNP			
Game 2	DNP			
Game 3	DNP			
Game 4	DNP			
Sweden 1	DNP			
Sweden 2	1	0	1	0
Game 5	DNP			
Game 6	DNP			
Game 7	DNP			
Game 8	DNP			
Prague	DNP			
SS Totals	**DNP**			

STAN MIKITA

CHICAGO BLACK HAWKS

b. Sokolce, Czechoslovakia (Slovakia), May 20, 1940 | 32 years old | #21 Forward | 5'9" 165 lbs.

		G	A	P	PIM
Game 1		DNP			
Game 2		**0**	**1**	**1**	**0**
Game 3		**0**	**0**	**0**	**0**
Game 4		DNP			
Sweden 1		DNP			
Sweden 2		DNP			
Game 5		DNP			
Game 6		DNP			
Game 7		DNP			
Game 8		DNP			
Prague		0	0	0	2
SS Totals	**2**	**0**	**1**	**1**	**0**

BOBBY ORR

BOSTON BRUINS

b. Parry Sound, Ontario, March 20, 1948 | 24 years old | #4 Defence | 5'11" 180 lbs.

	G	A	P	PIM
Game 1	DNP			
Game 2	DNP			
Game 3	DNP			
Game 4	DNP			
Sweden 1	DNP			
Sweden 2	DNP			
Game 5	DNP			
Game 6	DNP			
Game 7	DNP			
Game 8	DNP			
Prague	DNP			
SS Totals	**DNP**			

J-P PARISE

MINNESOTA NORTH STARS

b. Smooth Rock Falls, Ontario, December 11, 1941 | 30 years old | #22 Forward | 5'9" 175 lbs.

		G	A	P	PIM
Game 1		DNP			
Game 2		0	0	0	0
Game 3		1	1	2	2
Game 4		DNP			
Sweden 1		0	1	1	0
Sweden 2		0	0	0	4
Game 5		1	0	1	0
Game 6		0	0	0	0
Game 7		0	1	1	2
Game 8		0	0	0	32
Prague		0	0	0	0
SS Totals	6	2	2	4	36

BRAD PARK

NEW YORK RANGERS

b. Toronto, Ontario, July 6, 1948 | 24 years old | #5 Defence | 6' 190 lbs.

		G	A	P	PIM
Game 1		0	0	0	0
Game 2		0	2	2	2
Game 3		0	0	0	0
Game 4		0	0	0	0
Sweden 1		1	0	1	0
Sweden 2		0	0	0	0
Game 5		0	0	0	0
Game 6		0	0	0	0
Game 7		0	0	0	0
Game 8		1	2	3	0
Prague		0	2	2	0
SS Totals	8	1	4	5	2

GILBERT PERREAULT

BUFFALO SABRES

b. Victoriaville, Quebec, November 13, 1950 | 21 years old | #33 Forward | 6' 195 lbs.

	G	A	P	PIM
Game 1	DNP			
Game 2	DNP			
Game 3	DNP			
Game 4	**1**	**0**	**1**	**0**
Sweden 1	DNP			
Sweden 2	0	1	1	0
Game 5	**0**	**1**	**1**	**0**
Game 6	DNP			
Game 7	DNP			
Game 8	DNP			
Prague	DNP			
SS Totals	**2**	**1**	**1**	**2**	**0**

JEAN RATELLE

NEW YORK RANGERS

b. Lac St. Jean, Quebec, October 3, 1940 | 31 years old | #18 Forward | 6'1" 175 lbs.

	G	A	P	PIM
Game 1	**0**	**0**	**0**	**0**
Game 2	DNP			
Game 3	**1**	**0**	**1**	**0**
Game 4	DNP			
Sweden 1	0	0	0	0
Sweden 2	0	0	0	2
Game 5	**0**	**0**	**0**	**0**
Game 6	**0**	**0**	**0**	**0**
Game 7	**0**	**1**	**1**	**0**
Game 8	**0**	**2**	**2**	**0**
Prague	DNP			
SS Totals	**6**	**1**	**3**	**4**	**0**

MICKEY REDMOND

DETROIT RED WINGS

b. Kirkland Lake, Ontario, December 27, 1947 | 24 years old | #24 Forward | 5'11" 185 lbs.

		G	A	P	PIM
Game 1		0	0	0	0
Game 2		DNP			
Game 3		DNP			
Game 4		DNP			
Sweden 1		0	0	0	0
Sweden 2		DNP			
Game 5		DNP			
Game 6		DNP			
Game 7		DNP			
Game 8		DNP			
Prague		0	0	0	2
SS Totals	1	0	0	0	0

SERGE SAVARD

MONTREAL CANADIENS

b. Montreal, Quebec, January 22, 1946 | 26 years old | #23 Defence | 6'2" 200 lbs.

		G	A	P	PIM
Game 1		DNP			
Game 2		0	0	0	0
Game 3		0	0	0	0
Game 4		DNP			
Sweden 1		DNP			
Sweden 2		DNP			
Game 5		DNP			
Game 6		0	0	0	0
Game 7		0	2	2	0
Game 8		0	0	0	0
Prague		2	0	2	0
SS Totals	5	0	2	2	0

ROD SEILING

NEW YORK RANGERS

b. Elmira, Ontario, November 14, 1944 | 27 years old | #16 Defence | 6' 180 lbs.

		G	A	P	PIM
Game 1		0	0	0	0
Game 2		DNP			
Game 3		DNP			
Game 4		0	0	0	0
Sweden 1		DNP			
Sweden 2		0	0	0	0
Game 5		0	0	0	0
Game 6		DNP			
Game 7		DNP			
Game 8		DNP			
Prague		0	0	0	0
SS Totals	3	0	0	0	0

PAT STAPLETON

CHICAGO BLACK HAWKS

b. Sarnia, Ontario, July 4, 1940 | 32 years old | #3 Defence | 5'8" 185 lbs.

		G	A	P	PIM
Game 1		DNP			
Game 2		0	0	0	2
Game 3		0	0	0	0
Game 4		0	0	0	0
Sweden 1		0	0	0	0
Sweden 2		0	0	0	0
Game 5		0	0	0	0
Game 6		0	0	0	0
Game 7		0	0	0	2
Game 8		0	0	0	2
Prague		DNP			
SS Totals	7	0	0	0	6

DALE TALLON

VANCOUVER CANUCKS

b. Rouyn-Noranda, Quebec, October 19, 1950 | 21 years old | #32 Defence | 6'1" 195 lbs.

	G	A	P	PIM
Game 1	DNP			
Game 2	DNP			
Game 3	DNP			
Game 4	DNP			
Sweden 1	DNP			
Sweden 2	0	0	0	4
Game 5	DNP			
Game 6	DNP			
Game 7	DNP			
Game 8	DNP			
Prague	0	1	0	2
SS Totals	**DNP**			

BILL WHITE

CHICAGO BLACK HAWKS

b. Toronto, Ontario, August 26, 1939 | 33 years old | #17 Defence | 6'2" 190 lbs.

	G	A	P	PIM
Game 1	DNP			
Game 2	**0**	**0**	**0**	**0**
Game 3	**0**	**1**	**1**	**2**
Game 4	**0**	**0**	**0**	**0**
Sweden 1	0	0	0	0
Sweden 2	DNP			
Game 5	**0**	**0**	**0**	**2**
Game 6	**0**	**0**	**0**	**0**
Game 7	**0**	**0**	**0**	**2**
Game 8	**1**	**0**	**1**	**2**
Prague	DNP			
SS Totals	**7**	**1**	**1**	**2**	**8**

APPENDIX 2

SERIES PLAYER STATISTICS – SOVIET UNION

VYACHESLAV ANISIN

KRYLYLA SOVIETOV MOSCOW

b. Moscow, Soviet Union, July 11, 1951 | 21 years old | #22 Forward | 5'8" 163 lbs.

		G	A	P	PIM
Game 1		DNP			
Game 2		0	0	0	0
Game 3		0	2	2	0
Game 4		0	0	0	0
Game 5		1	1	2	0
Game 6		0	0	0	0
Game 7		0	0	0	2
Game 8		0	0	0	0
SS Totals	7	1	3	4	2

VLADIMIR ASTAFIEV

TORPEDO

b. February 1, 1950 | 22 years old

	G	A	P	PIM
Game 1	DNP			
Game 2	DNP			
Game 3	DNP			
Game 4	DNP			
Game 5	DNP			
Game 6	DNP			
Game 7	DNP			
Game 8	DNP			
SS Totals	**DNP**			

YURI BLINOV

CSKA MOSCOW

b. Moscow, Soviet Union, January 13, 1949 | 23 years old | #9 Forward | 5'6" 154 lbs.

		G	A	P	PIM
Game 1		0	1	1	0
Game 2		DNP			
Game 3		DNP			
Game 4		1	0	1	0
Game 5		1	0	1	2
Game 6		DNP			
Game 7		0	0	0	0
Game 8		0	0	0	0
SS Totals	5	2	1	3	2

ALEXANDER BODUNOV

KRYLYLA SOVIETOV MOSCOW

b. Moscow, Soviet Union, June 3, 1951 | 21 years old | #24 Forward | 5'10" 174 lbs.

		G	A	P	PIM
Game 1		DNP			
Game 2		DNP			
Game 3		**1**	**0**	**1**	**0**
Game 4		**0**	**0**	**0**	**0**
Game 5		DNP			
Game 6		**0**	**0**	**0**	**0**
Game 7		DNP			
Game 8		DNP			
SS Totals	**3**	**1**	**0**	**1**	**0**

VITALI DAVYDOV

DYNAMO MOSCOW

b. Moscow, Soviet Union, April 3, 1939 | 33 years old

	G	A	P	PIM
Game 1	DNP			
Game 2	DNP			
Game 3	DNP			
Game 4	DNP			
Game 5	DNP			
Game 6	DNP			
Game 7	DNP			
Game 8	DNP			
SS Totals	**DNP**			

ANATOLI FIRSOV

CSKA MOSCOW

b. Moscow, Soviet Union, February 1, 1941 | d. Moscow, Russia, July 24, 2000 | 31 years old

	G	A	P	PIM
Game 1	DNP			
Game 2	DNP			
Game 3	DNP			
Game 4	DNP			
Game 5	DNP			
Game 6	DNP			
Game 7	DNP			
Game 8	DNP			
SS Totals	**DNP**			

ALEXANDER GUSEV

CSKA MOSCOW

b. Moscow, Soviet Union, January 21, 1947 | 25 years old | #2 Defence | 5'11" 176 lbs.

		G	A	P	PIM
Game 1		0	0	0	0
Game 2		0	0	0	2
Game 3		0	0	0	0
Game 4		DNP			
Game 5		1	0	1	0
Game 6		DNP			
Game 7		0	0	0	0
Game 8		0	0	0	0
SS Totals	6	1	0	1	2

VALERI KHARLAMOV

CSKA MOSCOW

b. Moscow, Soviet Union, January 14, 1948 | d. Moscow, Soviet Union, August 27, 1981 | 24 years old | #17 Forward | 5'6" 164 lbs.

		G	A	P	PIM
Game 1		2	0	2	2
Game 2		0	0	0	10
Game 3		1	0	1	0
Game 4		0	1	1	0
Game 5		0	2	2	4
Game 6		0	0	0	0
Game 7		DNP			
Game 8		0	1	1	0
SS Totals	7	3	4	7	16

VIKTOR KUZKIN

CSKA MOSCOW

b. Moscow, Soviet Union, July 6, 1940 | d. Sochi, Russia, June 24, 2008 | 32 years old | # 4 Defence | 6' 187 lbs.

		G	A	P	PIM
Game 1		0	0	0	0
Game 2		0	0	0	0
Game 3		0	0	0	0
Game 4		0	0	0	2
Game 5		0	1	1	0
Game 6		DNP			
Game 7		0	0	0	4
Game 8		0	0	0	2
SS Totals	7	0	1	1	8

YURI LEBEDEV

KRYLYLA SOVIETOV MOSCOW

b. Moscow, Soviet Union, March 1, 1951 | 21 years old | #23 Forward | 5'10" 159 lbs.

		G	A	P	PIM
Game 1		DNP			
Game 2		DNP			
Game 3		**1**	**0**	**1**	**2**
Game 4		**0**	**0**	**0**	**0**
Game 5		DNP			
Game 6		**0**	**0**	**0**	**0**
Game 7		DNP			
Game 8		DNP			
SS Totals	**3**	**1**	**0**	**1**	**2**

VLADIMIR LUTCHENKO

CSKA MOSCOW

b. Moscow, Soviet Union, January 2, 1949 | 23 years old | #3 Defence | 6'2" 190 lbs.

		G	A	P	PIM
Game 1		**0**	**0**	**0**	**0**
Game 2		**0**	**0**	**0**	**0**
Game 3		**0**	**0**	**0**	**0**
Game 4		**0**	**2**	**2**	**0**
Game 5		**0**	**0**	**0**	**0**
Game 6		**0**	**0**	**0**	**0**
Game 7		**0**	**1**	**1**	**0**
Game 8		**1**	**0**	**1**	**0**
SS Totals	**8**	**1**	**3**	**4**	**0**

YURI LYAPKIN

SPARTAK MOSCOW

b. Moscow, Soviet Union, January 21, 1945 | 27 years old | #25 Defence | 5'11" 172 lbs.

		G	A	P	PIM
Game 1		0	0	0	0
Game 2		0	1	1	0
Game 3		DNP			
Game 4		DNP			
Game 5		0	1	1	0
Game 6		1	1	2	0
Game 7		0	1	1	0
Game 8		0	1	1	0
SS Totals	6	1	5	6	0

ALEXANDER MALTSEV

DYNAMO MOSCOW

b. Setkovskaya, Soviet Union, April 20, 1949 | 23 years old | #10 Forward | 5'9" 161 lbs.

		G	A	P	PIM
Game 1		0	2	2	0
Game 2		0	0	0	0
Game 3		0	0	0	0
Game 4		0	1	1	0
Game 5		0	0	0	0
Game 6		0	0	0	0
Game 7		0	1	1	0
Game 8		0	1	1	0
SS Totals	8	0	5	5	0

ALEXANDER MARTINYUK

SPARTAK MOSCOW

b. Moscow, Soviet Union, September 11, 1945 | 26–27 years old | #29 Forward | 5'10" 176 lbs.

		G	A	P	PIM
Game 1		DNP			
Game 2		DNP			
Game 3		DNP			
Game 4		DNP			
Game 5		**0**	**0**	**0**	**0**
Game 6		DNP			
Game 7		DNP			
Game 8		DNP			
SS Totals	**1**	**0**	**0**	**0**	**0**

BORIS MIKHAILOV

CSKA MOSCOW

b. Moscow, Soviet Union, October 6, 1944 | 27 years old | #13 Forward | 5'10" 165 lbs.

		G	A	P	PIM
Game 1		**1**	**1**	**2**	**2**
Game 2		**0**	**0**	**0**	**0**
Game 3		**0**	**0**	**0**	**0**
Game 4		**2**	**1**	**3**	**0**
Game 5		**0**	**0**	**0**	**0**
Game 6		**0**	**0**	**0**	**0**
Game 7		**0**	**0**	**0**	**7**
Game 8		**0**	**0**	**0**	**0**
SS Totals	**8**	**3**	**2**	**5**	**9**

YEVGENI MISHAKOV

CSKA MOSCOW

b. Moscow, Soviet Union, February 22, 1941 | d. Moscow, Russia, May 30, 2007 | 31 years old | #12 Forward | 5'8" 176 lbs.

		G	A	P	PIM
Game 1		0	0	0	0
Game 2		0	0	0	0
Game 3		0	0	0	2
Game 4		DNP			
Game 5		0	0	0	0
Game 6		DNP			
Game 7		0	0	0	4
Game 8		0	0	0	5
SS Totals	6	0	0	0	11

YEVGENI PALADIEV

SPARTAK MOSCOW

b. Ust-Kamenogorsk, Soviet Union, May 12, 1948 | 24 years old | #26 Defence | 5'10" 176 lbs.

		G	A	P	PIM
Game 1		0	0	0	0
Game 2		0	0	0	0
Game 3		DNP			
Game 4		0	0	0	0
Game 5		DNP			
Game 6		DNP			
Game 7		DNP			
Game 8		DNP			
SS Totals	3	0	0	0	0

ALEXANDER PASHKOV

b. Moscow, Soviet Union, August 28, 1944 | 28 years old | #26 Goalie

Game 1	DNP
Game 2	DNP
Game 3	DNP
Game 4	DNP
Game 5	DNP
Game 6	DNP
Game 7	DNP
Game 8	DNP
SS Totals	**DNP**

VLADIMIR PETROV

CSKA MOSCOW

b. Krasnogorsk, Soviet Union, June 30, 1947 | 25 years old | #16 Forward | 5'10" 168 lbs.

		G	A	P	PIM
Game 1		1	0	1	0
Game 2		0	0	0	0
Game 3		1	0	1	2
Game 4		0	3	3	2
Game 5		0	1	1	0
Game 6		0	0	0	0
Game 7		1	0	1	0
Game 8		0	0	0	6
SS Totals	8	3	4	7	10

ALEXANDER RAGULIN

CSKA MOSCOW

b. Moscow, Soviet Union, May 5, 1941 | d. Moscow, Russia, November 17, 2004 | 31 years old | #5 Defence | 6'2" 220 lbs.

		G	A	P	PIM
Game 1		0	0	0	2
Game 2		0	0	0	0
Game 3		DNP			
Game 4		0	0	0	0
Game 5		0	1	1	0
Game 6		0	0	0	2
Game 7		0	0	0	0
Game 8		DNP			
SS Totals	6	0	1	1	4

VLADIMIR SHADRIN

SPARTAK MOSCOW

b. Moscow, Soviet Union, June 6, 1948 | 24 years old | #19 Forward | 5'10" 161 lbs.

		G	A	P	PIM
Game 1		0	2	2	0
Game 2		0	0	0	0
Game 3		0	0	0	0
Game 4		1	0	1	0
Game 5		1	0	1	0
Game 6		0	2	2	0
Game 7		0	1	1	0
Game 8		1	0	1	0
SS Totals	8	3	5	8	0

YURI SHATALOV

KRYLYA SOVIETOV MOSCOW

b. Omsk, Soviet Union, June 13, 1945 | 27 years old | #14 Defence | 5'8" 178 lbs.

	G	A	P	PIM
Game 1	DNP			
Game 2	DNP			
Game 3	**0**	**0**	**0**	**0**
Game 4	DNP			
Game 5	DNP			
Game 6	**0**	**0**	**0**	**0**
Game 7	DNP			
Game 8	DNP			
SS Totals	**2**	**0**	**0**	**0**	**0**

ALEXANDER SIDELNIKOV

KRYLYLA SOVIETOV MOSCOW

b. Moscow, Soviet Union, August 12, 1950 | d. June 23, 2003 | 22 years old | #27 Goalie

Game 1	DNP
Game 2	DNP
Game 3	DNP
Game 4	DNP
Game 5	DNP
Game 6	DNP
Game 7	DNP
Game 8	DNP
SS Totals	**DNP**

VYACHESLAV SOLODUKHIN

SKA LENINGRAD

b. Leningrad, Soviet Union, November 11, 1950 | 21 years old | #21 Forward | 5'11" 194 lbs.

		G	A	P	PIM
Game 1		DNP			
Game 2		DNP			
Game 3		**0**	**0**	**0**	**0**
Game 4		DNP			
Game 5		DNP			
Game 6		DNP			
Game 7		DNP			
Game 8		DNP			
SS Totals	1	0	0	0	0

VYACHESLAV STARSHINOV

SPARTAK MOSCOW

b. Moscow, Soviet Union, May 6, 1940 | 32 years old | #8 Forward | 5'8" 183 lbs.

		G	A	P	PIM
Game 1		DNP			
Game 2		**0**	**0**	**0**	**0**
Game 3		DNP			
Game 4		DNP			
Game 5		DNP			
Game 6		DNP			
Game 7		DNP			
Game 8		DNP			
SS Totals	1	0	0	0	0

VLADISLAV TRETIAK

CSKA MOSCOW

b. Dmitrovo, Soviet Union, April 25, 1952 | 20 years old | #20 Goalie | 6'1" 172 lbs.

	Min	W–L–T	GA	SO	GAA
Game 1	60	W	3		
Game 2	60	L	4		
Game 3	60	T	4		
Game 4	60	W	3		
Game 5	60	W	4		
Game 6	60	L	3		
Game 7	60	L	4		
Game 8	60	L	6		
SS Totals 8	480:00	3–4–1	31	0	3.87

GENNADI TSYGANKOV

CSKA MOSCOW

b. Vanino, Soviet Union, August 16, 1947 | d. St. Petersburg, Russia, February 16, 2006 | 25 years old | #7 Defence | 5'11" 174 lbs.

	G	A	P	PIM
Game 1	0	0	0	0
Game 2	0	0	0	2
Game 3	0	1	1	0
Game 4	0	0	0	0
Game 5	0	0	0	2
Game 6	0	0	0	0
Game 7	0	1	1	0
Game 8	0	0	0	2
SS Totals 8	0	2	2	6

VALERI VASILIEV

DYNAMO MOSCOW

b. Gorky, Soviet Union, August 3, 1949 | d. Moscow, Russia, April 19, 2012 | 23 years old | #6 Defence
| 5'11" 187 lbs.

		G	A	P	PIM
Game 1		0	0	0	0
Game 2		DNP			
Game 3		0	1	1	2
Game 4		0	1	1	0
Game 5		DNP			
Game 6		0	0	0	2
Game 7		0	0	0	0
Game 8		1	0	1	2
SS Totals	6	1	2	3	6

VLADIMIR VIKULOV

CSKA MOSCOW

b. Moscow, Soviet Union, July 20, 1946 | 26 years old | #18 Forward | 5'10" 165 lbs.

		G	A	P	PIM
Game 1		0	0	0	0
Game 2		DNP			
Game 3		DNP			
Game 4		1	0	1	0
Game 5		1	0	1	0
Game 6		0	0	0	0
Game 7		0	1	1	0
Game 8		0	0	0	0
SS Totals	6	2	1	3	0

ALEXANDER VOLCHKOV

CSKA MOSCOW

b. Moscow, Soviet Union, January 11, 1952 | 20 years old | #30 Forward | 6' 198 lbs.

		G	A	P	PIM
Game 1		DNP			
Game 2		DNP			
Game 3		DNP			
Game 4		DNP			
Game 5		DNP			
Game 6		0	0	0	0
Game 7		0	0	0	0
Game 8		0	0	0	0
SS Totals	3	0	0	0	0

ALEXANDER YAKUSHEV

SPARTAK MOSCOW

b. Moscow, Soviet Union, January 2, 1947 | 25 years old | #15 Forward | 6'3" 178 lbs.

		G	A	P	PIM
Game 1		1	1	2	2
Game 2		1	0	1	0
Game 3		0	0	0	0
Game 4		0	1	1	0
Game 5		0	1	1	2
Game 6		1	1	2	0
Game 7		2	0	2	0
Game 8		2	0	2	0
SS Totals	8	7	4	11	4

YEVGENI ZIMIN

SPARTAK MOSCOW

b. Moscow, Soviet Union, August 6, 1947 | 25 years old | #11 Forward | 5'8" 165 lbs.

		G	A	P	PIM
Game 1		2	0	2	0
Game 2		0	1	1	0
Game 3	DNP				
Game 4	DNP				
Game 5	DNP				
Game 6	DNP				
Game 7	DNP				
Game 8	DNP				
SS Totals	2	2	1	3	0

VIKTOR ZINGER

SPARTAK MOSCOW

b. Moscow, Soviet Union, October 29, 1941 | 30 years old | #1 Goalie

Game 1	DNP
Game 2	DNP
Game 3	DNP
Game 4	DNP
Game 5	DNP
Game 6	DNP
Game 7	DNP
Game 8	DNP
SS Totals	**DNP**

APPENDIX 3

SUMMIT SERIES FINAL STANDINGS

	GP	W	L	T	GF	GA
CANADA	8	4	3	1	31	32
SOVIET UNION	8	3	4	1	32	31

GAME 1	September 2	Montreal	Soviet Union 7	Canada 3
GAME 2	September 4	Toronto	Canada 4	Soviet Union 1
GAME 3	September 6	Winnipeg	Canada 4	Soviet Union 4
GAME 4	September 8	Vancouver	Soviet Union 5	Canada 3
GAME 5	September 22	Moscow	Soviet Union 5	Canada 4
GAME 6	September 24	Moscow	Canada 3	Soviet Union 2
GAME 7	September 26	Moscow	Canada 4	Soviet Union 3
GAME 8	September 28	Moscow	Canada 6	Soviet Union 5

APPENDIX 4

GAME RECORDS BY PLAYER

CANADA	W–L–T
Serge Savard	4–0–1
J-P Parise	4–1–1
Guy Lapointe	4–2–1
Peter Mahovlich	4–2–1
Pat Stapleton	4–2–1
Bill White	4–2–1
Gary Bergman	4–3–1
Bobby Clarke	4–3–1
Yvan Cournoyer	4–3–1
Ron Ellis	4–3–1
Phil Esposito	4–3–1
Paul Henderson	4–3–1
Brad Park	4–3–1
Dennis Hull	3–1–0
Jean Ratelle	3–2–1
Rod Gilbert	3–3–0
Tony Esposito	2–1–1
Bill Goldsworthy	2–1–0
Ken Dryden	2–2–0

CANADA (cont'd)	W–L–T
Frank Mahovlich	2–3–1
Wayne Cashman	1–0–1
Stan Mikita	1–0–1
Red Berenson	1–1–0
Mickey Redmond	0–1–0
Don Awrey	0–2–0
Vic Hadfield	0–2–0
Gilbert Perreault	0–2–0
Rod Seiling	0–3–0

SOVIET UNION	W–L–T
Yuri Blinov	3–2–0
Valeri Kharlamov	3–3–1
Viktor Kuzkin	3–3–1
Alexander Ragulin	3–3–0
Vladimir Vikulov	3–3–0
Vladimir Lutchenko	3–4–1
Alexander Maltsev	3–4–1
Boris Mikhailov	3–4–1
Vladimir Petrov	3–4–1
Vladimir Shadrin	3–4–1
Vladislav Tretiak	3–4–1
Gennadi Tsygankov	3–4–1
Alexander Yakushev	3–4–1
Yevgeni Paladiev	2–1–0
Alexander Gusev	2–3–1
Yevgeni Mishakov	2–3–1
Valeri Vasiliev	2–3–1
Vyacheslav Anisin	2–4–1
Yuri Lyapkin	2–4–0

SOVIET UNION (cont'd)   W–L–T

	W–L–T
Alexander Martiniuk	1–0–0
Yevgeni Zimin	1–1–0
Alexander Bodunov	1–1–1
Yuri Lebedev	1–1–1
Yuri Shatalov	0–1–1
Vyacheslav Solodukhin	0–1–1
Vyacheslav Starshinov	0–1–0
Alexander Volchkov	0–3–0

REFEREES

Franz Bader (FRG)	1 game
Rudy Bata (TCH)	3 games
Uwe Dahlberg (SWE)	2 games
Steve Dowling (USA)	1 game
Len Gagnon (USA)	3 games
Josef Kompalla (FRG)	2 games
Frank Larsen (USA)	1 game
Gord Lee (USA)	3 games

Paul Henderson's 1972 sweater was repatriated in 2010 and has been touring Canada ever since.

APPENDIX 5

A MOST TREASURED SWEATER

On June 23, 2010, Paul Henderson's white Team Canada sweater sold at auction for US$1,067,538. The winning bid came from Mitchell Goldhar, owner of SmartCentres, a real-estate development company in Vaughan, Ontario.

"I just got very excited about it and decided that I wanted to bring it back to Canada, and I wanted to make it available to the country," said Goldhar. "I feel like it's everybody's jersey." To that end, he promised to have the sweater travel the country, to museums and malls in towns large and small, so Canadians from coast to coast could see it up close and recall the Summit Series and the hero Henderson, who scored the winning goals in games six, seven, and eight wearing the white sweater with red maple leaf.

Henderson gave it to trainer Joe Sgro soon after the Summit Series ended, and Sgro later sold it to an American, who wished to remain anonymous when he put it up for auction in 2010.

Henderson also donated his red sweater from the first four games in Canada to the Hockey Hall of Fame in Toronto.

ACKNOWLEDGEMENTS

The author would like to thank the many people who have helped make this book a wonderful celebration of an historic event.

First, to publisher Doug Pepper at M&S and to Jordan Fenn, publisher of the Fenn/M&S imprint, for their enthusiasm from day one. To Horst Streiter at Ficel Marketing for coordinating everything at the Team Canada end of things. But, of course, the biggest thanks and credit goes to the players themselves. It was an honour to have spoken to every one of them, and their pleasure in discussing the games and their recollections of events forty years later is inspiring in itself. Further thanks go to designer Andrew Roberts and to editors Michael Melgaard and Linda Pruessen at M&S. Together they helped take word and photo files and turned them into an impressive book worthy of the Summit Series. As well, to my agent Dean Cooke and his expert team at The Cooke Agency.

Lastly, to my family, notably my mom, who put me on skates (a few years ago) and let me go; to Liz, Ian, and the kids who aren't kids anymore, Zac and Emily; and lastly to my wife Jane who is too busy saving lives to watch the eight games over and over with me, but who would recognize Foster Hewitt's voice anywhere all the same.

PHOTO CREDITS

GRAPHIC ARTISTS/HOCKEY HALL OF FAME: 12-13, 15, 17, 18, 25, 28, 36, 40, 44, 48, 56, 59, 62, 66, 70, 80, 84, 96, 100, 112, 116, 118, 122, 126, 130, 134, 146, 150, 162, 166, 170, 174, 186, 190, 202, 206, 212, 216, 220, 222, 232, 235, 238, 242, 244, 246, 248

FRANK PRAZAK/HOCKEY HALL OF FAME: 34, 60, 205

HOCKEY HALL OF FAME ARCHIVES: 144, 199, 226-27

FRANK ARNOLD/HOCKEY HALL OF FAME: 7 (top)

GETTY IMAGES: viii, 7 (bottom), 14, 22, 30-31, 32, 38, 43, 46, 50, 53, 54-55, 64, 68, 73, 74-75, 76, 78, 87, 88-89, 90, 93, 94, 98, 103, 104-5, 106, 110, 115, 120, 125, 129, 133, 138-39, 140 (all), 142, 143, 149, 152, 154-55, 156, 159, 160, 164, 168, 172, 177, 180-81, 182, 184, 189, 193, 194-95, 196, 200, 208, 214, 219, 229, 230, 236-37, 241, 250

Sharp Canada Congratulates Team Canada 1972 on this Historic Anniversary.

100th
ANNIVERSARY

SHARP

A proud partner of Canada's Team of the Century.

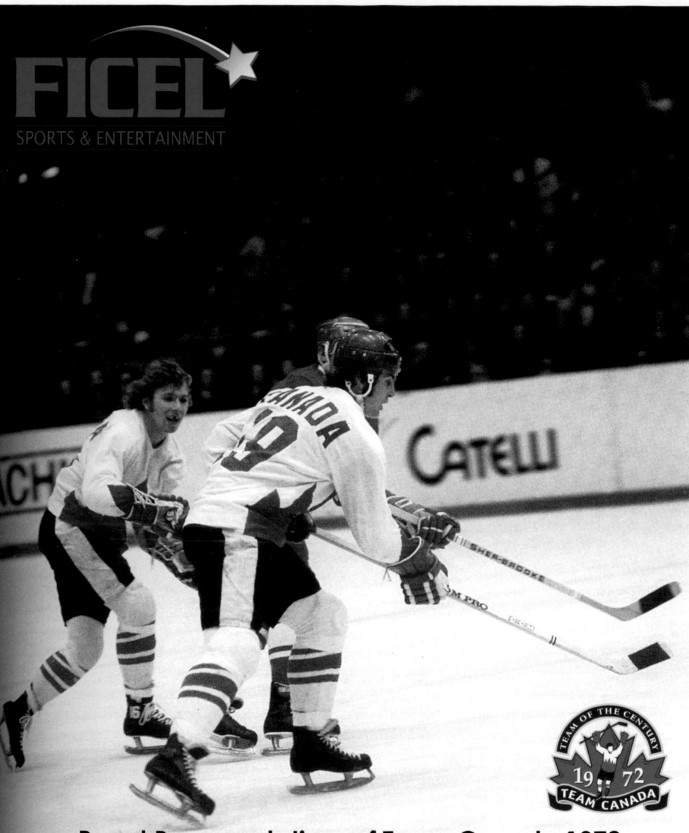

Proud Representatives of Team Canada 1972
www.heritagehockey.com